A REGIONAL HISTORY OF
THE RAILWAYS OF GREAT BRITAIN

General Editor: DAVID ST JOHN THOMAS

VOLUME IV

THE NORTH EAST

THE NER COAT OF ARMS

A REGIONAL HISTORY OF
THE RAILWAYS OF GREAT BRITAIN

Volume IV

THE NORTH EAST

by
K. Hoole

WITH 44 PLATES
9 ILLUSTRATIONS IN TEXT
INCLUDING REGIONAL MAPS
AND LARGE FOLDING MAP

DAVID & CHARLES

NEWTON ABBOT   LONDON

Set in 11 on 12 point Intertype Baskerville and
printed in Great Britain by The Garden City
Press Limited Letchworth Hertfordshire SG6
1JS for David & Charles (Holdings) Limited
South Devon House Newton Abbot Devon

Contents

Illustrations

IN TEXT

Sources of the Photographs

Thanks are due to the following for providing material: J. W. Armstrong, Esq.; British Railways; H. C. Casserley, Esq.; other photographs by the late Leslie Good and the author.

Note on the Maps

All the maps in this book have been drawn specially. The
three-colour folding map at the back is the most comprehensive
yet prepared of the railways of North East England, but owing
to the complexity of the system in certain areas it has proved
impossible to include all lines. Certain of the more complicated
areas are the subject of separate maps in the text. These give
more detail, but still do not profess to show all the lines concerned. Neither do they show the position at any particular
point in time. They are intended to be a basic guide to be used
in conjunction with the text.

CHAPTER I

The North East

Nowhere have railways had a greater impact than in the North East. The North East: the cradle of railways whose primitive beginnings go back over 350 years. The North East: criss-crossed by an intricate network of lines, including some of the busiest mineral routes in Britain, the trunk east coast main line from Scotland to London, some of the country's quietest rural byways, and coastal holiday routes as busy as any on summer Saturdays. Here railways were not merely big business; they were the very way of life. They directly employed many thousands of workers, not only on their trains and in their stations, but in their vast workshops and their docks. Indirectly, almost every man employed in the region's great coal industry owed his job to railway transport, as of course did the seaside landladies of Scarborough and Bridlington, the workers in many remote quarries, and farmers who switched to producing milk taken daily to the big centres of population.

In the North East, perhaps more than in any other comparable part of Britain, it is hard to talk of railways in a general sense. A very particular railway is usually implied: the North Eastern, one of the greatest of the trunk lines of the pre-1923 era, a railway whose fortunes were built on coal and steam but much of whose individual atmosphere survived the 1923–47 'grouping' era only to be killed off in today's British Railways' diesel age. The greater part of this book is inevitably devoted to the North Eastern, but this is not a company history. On the one hand it includes only a small part of the detail incorporated by William Weaver Tomlinson in his famous *The North Eastern Railway, Its Rise and Development*, published in 1914. On the other hand, it brings the story down to the present time, it includes those lines which never came under North Eastern ownership, and as are all volumes in this series, it is concerned to portray the railways against their geographical, social and economic background.

As far as can be ascertained the earliest wagonway in North East England was near Blyth, in Northumberland, probably opened in 1609 to carry coal from mines near Bedlington to the River Blyth. The venture was not a success and closed down about 1614. However, once the advantage of running wagons on rails – primitive though they were – had been demonstrated, the mine owners of Durham and Northumberland rapidly took up the idea. Wagonways multiplied rapidly and by the end of the eighteenth century an extensive network of lines existed, particularly in southern Northumberland and northern Durham.

The object in each case was the same, namely to get coal to the nearest navigable river as quickly and as economically as possible. Thus many of the early lines ran down to the River Tyne between its mouth and a point some six or seven miles upstream from Newcastle and Gateshead, which face each other across the river. A major concentration of wagonways also accumulated on both banks of the Wear in the Penshaw area, approximately five miles upstream from Sunderland. Where the mines were adjacent to the rivers only a short wagonway was required but lines seven or eight miles long had to be laid to provide an outlet from the Pontop area to the Tyne, and from the Beamish area to the Wear.

But it was not until the opening years of the nineteenth century that the wagonways began to bear some resemblance to the complicated network we know today. The change was brought about by the introduction, almost simultaneously, of the steam locomotive and the iron rail for it to run upon. From this period emerges one of the best-known characters connected with railway development, George Stephenson. Stephenson began building locomotives in 1814 and eight years later his first major task was completed when the Hetton Colliery Railway was opened on 18 November 1822. Locomotives could work less than half the length of this eight-mile line, the remainder being worked by winding engines and self-acting inclines (Chapter VII).

George Stephenson was not, of course, the inventor of the steam locomotive; he was mainly concerned with improving the ungainly machines of the early nineteenth century. Much of his fame was due to his connection with the Stockton & Darlington

Railway – the first public railway to use steam power – and it was on the historic opening day of that railway, on 27 September 1825, that our present railway system was born. It seems regrettable that the s&d could not absorb the other railways which grew in the North East but had itself to be taken over by the NER, thirty years its junior. Fortunately the NER and the LNE never forgot the part the s&d played in the development of railways and fiftieth and hundredth anniversaries were suitably celebrated.

It was due to the foresight of Edward Pease that the Stockton & Darlington was built : for years there had been talk of a canal between the two towns and it was this Darlington mill owner – a Quaker – who advocated and fought for a railway. Fierce opposition was encountered from the landowners on the route but Pease succeeded in enlisting the help of some influential families, such as the Backhouses, the Meynells, and the Stobarts; even so the bill was rejected on its first passage through Parliament in 1819. A further bill was submitted in 1821 and this time it was successful, although not without some anxious moments when it was found that insufficient capital had been subscribed. The day was saved when Edward Pease himself put up the £10,000 necessary.

Various accounts exist as to when Edward Pease first met George Stephenson, but there is no doubt that it was in July 1821 that Stephenson was asked by Pease (on behalf of the s&d Committee) to carry out a survey, thus bringing about an association which was eventually to have world-wide repercussions. The original Act of 1821 was vague about the form of motive power to be used but the Act of May 1823 specifically mentioned stationary and locomotive engines.

The s&d was soon faced with the need for expansion at both its extremities – at the western end to serve more collieries and quarries, and at the eastern end to provide improved shipping facilities. Many of the lines in the west were built nominally by separate companies, but their directors were also directors of the Stockton & Darlington and their creation was to ensure that if one root died then the whole tree did not perish.

In the east the s&d was extended from Stockton to Middlesbrough in 1830, crossing the River Tees into Yorkshire on an unsuccessful suspension bridge. Stockton, on the north bank of the river, was an established town, but its shipping facilities were becoming inadequate for the rapidly increasing coal trade and so search was made for a site nearer the sea, offering a greater depth of water and suitable for docks. The area chosen, then a mere collection of huts on the banks of the Tees, is today the thriving town of 160,000 inhabitants we know as Middlesbrough, the centre of a tremendous industrial area specializing in chemicals and steel.

Although the principal business of the s&D was undoubtedly the carriage of minerals, it also had an eye on developing its passenger traffic – once it had realized the possibilities. Until the 1830s the company allowed contractors to handle the passengers. Later, to further this side of the business, a development company was formed to build the nucleus of the town of Saltburn which, in the century since its birth, has grown into a seaside resort and residential area warranting a half-hourly service of railcars to Middlesbrough and Darlington for eighteen hours a day.

Eventually the s&D extended almost across County Durham, from Stockton in the south east to Consett in the north west, with tentacles reaching into Westmorland to Tebay and Penrith, and into Yorkshire to Saltburn and Guisborough. Whilst the s&D remained independent, the North Eastern Railway was not safe from invasion from the west and in 1860 – only six years after the formation of the NER – approaches were made to the s&D with a view to amalgamation. Although formal amalgamation did not take place until July 1863 the two companies began working together from 1 January 1861. After the amalgamation the s&D carried on almost as a separate concern for a further ten years, under the direction of a committee, with power to appoint its own secretary, solicitor and all officers and servants, and to fix the times and number of trains, fares and rates. Eventually it became known as the Central Division of the NER and this term is still used occasionally today.

The full anatomy of the complex railway system of the North East can only emerge in the book as a whole, but for the benefit of readers who may not be railway experts the importance of the east coast main line may now be emphasized.

Commencing at the southern end – and for the sake of clarity starting off the North Eastern – the original course between Doncaster and York was via Great Northern Railway metals to

Askern Junction (four miles north of Doncaster) where an end-on junction was made with the Lancashire & Yorkshire Railway, which was used as far as Knottingley. Knottingley was one of the southern extremities of the York & North Midland Railway and the journey to York was completed over the Knottingley branch of the company as far as Burton Salmon, thence over its main line via Milford Junction and Church Fenton.

Until 1877 reversal was necessary at York before the forty-four level miles across the Plain of York to Darlington could be covered over Great North of England Railway lines. North of Darlington the position was complicated: originally it had been planned to continue the GNE to Gateshead, but this fell through and the forty-mile gap was eventually closed in 1844 by running over the metals of four companies – Newcastle & Darlington Junction, Durham Junction, Pontop & South Shields and Brandling Junction, all of which became part of the York & Newcastle Railway.

North of the Tyne only one company was concerned, namely the Newcastle & Berwick, and here the route is exactly the same as when it was opened 126 years ago. However, south of York, and between Ferryhill and Newcastle the line has undergone changes as improved routes have been opened. At the southern end the route via Knottingley has been replaced by the present line from Chaloner Whin Junction – two miles south of York – to Shaftholme Junction – four miles north of Doncaster. Of course it must be remembered that until the Knottingley route was opened passengers from York to London travelled via Normanton, Derby and Rugby into Euston station.

North of Ferryhill the original route via Brockley Whins (now Boldon Colliery) was replaced in 1850 by a more direct route from Washington to Pelaw; this in turn was superseded by the Team Valley line from Gateshead to Ferryhill in 1872, and this latter route remains the main line of today.

Following the general plan of the Regional History series each chapter covers a specific area. The detailed history of the east coast main line will be found as follows:

The formation of the North Eastern Railway in 1854 was the most important event in the history of the railways of the North East – and possibly in the history of North East England itself. Before considering the North Eastern itself, it may be helpful to describe its constituents and the joint lines with which it worked. Four companies amalgamated to form the North Eastern :

1. York & North Midland. This ran southwards from York to join the North Midland Railway at Altofts Junction, a short distance north of Normanton, thus providing a link in the first railway route from York to London, and much of its development was due to the famous (or infamous) George Hudson. At the time of the amalgamation the company controlled (in addition to its original line) most of the railways in the area bounded by York, Whitby, Hull and Leeds, including the extremely important connection between Burton Salmon and Knottingley which gave access to the Great Northern route to London.

2. The York, Newcastle & Berwick. As its name implied, this controlled the lines from York to the north, together with various country branches and a network of lines on both banks of the River Tyne. It had grown mainly out of the Great North of England Railway (York–Darlington), the Newcastle & Darlington Junction and the Newcastle & Berwick, but it also included the Newcastle & North Shields, Brandling Junction (Gateshead–Sunderland), the Pontop & South Shields (successor to the Stanhope & Tyne) and the Durham Junction (Washington–Rainton Meadows).

3. The Leeds Northern. Mainly concerned with the services between Leeds, Harrogate, Thirsk, Northallerton and Stockton.

4. The Malton & Driffield.

The formal amalgamation took place on 31 July 1854, when Parliament passed an Act, but the companies had already worked together for a short period. This still left some other lines not yet in the net of one of the three major partners, the most important being the Blyth & Tyne, the West Durham, the West Hartlepool Harbour & Railway and, of course, the Stockton & Darlington; but these were all taken over in the course of the twenty years 1854–74.

Thenceforward the NER was mainly concerned with taking over lines which had been constructed by small companies but which it had itself worked from the outset, such as the Scar-

STOCKTON AND DARLINGTON REMAINS
(1) *Coal drops at Shildon*
(2) *Ruins of Stanley incline engine house of 1858*
(now demolished)

TYPICAL 19TH CENTURY TRAINS

(3) *Richmond station c. 1860 with 2-2-2 No. 69*
(4) *Masham station c. 1880 with 2-4-0T No. 84*

borough & Whitby, Whitby, Redcar & Middlesbrough Union (Whitby–Loftus), Scarborough, Bridlington & West Riding Junction (Driffield–Market Weighton), and the Tees Valley (Barnard Castle–Middleton in Teesdale), as well as such minor lines as the Merrybent & Darlington, and the Cawood Wistow & Selby Light. In its own right the NER continued to expand by filling in gaps in the network.

The NER was a partner in five joint railways:

Swinton & Knottingley	With MR	
Methley	With GN and L&Y	GN worked passenger traffic
Otley & Ilkley	With MR	
Axholme	With L&Y	L&Y worked passenger traffic
South Yorkshire		

Although the North Eastern came closer to having a monopoly over a large and important area than did any other British railway, it was always willing to negotiate with other companies who wanted to use its lines: witness the number of companies which worked to York over North Eastern lines – everyone was welcome who would feed passengers and freight to the North Eastern.

In its heyday at the turn of the century York was one of the most cosmopolitan of railway centres, where engines from six different companies could be seen side by side, all hauling their own rolling stock. These companies reached York under various running powers agreements granted at various times for various reasons. The points from which these powers commenced were:

MR	Ferrybridge Junction	Commenced 1879
GCR	Ferrybridge Junction	Commenced 1899
LNW	Leeds	Commenced 1893
L&Y	Altofts Junction	Commenced 1884
GER	Shaftholme Junction	Commenced 1892
GNR	Shaftholme Junction	Commenced 1871
GNR	Knottingley Junction	Commenced 1850

Other NER stations which regularly saw the engines and trains of different companies were Hull, Harrogate and Newcastle; at the latter the North British was the only company to manage to invade the NER stronghold, although the latter more than made up for this indignity by its powers to work all east-coast expresses between Berwick and Edinburgh over 57½ miles of NBR track. Whether this concession was a profitable one for the NER is doubtful, as it meant maintaining a stud of locomotives and staff at Edinburgh and replacements and reliefs could only be provided from Tweedmouth or Gateshead. The flow of traffic was largely seasonal and involved a large amount of light engine and empty stock working. However, the NER was very jealous of this right; in 1894 it strongly opposed a North British company challenge to its legality, and was eventually allowed to provide the motive power for ten trains per day against the eight allocated to the North British. It would appear, however, that the North British eventually regretted its protracted struggle to obtain this privilege, because in 1904 it reached an agreement with the North Eastern whereby the latter worked all the through Anglo-Scottish trains north of Berwick, subject to the payment by the NBR of a fixed sum per train.

The North Eastern owned some 1,700 miles of line and worked over a further 300, either by virtue of lease, joint ownership, or running powers. In the last normal year (1913) the number of first-class passengers carried reached 1,219,180, and third class 59,834,885, coming from more than 500 stations. In the same year the receipts amounted to £11,315,129, whilst expenditure was £7,220,784 – and a dividend of 7 per cent was being paid!

It was, of course, its handling of gigantic quantities of mineral traffic that made the North Eastern famous throughout the world: Northumberland and Durham alone were producing more than *fifty million tons* of coal a year prior to World War I. The actual northern coalfield covers an area of approximately 700 square miles and it is contained roughly in a district bounded by Hartlepool, Shildon, Hexham and Amble, being about fifty miles long and up to twenty-five miles wide. Coal is found at varying depths with seams varying in thickness from 18 in. to 7 ft, the average being between 3 and 5 ft. In general coal from the northern part of the field is 'hard' and therefore suitable for steam-raising purposes; that from around the Tyne is especially suitable for household use and for gas and coke making; West Durham coal is also used for coking, and coal from east and south Durham is suitable for all purposes. Outside this main producing area mines have also been established at one time or another at points north-west of Alston (Lambley Fell, Midgeholme, etc) and south of Berwick (Scremerston).

The development of the coal-mining industry was contemporaneous with the growth of the railway system to which, indeed, it gave birth, and in the years before the Great War the amount of coal mined in Durham and Northumberland doubled. The NER had to expand to keep pace.

	TONS MINED		
Year	Northumberland	Durham	Total
1870	5,840,254	21,773,275	27,613,529
1880	6,850,162	28,063,346	34,913,508
1890	9,446,035	30,265,241	39,711,276
1900	11,514,521	34,800,719	46,315,240
1910	13,121,691	39,431,598	52,553,289

In 1910 the amount of Durham and Northumberland coal exported totalled 18,981,000 tons: this was 36 per cent of the output, whereas the national average at that time was 23 per cent.

The east coast ports, at many of which the dock installations were owned by the NER, handled not only coal but many other commodities as well. Hull, or to give the city its full title, Kingston upon Hull, is not only one of the country's leading fishing ports but it handles also wool for the West Riding; large amounts of soft fruits and vegetables; timber; vegetable and mineral oils; and general cargo. Fishing ports extend the whole way up the coast – Bridlington, Flamborough, Filey, Scarborough, Whitby, Staithes, Hartlepool, North Shields, Seahouses, etc, all contributing to the flow of traffic, although unfortunately much of this now passes by road. Middlesbrough – a town that, as mentioned earlier, grew from nothing with the coming of the railway – now handles large quantities of chemicals to and from the giant Imperial Chemical Industries empire on both sides of the Tees, and a large oil refinery, recently established in the area, is rapidly developing. West Hartlepool had its timber; Sunderland its coal and shipbuilding; while the Tyne could handle almost anything.

In many cases the carriage of passengers developed from the

transport of the miners and their families, often isolated in some valley or on bleak moorland where the mineral wealth could be easily worked. To reach the nearest market town or village for provisions or recreation they were allowed to ride on the wagons of the mineral trains; later a rough coach was provided and a branch service was born. Some of the services run solely for miners survived until recently in the North East, latterly used to enable miners to reach distant collieries, the largest system being at Ashington in Northumberland.

The position of the Pennine Chain largely affected the railways of North East England. The water draining from the eastern slopes formed valleys running generally east and west, along which the market towns and villages naturally developed, and consequently the railways followed the valleys for ease of construction and to serve the population. Most of the lines terminated in the valleys (the lines along Swaledale, Nidderdale, Weardale, etc) but the Wensleydale branch broke through to the west and connected with the Midland main line between Leeds and Carlisle. The South Durham & Lancashire Union surmounted Stainmore to reach Tebay and Penrith, which it managed without a tunnel, and the Newcastle & Carlisle utilized the Tyne valley to become the first railway across England.

Wherever possible the early surveyors took advantage of the gaps in the hills, both to save expense and to keep the gradients within the capabilities of the early locomotives. An example of this is the line between York and Scarborough, which follows every twist and turn of the river for some miles as it runs through the Howardian hills; unfortunately the twisting and turning has necessitated a speed restriction ever since the opening in 1845! Other examples are the line from Battersby to Whitby, along the Esk valley, and the western outlet from Hull along the shores of the River Humber. It was the occupation of this strategic position by the Hull and Selby Railway (later NER) that many years later forced the Hull & Barnsley to climb over, and burrow through, the Yorkshire Wolds at great expense.

Often the most awkward lines to construct and work have been those running north and south along the coast: the valleys running down to the sea have had to be bridged or else the railway had to descend one side and climb up the other. For example, on the coast route north of Scarborough large viaducts had to be built at Whitby and Staithes, with smaller ones at Upgang, Newholm Beck, East Row and Sandsend. At Fylingdales, however, the line had to drop down from Ravenscar (631 ft above sea level) on a gradient of 1 in 39 and then climb up through Robin Hood's Bay at 1 in 43. The Seaham–West Hartlepool line is another case where numerous valleys had to be bridged.

The NER had an atmosphere of its own. The main line was always busy carrying its unending stream of travellers southwards to seek fame and fortune in London, and its seasonal flow northwards of tourists and holidaymakers bound for Edinburgh and 'bonnie Scotland' generally, not forgetting the exodus from London and the south for 'the glorious twelfth', bringing sudden death to many an unsuspecting game bird!

On the country branches life was unhurried, with all the passengers knowing one another and the staff. As the train progressed along the fertile valleys, stopping at each station, discussion would range from Farmer Brown's old sow and her latest litter to Mrs Smith's recently delivered twins. On Tyneside, agriculture entered less into the picture, the miners and their families travelled for a day out on the coast at Whitley Bay, Cullercoats or Newbiggin, and talk was more of whippets and horticultural achievements. Instead of the broad dialects of Yorkshire one heard the unadulterated Geordie tongue, so difficult for a stranger to understand that a southerner could easily be misled into thinking that he had entered a compartment full of foreigners.

The North Eastern Railway was well served by its staff, from the lowest grade junior porter sweeping the platform at some small station, to the officers secure in the magnificent headquarters at York. Prior to World War I the railwayman was a respected person, and at the country places the stationmaster often ranked with the doctor, the parson and the schoolmaster. Particularly envied were the footplate staff on the main-line turns, with their secure employment and a top rate of 7s 6d per day in 1883. The older drivers were often a law unto themselves, with their firemen as their slaves, and many are the tales of these martinets who insisted on things being done their way and no other.

A practice peculiar to the NER was that of allowing country

stationmasters to act as coal merchants for their own areas. This scheme appears to have originated way back in the company's early days, or probably even back in Stockton & Darlington days. The stationmaster could purchase coal direct from the colliery by the wagon-load, weigh and bag it – he would often pay the porter a small sum to do this – and distribute it to any customer he could find in the locality.

The business was carried on in the company's time provided it did not conflict with running the railway efficiently. Before the first World War it was bringing stationmasters on average about £1 per week, but by 1920 some were making up to £5–£7 per week at such places at Tadcaster, Pickering, Driffield, etc – stations which served small towns and rich agricultural areas. In fact some stationmasters refused promotion in order to retain a station with particularly lucrative coal sales.

The scheme was continued under the LNE, and in the late 1930s its extension to other areas was considered; war stopped further development, however, and it remained the sole privilege of the North Eastern Area men. Even under British Railways the privilege has continued, but with the mass closure of country stations the number of qualifying stationmasters is rapidly decreasing.

Although the scheme was a private venture by the stationmaster his books were inspected by the railway company's auditor, and woe betide any man caught 'fiddling'. The company was so jealous of its public image – to use a modern term – that an employee found carrying on any dubious trading practices was severely reprimanded or, in extreme cases, dismissed.

Although its main traffics were among the heaviest in the country, the NER never neglected small additions to its income. Between 1840 and 1860 the practice grew up of trains stopping at certain level crossings to collect farmers and their wives going to market. In some cases this was the birth of a proper station, but in others the calling-place continued to open on market days only well into the British Railways' era. Then, though the number of stations without goods-handling facilities was small – such stations were normally in an urban area served by a central goods depot, or near another station which could handle freight more conveniently – there were numerous sidings, usually unstaffed, where traders and farmers might load and unload their goods; they were saved the need to traverse a long, and perhaps tortuous, road to the nearest fully equipped station. Under the rationalization schemes of B R most of these sidings have been closed. All these 'drops in the ocean' were characteristic of the company, which was prepared to give a service, however small, even when its main concern was the carrying in bulk loads of 1,000 tons or more.

Even the NER stations themselves had their own distinctive flavours. York was largely an interchange station, with barrow-loads of luggage being taken from platform to platform, often followed by father, mother, and two or three children clutching their buckets and spades and fretfully asking if they would reach the sands before the tide came in. Also bound for the sea-side and a good day out were parties from factories and mills in the West Riding, travelling in reserved saloons well stocked with bottled beer or barrels of ale; it was not unusual for a few people to be drunk by the time the train reached Bridlington or Scar-borough. Transferring the saloons to trains bound for the coast kept occupied four or five pilot engines, which also handled the numerous regular 'through coaches' now, alas, only a memory.

The feeling of being in a railway town could be sensed at many places in the North East, particularly in York, Darlington, Gateshead and Shildon, where almost every family had some member or near relation working for the NER. Latterly York's railway atmosphere has suffered an eclipse because of the num-ber of people employed at the two large chocolate factories – Rowntree's and Terry's. Although the majority of these em-ployees are women, the factories have played a part in the neglect of York as a main-line locomotive centre because with their wives working the footplate staff had sufficient money to resist the plans to make York the half-way house on the east coast main line. It was envisaged that York drivers and fire-men would lodge overnight at London or Edinburgh and that the depot would share the main-line workings with engines and men from King's Cross and Haymarket sheds, allowing Gran-tham and Gateshead to be reduced in status. However, the York men's opposition led to the 'lodging turns' strike of 1949 and the scheme was dropped, so York had few important trains to work, their main turns being restricted to York–Newcastle out and home jobs.

Sunderland, Bishop Auckland and Durham were the Saturday-night targets for the miners after their long and dirty work underground : they believed in working hard and playing hard and much of their well-earned wages went on drink, so that often they had to be delivered at their home station by the guard. At the turn of the century the NER inherited the Londonderry Railway station at Seaham – with the entrance to the 'local' straight off the station platform. At closing time the inebriated were bundled out of the hotel, across the platform and into the train bound for Sunderland – even if they lived in the opposite direction !

Prim and proper Harrogate would have been shocked by such goings-on. There the station was kept spotlessly clean, with a display of flowers to welcome the travellers arriving to take the waters. Until 1939 a number of people wintered in Harrogate and spent the summer at Scarborough and, in fact, the two towns are very similar : it is said that strangers have arrived in Harrogate and asked to be directed to the sea. Scarborough's rise from a small fishing port to a major holiday resort has been greatly helped by the railway which, under the auspices of George Hudson, reached the coast in July 1845, despite the warning published in 1840 that the town had 'no wish for a greater influx of vagrants', and that the chief claim to the estimation of the fashionable public should lie in the novelty of it not having a railroad.

At Newcastle, the North Eastern's busiest station, the flood of suburban traffic almost engulfed the long-distance travellers, who consequently were not as noticeable as at York. The largest flow of passengers could be seen on a hot summer weekend when everyone in the city seemed to have one thought in mind, to get to the coast and on to the sands, away from the sweltering city streets. Early in the century the NER was rapidly losing traffic to the electric trams and it was decided to electrify the lines to the coast, both from Newcastle Central and New Bridge Street. Actually these two lines formed an almost complete circle, broken only by the few hundred yards separating the old Blyth & Tyne terminus at New Bridge Street from the East Coast main line at Manors. The electrification was completed in 1904, and increasing traffic necessitated additional rolling stock in 1905, 1908, 1912 and 1915. The missing link between New Bridge

Street and Manors was installed in 1909 but circular running did not commence until 1917, when trains commenced and terminated at Central station.

The entrance to Newcastle from the south was also far more interesting than that to York: as the train squealed its way round the curve on to the King Edward Bridge it was possible to get a glimpse of the array of locomotives outside Gateshead shed, with perhaps some old engine waiting its fate standing on Chater's Bank, on the opposite side of the line. Then over the 'coaly Tyne', with perhaps a dirty collier passing below, and then another curve into Central itself, with its huge gantries of pneumatically operated signals. Or there was the old route in from the south, actually passing Gateshead shed and works, then curving sharply through Gateshead West station on to Stephenson's famous High Level Bridge, with its three-track railway on the top deck and the road below – a road where the toll was collected by NER employees resplendent in a 'Ticket Collector's Double Breasted Frock Coat Suit' in winter, and a 'Ticket Collector's Double Breasted Jacket Suit' in summer.

Finally, it is perhaps hard for us to remember that railways did not just happen! First of all an influential committee had to be formed to engage an engineer to survey the route and give an estimate of the cost. The promise of the necessary capital had to be ensured and the bill had to be piloted through Parliament, often in the face of fierce opposition from other companies. Once the Royal Assent had been obtained it might be thought that everything would be plain sailing, but 1,001 things could still go wrong. For instance the contractor engaged to build the line often found that he had bitten off more than he could chew, or his sub-contractors let him down; strikes amongst the navvies for better pay were common, and if they did not get it they would walk off to some other line where the pay was better.

Newly erected bridges collapsed, cuttings and embankments turned out to be unstable, or a contractor engaged on building a tunnel – which he imagined, or the surveyor had told him, would be easy going – struck water, rock, or running sand: that meant extra expense and delay, with the shareholders pestering the directors, the directors badgering the engineer and the engineer cajoling and pleading with the contractor to get a move on. When not properly supervised some contractors would try to save money by carrying out work of a standard below that specified in the contract – this happened to the Whitby, Redcar & Middlesbrough Union Railway when its line was started between Whitby and Loftus. Construction actually commenced in 1871 but ceased when the company was unable to bear the extra cost caused by unexpected cliff falls and landslips. In 1875 'an agreement was come to with the NER company to take over the new line on lease, to finish it in a substantial and satisfactory manner, and to work it in perpetuity, they to receive 50 per cent of the gross receipts of the line'. In 1883, just prior to the opening of the line (more than two years after the target date), T. E. Harrison, the NER engineer, issued a report on the difficulties encountered :

> I have never seen work so thoroughly scamped, with the viaducts and ordinary bridges so badly designed and as badly executed as to be in a dangerous condition. Over £30,000 has been spent on putting the viaducts in a proper state and the roadway for the permanent way over the viaducts was of the flimsiest character and such as no Government Inspector would under any circumstances have passed. All the bridges with the exception of one were so defective and in such a dangerous state that three were obliged to be taken down and rebuilt before the contract was let, and plans had to be prepared for rebuilding or strengthening others, and nearly every abutment of the viaducts had to be taken down and rebuilt.

Holes were cut in the metal piers of the viaducts to examine the concrete within and it was discovered that some were filled with gravel, without any cement. Several of the piers were not perpendicular, and 600 bushels of cement had to be injected into the piers under pressure by means of a special machine devised by the NER engineers. The holes bored could still be seen when the viaducts were demolished in 1960.

And what of the engines themselves? Many NER passenger engines had a life of forty to fifty years, or even more, starting on the main-line expresses and gradually losing status until they ended their days quietly on some branch line. Many of the goods and shunting engines lasted even longer, some reaching the ripe old age of three score years and ten before going to the scrap heap. On many lines engines built in the last century appeared in the 1950s to be old-fashioned, but not so the North Eastern engines: the tender locomotives with their double side window cabs did not 'date' so much, and even the tank engines gave no outward sign of their age. Now, alas, all the N E R engines have been withdrawn, although many 0–6–0 and 0–8–0 locomotives were hard at work in Northumberland and Durham, handling coal traffic, until 1967.

In this book frequent reference will be made to coal, and it is surely appropriate that the last of a very long line of steam locomotives should die in harness, still toiling with loads of coal to the east coast ports as their ancestors did when they started life a century and a half ago.

On the west side of the 140-mile stretch of the east coast main line between York and Berwick there is now only one complete North Eastern branch, namely that between Newcastle and Carlisle.

The York to Harrogate branch still carries passengers but services to stations between Harrogate and Northallerton have gone with the closure of the Leeds Northern line through Ripon. From Northallerton the truncated Wensleydale branch is open as far as Redmire for stone traffic, whilst from Darlington the few remaining remnants of the Stockton & Darlington Railway system carry a passenger service as far as Bishop Auckland. Beyond there part of the branch along Weardale is open as far as Eastgate for cement traffic. Finally, there is the service to Consett, mainly for ironworks traffic. North of the Tyne there is not a single branch line remaining on the west side of the main line!

Thus in the gigantic area bounded by York, Harrogate, Ilkley, Skipton, Carlisle and Newcastle there is no passenger train service of any kind. Certainly much of this area is used solely for agricultural purposes, and much of it is wild moorland, but is it right that the inhabitants should be denied regular and reliable rail transport?

CHAPTER II

The West Riding

THE LEEDS & SELBY RAILWAY

The North, East and West Ridings of Yorkshire, with their 3,890,000 acres, form Britain's largest county. In fact the West Riding alone could take the second county (Lincolnshire) and still have 70,000 acres to spare, while the North Riding is larger than Norfolk – itself England's fourth county. The word 'Riding' means 'a third' and thus, in spite of Winifred Holtby's novel, there is no South Riding. However, the Rotherham and Sheffield area is often referred to as South Yorkshire although actually situated in the West Riding. Except for a minor excursion over the border – in this case the River Ouse – into the East Riding all the lines dealt with in this chapter are in the north-eastern corner of the West Riding, bounded roughly by York, Wetherby (and the branch to Harrogate), Leeds (exclusive), Pontefract, Thorne, Goole, and back to York along the Ouse. Leeds and the industrial portion of the West Riding will be covered in a separate volume. The Leeds & Thirsk Railway is, however, covered in Chapter V as a 'Line to the North'.

Because of the River Ouse the first railway which we consider stopped short at Selby. The story starts in December 1824 when, at a meeting in Leeds, the Leeds & Hull Railroad Company was formed as part of a scheme to straddle the country with a railway from Liverpool to Hull (see Chapter III). George Stephenson was appointed engineer and a survey was started on 7 February 1825, most of the work actually being carried out by Joseph Locke. The scheme was insufficiently supported and remained in abeyance until 1828, when the citizens of Kingston upon Hull began to get alarmed at the rapidly increasing importance of Goole, the result of its improved communication with the hinterland after the opening of the Knottingley & Goole canal on 20 July 1826.

Hull's agitation had its effect in Leeds, and at two meetings held there in March 1829 it was decided to form a company to build a railway from Leeds to Selby. The argument against extending the line to Hull was that as a free tidal river was available between Selby and Hull, why go to the expense of constructing a railway!

Stephenson's survey of 1825 included three inclined planes, and in an effort to avoid this inconvenience another survey was carried out in 1829, this time by James Walker. At a further meeting, held on 31 July 1829, at which George Stephenson was present, Walker's route was unanimously adopted. A bill was promoted in Parliament, and it received the Royal Assent on 29 May 1830.

A start on building the line was made on 1 October 1830 but because of some doubt about the location of the terminus at Leeds little was done until the end of February 1831. Such good progress was made with the 700 yard long tunnel through Richmond Hill, situated immediately east of the site eventually chosen for the terminus at Marsh Lane, that it was completed some fifteen months before the remainder of the line. In the mid-1890s the tunnel was opened out and widened to allow five tracks. On 18 September 1834 the completed railway was inspected by the directors and their friends; it was opened to the public four days later.

At this time Leeds was 'the largest and most flourishing town of Yorkshire', but as the city is not being dealt with in this volume we must look at Selby, at the opposite end of the line. This country market town is famous for its Abbey, its flour and oil-cake mills, and its ship-building activities. Although far from the sea many trawlers have been launched sideways into the Ouse, to sail from Hull to the Faroe Islands, Greenland and Iceland in search of prime fish for the English table. However, perhaps at the present time Selby is better known for its frustrating ancient wooden toll bridge which carries the main road (A19) from Doncaster to York across the river. It was originally intended to have the station adjacent to the old bridge, but to allow for future development, it was built some 200 yards down river. There was, of course, no railway bridge across the river until 1840, when the Hull & Selby Railway arrived from the East Riding bank over a cast iron bascule bridge. The erection of a new through station at the same time enabled the Leeds & Selby station to be converted into the goods station, which still remains. The original bridge was used until 1891, carrying east coast main line traffic in addition from 1871 : the new swing bridge, which is still in use, was built slightly to the east of the original.

For many years the two up and two down lines were gauntleted across the bridge. The signal box was at the south end and in the down direction the fast and slow lines diverged immediately after crossing the bridge, with the point blades on the south side and the frogs on the north, thus avoiding a complicated system which would have been necessary if the points had been on the north side. In the up direction the gauntleting was abolished some years ago when the slow line was altered to join the fast line north of the bridge, utilizing spring points, and that on the down line was done away with in 1960 when electrically operated points were installed at the north end of the bridge.

ENTER GEORGE HUDSON

Originally the Leeds & Selby connected with no other railway, but in 1839 it became entangled in the web so cunningly being spun by George Hudson when, on 29 May, it was joined at York Junction (now Gascoigne Wood Junction) by the York & North Midland from York.

For almost ten years there had been agitation for a railway from York to London and various routes had been discussed, but the formation in September 1835 of the North Midland Railway to construct a line from Leeds to Derby pointed the way. By building a line from York to Normanton the North Midland could be used to Derby, and thence over the Midland Counties Railway and the London & Birmingham into Euston. The Y&NM, therefore, was formed on 13 October 1835 to construct this York–Normanton link, with George Stephenson as engineer.

Two routes were proposed by the Provisional Committee, one via Tadcaster and the other via Bolton Percy, the latter being chosen on 28 October 1835. The necessary survey was rapidly completed and the bill prepared, so that within eight months the Royal Assent was received: it was on the very same day that the Hull & Selby was authorized.

The first meeting of the Y&NM was held on 10 August 1836 and George Hudson was elected chairman, a position which before the middle of the century was to bring about his downfall. The first section of the line from York to a connection with the Leeds & Selby at Milford was formally opened on 29 May 1839 with the festivities usually associated with such happenings. The day commenced with a breakfast 'of the most sumptuous description' at the Guildhall in York, to which were invited the directors of the North Midland Railway and the Great North of England Railway; the North Midland has already been mentioned as the line with which the Y&NM was to connect at Normanton, and the GNE was similarly to give access to the north. From the Guildhall the Y&NM directors and their guests passed in procession to a temporary station outside the city walls, just south of the present Queen Street bridge, as the station inside the walls was not ready. At this time Hudson was Lord Mayor of York and riding on the crest of a wave of great popularity.

The two remaining major sections of the Y&NM were opened in 1840, together with two curves which were to play an important part in the company's history. First the main line was extended to Burton Salmon on 11 May, and on to the junction with the North Midland at Altofts (one mile north of Normanton) on 1 July; a curve to the North Midland Railway at Methley to allow through running from the Y&NM to Leeds followed on 27 July. Finally, on 9 November 1840 a second connection with the Leeds & Selby at Milford was opened. The opening from York to Altofts was timed to coincide with the opening of the North Midland, and from that date rail travel between York and London finally became a reality.

The curve between Whitwood Junction on the Y&NM and Methley Junction on the NMR gave Hudson the opportunity to compete with the Leeds & Selby between Milford and Leeds, although his route was $4\frac{1}{2}$ miles longer. Naturally the passengers preferred the shorter route and those travelling from Selby to Leeds saw no point in changing from one train to another at Milford, just to please Hudson, when they could travel the whole distance in one coach. Hudson proposed, therefore, that trains between Leeds and Milford should run alternately via his route and via the direct Leeds & Selby route; this was declined by the L&S directors. Hudson realized that if left to its own devices the Leeds & Selby was going to prove an extremely prickly thorn in the side of the Y&NM. So he offered the Leeds & Selby a tempting lease (which it could not afford to decline) for thirty-one years at a rental of £17,000 per annum, with the option of purchase, and on 9 November 1840 he added control of this important fragment to his growing empire.

Hudson could now dictate which route should be used by passengers to Leeds from both Selby and York, and they had to travel via Methley whether they liked it or not, as passenger traffic was completely withdrawn west of Milford on the Leeds & Selby line. Freight continued to be worked to and from Marsh Lane, but in July 1848 it too was diverted via Methley : the reason given was that Marsh Lane station was isolated and did not connect with any other railway, whereas by using the North Midland route into Leeds goods traffic could easily be inter-changed with other lines. Local passenger traffic between Milford and Leeds was reinstated in 1850 but through traffic continued to travel via Methley until the Church Fenton–Mickle-field cut-off and Leeds New station were opened simultaneously on 1 April 1869.

Before leaving Milford it may be as well to explain the area in detail. Originally the Y&NM and the Leeds & Selby connected at York Junction, but the southern end of the east to south curve (completed in November 1840) also connected with the Y&NM main line, and it was here that Milford Junction station was erected; eventually the station at York Junction was closed. The latter was reopened in December 1850 as Old Junction but it became Milford Old Junction (from 1867) and finally Gascoigne Wood (in 1879). As Gascoigne Wood it remained open for nor-mal passenger traffic until 1 January 1902; five years later it was reopened with small wooden platforms for use by the staff employed at the remote marshalling yard of the same name. Their wives and families were also allowed to use the station – really a halt – and in this form it remained until the yards were closed on 2 November 1959. Milford Junction station was open until 1 October 1904, by which time its importance as an inter-change point had almost disappeared.

STANHOPE & TYNE RAILWAY
(5) *Ruins of Weatherhill engine house (now demolished)*
(6) *Looking down Nanny Mayor's incline at Waskerley. The S & D
loco worked line on embankment on right. Consett in distance*

YORK & NORTH MIDLAND RAILWAY
(7) *Carriage sidings for Y & NM station c. 1865*
(8) *As (7) today*

Until the engine shed at Selby closed in 1959 both Gascoigne Wood and Milford Junction were extensively used during the summer for engine-changing purposes: Selby engines used to take over from LMS (later LMR) engines and work to Bridlington and Scarborough via Market Weighton, thus relieving congestion at York. For a few years longer locomotives ran out light from York but the practice has now ceased. The station buildings at Milford Junction were demolished in October 1960 after standing empty and out of use for more than fifty years.

At the next junction to the south – Burton Salmon – the Knottingley branch diverges and this, only $2\frac{1}{2}$ miles long, played an important part in the development of the east coast main line. It was the connecting link which gave the Great Northern Railway access to York, utilizing running powers over the L&Y from Askern Junction to Knottingley.

The Y & N M section between Knottingley and Burton Salmon included one of Stephenson's lesser-known tubular bridges at Brotherton. This consisted of two tubes 20 ft 1 in. high to eaves and 12 ft 10 in. wide overall, with a clearance above the River Aire of 28 ft 3 in. The tube on the up line was 237 ft 3 in. long, that on the down line being 1 in. longer. One line was opened in April 1850 and Mr Sherriff of the Y&NM reported on the 19th that goods trains were working through between York and Doncaster. Permission to open the tube to passenger traffic was granted in July 1851, and on 1 October 1851 notice requesting permission to open the second tube was given to 'The Lords of Commissioners of the Privy Council for Trade'. Because of limited clearance permission was refused, and after a number of unsuccessful inspections the Board of Trade complained to the Y&NM that 'the repetitions of Inspecting by their Officers' were 'productive of inconvenience'. A further inspection in March 1852 still did not satisfy the Inspecting Officer and it was not until October 1852 that permission was finally given.

Towards the end of the nineteenth century it was decided to replace the two tubes by a girder bridge, and in 1898 the engineer of the NER gave an estimate of £16,000; nothing was done until 1900, when a revised estimate was for £21,500. Tenders for the new bridge varied between £17,700 and £27,032 and the lowest – that of the Cleveland Bridge & Engineering Co. Ltd – was accepted.

In 1871 the direct line from Shaftholme Junction to York via Selby was opened, and since then main-line traffic via Knottingley has largely disappeared, although the route is still used in times of emergency.

It was from the Burton Salmon–Knottingley branch that the Swinton & Knottingley Joint line (NE and MR) struck off southwards; the name of this joint line is misleading as it does not pass through Knottingley station. It was opened in 1879, and three years later a station was opened immediately north of the junction: this was at first called Ferrybridge but in 1901 it had 'for Knottingley' added to its title.

From Burton Salmon the main line of the Y&NM continues through Castleford, with the line from Garforth coming in on the right half a mile before the present station; on the opposite side of the line to this junction is the site of the original Castleford station, replaced in 1871. Beyond the present station another spur goes off to the left to join the L&Y Methley–Pontefract (Monkhill) line at Cutsyke Junction. This curve carried trains between Leeds (New) and Pontefract (Baghill) via Garforth and Pontefract (Monkhill) until 1 November 1926, when they were cut back to Castleford. However, the service over the Cutsyke curve was resumed on 5 May 1958 when diesel railcars commenced running between Leeds (Central) and Pontefract (Monkhill) via the Methley Joint line; having to reverse at Castleford. From 4 January 1960 the railcars continued from Pontefract (Monkhill) to Baghill to connect with trains on the S&K joint line; but the whole service was withdrawn on 2 November 1964. The former NER station at Castleford had 'Central' added in 1953 to distinguish it from the former L&Y station, which became Castleford (Cutsyke).

In another mile the line forks again at Whitwood Junction: the left fork is the Y&NM main line to Altofts Junction, while on the right is the historically interesting Y&NM curve to Methley Junction over which Hudson diverted the York and Selby to Leeds traffic. Regular passenger services over this latter curve ceased on 1 April 1869 when the Church Fenton–Micklefield cut-off was opened, but six months later a new passenger service commenced over the southern part of the curve, which the Methley Joint line joined mid-way; the section between this Methley Joint Junction and Methley Junction remained intact until 1930-1, when the latter connection was removed. The track north of Methley Joint Junction was left in place to serve a colliery, but was finally lifted in 1943. So that freight trains from a proposed new marshalling yard at Stourton could reach former NER lines without reversing, the track was restored, together with the junction at the Methley Junction end, but due to another change of plans the scheme has been abandoned.

YORK & NORTH MIDLAND BRANCHES

In 1845 the Y&NM received permission to construct a branch from Church Fenton to Harrogate, via Tadcaster and Wetherby, and this was opened as far as Spofforth on 10 August 1847. On completion of Prospect Hill tunnel (also known as Crimple tunnel), 825 yd long, and Crimple viaduct, the line was extended to the small Brunswick station on the Stray at Harrogate on 20 July 1848. The station was reached via a tunnel under part of Harrogate, and the southern portal can still be seen from trains entering Harrogate from the south; during World War II it was used as an air-raid shelter. In 1862 Harrogate was given a new centrally sited station, Brunswick and the tunnel leading to it becoming redundant; all traces of the station have now vanished although a plaque marks the site.

Crimple viaduct is a magnificent structure 1,873 ft long, crossing the Crimple valley at a height of 110 ft by means of 31 arches each 50 ft in span. Below it ran the Leeds & Thirsk line (later Leeds Northern), which was prevented from reaching Harrogate by Almscliff Bank and therefore had to go round by Starbeck. As part of the 1862 improvements, however, a connection was put in at the south end of Crimple viaduct between the Leeds Northern line and the Y&NM branch, to enable trains from Leeds via Arthington to reach the new central station at Harrogate (see Chapter V).

The section between Church Fenton and Wetherby has never been notable for its quantity of passenger traffic, and one intermediate station (Stutton) was closed as long ago as 1905 because of poor patronage and its proximity to Tadcaster. Perhaps the line's only claim to fame is the fact that between 1925 and 1928 it was used by the *Harrogate Pullman* – the forerunner of the *Queen of Scots Pullman*. In 1942 a large munitions factory was established at Thorp Arch (between Wetherby and Tadcaster), with its own railway system and stations, and an intensive train service was provided for the workpeople from the surrounding towns. This decreased after the war but did not finally cease until 1958.

On 1 May 1876 a branch from Cross Gates to Wetherby was opened; in 1902 it was doubled throughout and a new connection at Wetherby allowed through running between Leeds and Harrogate. The object was to divert Newcastle–Liverpool trains via Wetherby so that they could enter Leeds from the east instead of the west, thus avoiding the complicated area between Holbeck (Low Level) and Leeds (New) station, and also avoiding a reversal. The new connection between Wetherby South and West missed the original Wetherby station and a new one had to be built, leaving the old to be used for goods.

The heavy gradients caused the line to lose favour for all except local trains in the 1940s and 1950s, but the introduction of diesel-electric locomotives on the Newcastle–Liverpool trains in January 1961 brought expresses back again. The decision to use the Wetherby route was partly dictated by the desire to run the locomotives through from the Tyne to the Mersey. But in January 1964 all services between Cross Gates, Church Fenton and Harrogate were withdrawn and the Newcastle–Liverpool trains were diverted to the Arthington route. However, from March 1967 when the Leeds Northern line was closed north of Harrogate, these trains have run via York.

Because of a threatened invasion of its territory the Y&NM applied in 1845 for powers to construct 'a more direct line between York and Leeds' and received the necessary Act on 26 June 1846. This authorized the building of a route from the company's main line at Copmanthorpe to join its Church Fenton–Wetherby branch immediately north of Tadcaster station. After running south for a mile or so it was proposed to strike off near Stutton to join the Leeds & Selby line near Cross Gates. In addition it was planned to construct a new line from the Leeds & Selby at Osmondthorpe to join the Midland at Hunslet. The downfall of George Hudson and the financial straits in which the Y&NM found itself caused the suspension of operations on the direct line in 1849, by which time a magnificent stone viaduct over the River Wharfe at Tadcaster had been constructed. In 1883 a line was laid across the viaduct to serve a mill on the east bank of the Wharfe and this remained *in situ* until 1959, when it was deleted from the official instructions.

CHURCH FENTON–MICKLEFIELD CUT-OFF AND MAIN LINE IMPROVEMENTS

In an attempt to maintain a monopoly the NER deposited bills in 1863 for the improvement of its line into Leeds and also its main line southwards. The first covered the construction of a cut-off from Church Fenton to Micklefield and the projection west-wards from the Marsh Lane terminus of the Leeds & Selby to a new terminus (to be built jointly with the LNW) adjacent to the Midland station in the centre of Leeds.

The proposed main-line improvement was a new route from a point two miles south of York – later to become well-known as Chaloner Whin Junction – to join the Hull & Selby at Barlby, and then a second new line from a point immediately south of Selby station to join the Great Northern Railway at Owston – later to become famous as Shaftholme Junction. In addition there were two spurs; one from the new main line at Common Lane, Heck, to join the L&Y at Hensall Junction, and another to con-nect with the West Riding & Grimsby (Joan Croft Junction to Applehurst Junction). The Act for the main-line alterations re-ceived the Royal Assent on 23 March 1864 and that for the cut-off on 13 May 1864, but the extension beyond Marsh Lane was rejected. A modified route was, however, decided upon in time for submission later in 1864 and this received the Royal Assent on 5 July 1865 – on the same day as the new Leeds station was authorized.

The Church Fenton–Micklefield section, the extension from Marsh Lane, and the New station in Leeds, were all opened on 1 April 1869. At last there was a direct route from York to Leeds, with adequate interchange facilities at the latter station. From this date also the Milford Old Junction to Micklefield sec-tion was reopened to through passenger traffic, restoring once again the original route of 1834 and breaking the ties imposed by Hudson in 1840.

From Church Fenton the line climbs at gradients varying be-tween 1 in 133 and 1 in 150, and it was down the bank from

Micklefield that the NER 'single drivers' used to fly on the non-stop trains from Leeds to Scarborough, which were introduced on 1 June 1900 and timed to cover the 67½ miles in 75 minutes. At that time, however, the curve and junction at Church Fenton were not laid out for high speeds and after slowing down at this point the pace had to be regained over the almost straight and level section into York.

The section between Church Fenton and Chaloner Whin Junction was converted from double to quadruple track under Acts obtained in 1900 and 1901, and the new stations erected at Copmanthorpe, Bolton Percy and Ulleskelf were unusual (for the NER, at least) in being island platforms served only by one pair of tracks.

Until 1871 the east-coast main line included a section of L&Y-owned track between Knottingley and Askern Junction, where an end-on junction with the GNR was made. This was where the GNR 'ended in the middle of a ploughed field' and not as sometimes quoted at Shaftholme Junction, 220 yd to the south, where the NER made a true junction with the GNR in 1871.

With the opening of the new lines north and south of Selby on 2 January 1871 the east-coast main line as we know it today was taking shape, and it was completed in the following year when the section between Durham and Ferryhill was opened. The spur from Joan Croft Junction to join the West Riding & Grimsby at Applehurst Junction was opened on 1 July 1877, but the spur authorized from the main line at Common Lane, Heck, to join the L&Y at Hensall, although built was very little used, and NER records show it as being abandoned by 1905, although the earthworks are still visible.

The L&Y line at Hensall was promoted by the Wakefield, Pontefract & Goole Railway and opened on 1 April 1848, by which time the company had been absorbed by the L&Y. This and the branch from Pontefract to Methley (to allow access to Leeds over the Midland Railway) are the only L&Y lines which fall within the scope of this volume. The Pontefract–Methley line first saw passenger trains on 12 September 1849 when the L&Y ran race specials from Leeds to Doncaster; regular trains commenced on 18 October 1849 but from 10 March 1947 these terminated at Knottingley instead of continuing to Doncaster.

The Wakefield–Goole line gave the L&Y an outlet to the east,

and Goole is another town which owes its development and
growth to a railway company, although the original impetus
was given not by a railway but by the Knottingley & Goole
Canal; this was completed in July 1825, but had to wait another
year before the basins at Goole were completed.

Once the railway reached Goole in 1848 the port continued
to grow rapidly, in spite of its position some fifty miles from the
North Sea, via a treacherous channel up the River Ouse. Goole's
mainstay was coal shipments, and one dock alone was designed
to handle 1 million tons annually, but it also handled general
cargo and the L&Y operated its own fleet of steamers to Rotterdam, Amsterdam, Antwerp, Ghent, Dunkirk, Hamburg and
Copenhagen, with fares (in 1908) varying between £1 and £3
return.

Also at Hensall Junction the L&Y was joined by a curve from
Gowdall Junction on the Hull & Barnsley Railway, which had
crossed into the West Riding via the Ouse swing bridge, between
Barmby and Drax. The connection was regularly used by a day-
time freight train from Wakefield to Hull and back, and by a
similar night-time H&B freight in the opposite direction, booked
to leave Hull at 10.0 p.m. and to arrive at Wakefield at 1.0 a.m.,
returning to Hull at 2.30 a.m. Prior to World War I, H&B excursions from Hull (Cannon Street) to Leeds used the curve,
reaching Leeds via the Pontefract–Methley line and Midland
metals into Wellington station.

A mile north-east of Gowdall Junction the Hull & Barnsley
and Great Central joint Gowdall and Braithwell mineral line
branched off southwards from Aire Junction. This was opened
on 1 May 1916 and closed between Aire Junction and Bull-
croft Junction from 20 October 1958, followed on 29 November 1958 by the H&B main line. Over this latter section passenger
trains had been withdrawn from 1 January 1932.

In 1879, prior to the opening of the H&B, the Church Fenton,
Cawood & Wistow Railway was authorized, and in 1882 it was
proposed that this (on which no work had been done) should
be extended from Wistow, through Selby, to join the H&B at
Drax, and also be worked by the H&B. The NER petitioned
against this and the plan was rejected, but later the Cawood,
Wistow & Selby Light Railway was constructed on a portion
of the route.

The Cawood, Wistow & Selby Light Railway was commenced on 11 July 1896, when the first sod was cut by Mrs Henry Liversedge of York, wife of the chairman. The contractors actually started work at Selby on 12 September, and a connection was installed to allow material to pass from the NER. The line was opened on 16 February 1898 and in the first half-year carried 15,777 tons of freight and 6,819 passengers. Being an independent company the railway had its own terminus in Selby, adjacent to the Selby–Leeds line of the NER, but the buildings have now been demolished. Originally the trains were worked by the company's own 0-6-0 ST named *Cawood*, purchased from Messrs Manning, Wardle in 1897, but for many years before the branch closed to passenger traffic on 1 January 1930 they were worked by one of the NER petrol-electric railcars of 1904 and by a Leyland road bus converted to run on rails.

The branch was single line, laid across almost flat rich countryside which provided the staple traffic, agricultural produce. Unfortunately this dwindled to such an extent that the line was completely closed on 2 May 1960, and the track has since been lifted.

By its Act of 14 August 1903 the NER was authorized to build a 10½ mile branch between the Leeds–Selby line at Thorpe Willoughby and Goole, with its own connection to the York–Doncaster line to give access to Selby station. The Thorpe Willoughby connection was for goods traffic only and as the passenger trains ran between Selby and Goole they gave their name to the branch. Traffic never reached expectations and the branch was closed to passengers from 15 June 1964.

Finally mention must be made of the NER link put in between Staddlethorpe and Thorne to provide a through route between Hull and Doncaster. The old South Yorkshire Railway (later Manchester, Sheffield & Lincolnshire and eventually Great Central Railway) and the Lancashire & Yorkshire Railway both wished for rail access to Hull and the North Eastern also desired a shorter route. Accordingly in 1862 separate bills were introduced by these companies, all seeking power to construct a new line providing for better working to and from Hull. None of these proposals received Parliamentary sanction. In October of the same year, in order to save further Parliamentary contests, the three companies agreed that the NER should alone promote

a bill seeking powers to construct a railway between Staddlethorpe and Thorne. The Act was obtained on 28 July 1863 and
the Great Central and L&Y both obtained access to Hull by
means of running powers between Thorne and Hull, and between
Goole and Hull respectively, whilst the NER was granted powers
to run over the GCR line between Thorne and Doncaster.

The new line from Staddlethorpe through Goole to Thorne
largely supplanted what had previously been the chief route to
Hull through Milford Junction. It was destined to play an even
more important part in Hull's coal trade when the large collieries developed in South Yorkshire around the turn of the
century.

At Goole the L&Y station of 1848 was in the dock area but
the NER station of 1869 was some half mile to the north; a
connecting curve between the two was installed where they
crossed to the south-west of Goole, and in 1869 L&Y passenger
trains were diverted over this curve into the NER station. In 1910
a completely new route into the station from the west was
opened: it left the old L&Y route at Rawcliffe Bridge Junction,
three miles west of Goole, and after being joined by the new
North Eastern branch from Selby at Oakhill Junction took a
more northerly course to avoid the congested area west of the
docks. It joined the old route immediately west of Goole (NER)
station.

A notable feature of the line is the swing bridge across the
River Ouse, two miles east of Goole. This is 830 ft long, made up
of five fixed spans of 116 ft each, and one swinging portion 250
ft long which was originally estimated to weigh 670 tons but
which is now quoted as 800 or even 900 tons. The route between Saltmarshe and Goole, which includes the bridge, was
one of the first to receive colour-light signalling, brought into
use in May 1933, allowing a signal box at each end of the
bridge, and also one at Goole, to be closed.

Because of the industrial nature of the area, and its suitability
for power stations, some of the lines dealt with in this chapter
seem to have a more secure future than many others, although it
remains to be seen what effect the M62 motorway and the
Humber Bridge will have.

CHAPTER III

The East Riding

THE HULL AREA

Except between York and Stamford Bridge, and Ganton to just north of Filey, the boundary of the East Riding is formed by the rivers Humber, Ouse, and Derwent. Hull, on the Humber, some twenty miles from the sea, is the Riding's major city. With its 1961 population of 303,261, it is ten times larger than at the beginning of the nineteenth century, largely because of its development as a port with massive railway facilities.

One is reminded of the importance of shipping in the very centre of the city when catching a view of Prince's Dock although this, together with the adjacent Humber and Railway docks, is now disused, being too small and antiquated for modern needs. Hull has an atmosphere of the sea and many of its citizens are connected with it in one way or another. They handle the timber from Scandinavia, the grain from North America and Canada, the nuts from Africa to be ground for oil, the fruit and vegetables from the Channel Islands, the petroleum products brought alongside the Saltend jetties, whilst the manning, repairing and revictualling of the trawler fleet is an industry on its own.

Yet, though long Britain's third port, Hull often considers itself neglected. It has intense local activity, but because of its geographical position it literally is 'the end of the line', and is relatively unknown and unvisited by people from the rest of the country. The fact that during the 1939–45 war, its railway installations – and its inhabitants – were battered by more than 100 German air-raids was not appreciated by most of Britain.

Some idea of the scale of railway operations in the city may be gauged from figures of the daily number of trains. In 1847 twenty-two a day were already using the original Hull & Selby station on weekdays: seven each way to and from Selby, and

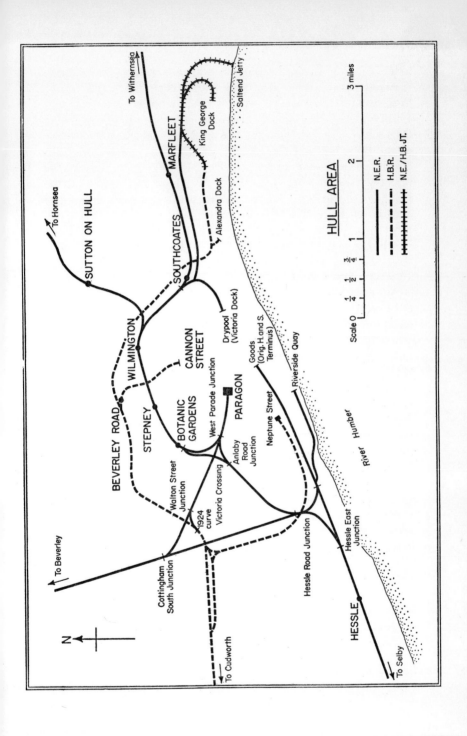

HULL AREA

Scale 0 ¼ ½ ¾ 1 2 3 miles

N.E.R.
H.B.R.
N.E./H.B. JT.

To Hornsea

SUTTON ON HULL

To Withernsea

MARFLEET

King George Dock

Salt end Jetty

SOUTHCOATES

Alexandra Dock

WILMINGTON

BEVERLEY ROAD

STEPNEY

BOTANIC GARDENS

CANNON STREET

Drypool (Victoria Dock)

West Parade Junction

PARAGON

Walton Street Junction

1924 curve

Victoria Crossing

Anlaby Road Junction

Neptune Street

Goods (Orig. H. and S. Terminus)

Riverside Quay

River Humber

Cottingham South Junction

To Beverley

To Cudworth

Hessle Road Junction

Hessle East Junction

HESSLE

To Selby

N

four each way on the Bridlington branch. By 1870, at the main
Paragon station alone the figure had grown to eighty-six trains
in and out; by 1904 to 192, and by 1931 to no less than 268.
In 1930, 579,648 passengers were booked. Since then there have
been many cuts, largely in the last ten years, including the closure
of the branches to Hornsea and Withernsea. The regular half-
hourly services to Beverley and Brough have disappeared, the
direct service to York via Market Weighton has gone, and the
Bridlington and Scarborough line is threatened with closure.

Most of Hull's growth was only made possible by railways.
First, the Hull & Selby, then the York & North Midland, the
North Eastern, the competing Hull & Barnsley, the London &
North Eastern, and now the Eastern Region of British Railways :
all have played their part.

Although the Leeds & Hull Railroad Company was formed in
1824, it was not until sixteen years later that Hull saw its first
train. In 1828 the shareholders at the Hull end of the proposed
line suddenly realized that if something was not done quickly
their trade would be abstracted by the fast-developing port of
Goole. As an immediate step it was decided to go ahead with
the Leeds to Selby section of the line (as described in Chapter
II) and to run connecting steam packets down the River Ouse,
thence along the Humber to Hull. But the Leeds & Hull became
the Leeds & Selby, and the inhabitants of Hull perceived that if
they wanted the railway to be extended from Selby to them, they
would have to do something about it.

In August 1834 they formed the Hull & Selby Railway Company, and in less than two years obtained an Act (21 June 1836)
authorizing a capital of £533,333. But although the 30¾ miles
separating the two towns were mostly level the line took four
years to construct. It was 1 July 1840 before the formal opening
took place, four trains totalling thirty-four coaches running from
Hull to Selby and back; public traffic began the following day.
The line followed the north bank of the Humber, avoiding the
Yorkshire Wolds – hills which sweep in an arc through the East
Riding. (This route already taken, the later Hull & Barnsley
Railway had no alternative but to go over and through the
Wolds at great expense and trouble.) West of the Wolds the land
is extremely flat and the line ran absolutely straight for many
miles, with no gradient steeper than 1 in 191, necessary to cross

the River Ouse at Selby. The difference in height above sea level between Hull and Selby is only 12 ft.

Hull's original station was in Manor House Street, on a site now swallowed up by the Central Goods Depot. When the line to Hull was originally planned it was intended to join up with the Manchester & Leeds Railroad, thus linking the heart of industrial Lancashire with Hull and its shipping outlets to northern Europe. Co-operation was always borne in mind, and from 1 January 1844 the traffic on the two lines was worked jointly. However, because of certain agreements entered into by the Manchester & Leeds there arose a split in the ranks of the Hull & Selby, the outcome being that the latter was leased to the York & North Midland from 1 July 1845; it was the Y&NM which fulfilled plans for a route from Hull to Bridlington described later in the chapter.

Before long Manor House Street was found inadequate and it was decided to build a station in what was becoming the new centre of Hull, away from the old town and the docks. An Act of 22 July 1847 authorized three new links to enable trains from the Selby and Bridlington directions to run into the new station. All were opened on 8 May 1848 and Manor House Street closed for passengers, although it was to reopen later for a purely suburban service.

The three earliest docks at Hull (Queen's Dock, Humber Dock and Prince's Dock – see page 48) were in the centre of the town and their freight traffic could easily be handled by the goods station remaining at Manor House Street. Subsequent expansion took place along the river frontage to the east and west. The first new dock was the Victoria, opened in 1850 and extended in 1852. The Y&NM realized that this must be served and on 30 June 1852 obtained powers for a line running in a semi-circle round the outskirts of Hull; due to the level nature of the land it was ready for opening to freight traffic on 16 May of the following year. It left the Selby–Hull line at Anlaby Road, crossed the Bridlington–Hull line on the level at Victoria Crossing and terminated at the new Victoria Dock station. Here a Mr Chaffers was appointed 'Foreman of Goods and Station Clerk of Passenger Traffic' at a wage of 24s per week.

The passenger service envisaged was solely for the convenience of the inhabitants of Hull. From 1 June 1853 trains commenced running not to Paragon Street but to the original terminus at Manor House Street where, the Minutes record, 'minor preparations must be made, such as providing a wooden box for booking passengers, laying in a siding, and the provision of a small platform'. The Minute added that stations were to be erected at Southcoates, Sculcoates and Stepney, but it would seem that passengers were also picked up where the line crossed the highway at Cemetery Gates, Anlaby Road and Hessle Road. Originally trains left the Old station every two hours from 6.0 a.m. to 6.0 p.m., and Victoria Dock on the odd hours from 7.0 a.m. to 7.0 p.m.: trains each way between 12 noon and 4.0 p.m. were for passengers only. Fares were 3d first class and 2d second class for any distance. Only one engine worked the branch but an instruction stated that if traffic necessitated the running of another 'special directions, as in the case of the Malton and Thirsk branch, will be given so as to avoid the possibility of accident'. In fact the first NER rule book, issued in October 1854, stated that the branch would be worked by a pilot guard wearing a special uniform.

This early suburban service does not appear to have been a success. Within six months it was cut from seven trains in each direction to four. Later it was altered to run to Paragon station, but even this could not save it and the passenger trains were withdrawn from 1 November 1854.

In the meantime, on 27 June 1854, the independent Hull & Holderness Railway opened from Withernsea to Hull and the Y&NM agreed to let it use Victoria Dock station for a payment of £4,000, with the working expenses divided between the two companies in proportion to the number of passengers carried by each line. As the Y & N M ceased to use the station for passengers from 1 November the Hull & Holderness had sole occupation. Running powers into Paragon Street under an 1853 Agreement do not seem to have been used. There were, therefore, two termini in use in Hull between 1854 and 1864. In the latter year the doubling of the Victoria Dock branch was completed, and with the construction of a connecting curve east of Victoria Dock station, trains from Withernsea commenced running into Paragon station from 1 June. On 28 March of the same year the Hull & Hornsea Railway was opened and for a few weeks its trains terminated at Wilmington before being extended to Paragon station from 1 July. Wilmington station remained in use until 9 June 1912, when a new station was opened further west, replacing both the original Wilmington and also Sculcoates.

In 1864, therefore, the NER railway system of Hull crystallized and it remains basically the same, over a hundred years later, with the main outlet running westwards along the banks of the wide River Humber, the Bridlington and Scarborough branch to the north, and the Hornsea and Withernsea branches (since closed) to the east. The Hessle Road Junction and Cottingham South Junction section, which was originally part of the Bridlington branch and which became redundant on the opening of Paragon station, was used until 1965 by passenger trains during the summer as it allowed through running to Bridlington, bypassing Paragon. There was for many years a station on this line at Newington, used for excursions to the giant pleasure fair held at Hull every autumn. In 1905, for instance, excursions from Bradford, Scarborough, York, Retford and Leeds all dropped their passengers at Newington and proceeded to Dairycoates for stabling. In the opposite direction trains from Nottingham, Manchester, Liverpool, Leeds, Halifax, Wakefield and Lincoln unloaded at Newington and ran on to Beverley or Driffield for stabling.

The origins of the station at Newington are unknown but it could possibly have resulted from a happening in 1896, for on 8 October the NER agreed that a special train from Buxton, conveying in a saloon a certain Mrs Jameson, might be run on the single goods line from Hessle Road Junction to Anlaby Road crossing. Mrs Jameson was an invalid – and also the wife of the owner of one of the oldest Hull timber firms who were, no doubt, good customers of the NER – and it was pointed out that if she could be detrained at the crossing it was only $\frac{1}{4}$ mile to her home. Mr Jameson was to be allowed to erect a platform with his own men and materials, under the supervision of a permanent way inspector and no charge was to be made!

OF RIVER, DOCKS AND LEVEL CROSSINGS

The muddy waters of the rivers Hull and Humber have always been the lifeblood of Kingston upon Hull but the Humber has also proved a troublesome barrier. For centuries the only direct means of reaching Lincolnshire has been by ferry: in 1845 the Great Grimsby & Sheffield Junction Railway purchased the Humber Ferries Company and, through various successors, has provided a service ever since.

Methods of crossing the Humber have been discussed for many years and today a bridge is at long last in the planning stage. However, in 1872 the Hull, South & West Junction Railway proposed to tunnel under the river to join the MS&L near Appleby and also near Brigg, both in Lincolnshire. With branches in Hull, the estimated cost was £960,000 and although supported by a petition signed by 10,000 citizens of Hull the scheme was rejected by the House of Lords, mainly on engineering grounds.

The first dock in Hull – Queen's Dock – was opened in 1778, long before the first railway arrived; Humber Dock and Prince's Dock followed in 1809 and 1829 respectively. Railway Dock, opened in 1846, was as its name implies mainly for goods carried by rail, and adjoined the original station in Manor House Street. Victoria Dock has already been mentioned and this was followed by Albert Dock (1869), William Wright Dock (1880) and St Andrew's Dock (1883). The latter (with subsequent extensions) has specialized in the handling of fish caught by the deep-water trawlers off Greenland, Iceland and Spitzbergen. Until recently much of it was rapidly sent away by braked freight trains and in the 1963–4 Working Timetable these were shown as running (Mondays to Fridays) to Plymouth, Banbury, Manchester, Normanton and King's Cross. Since then most of the traffic has changed to the roads.

All these docks came into the possession of the NER when the Hull Dock Company was taken over under an Act of 24 September 1893. (The Alexandra Dock of the Hull & Barnsley Railway, opened in 1885, remained H&B property until taken over by the NER in 1922.) The remaining dock – King George V – was a joint NER/H&B project, opened by the King in 1914. In addition there was the fine Riverside Quay opened by the NER in 1906, which suffered extensively during the bombing in World War II. Its primary use was for handling soft fruit and vegetables but a passenger station was also incorporated for those taking the joint NER/LYR service to the Continent.

Traffic to and from the larger docks on the eastern side of the

WHITBY & PICKERING RAILWAY

(9) *The old and new tunnels at Grosmont. Tunnel of 1836 for horse-drawn vehicles on left and 1847 tunnel for locos on right*

(10) *A rare photo of a NER autocar train in Beckhole station. This is the 1908 station opened for holiday traffic in summer months 1908–1914*

HULL

(11) *Engines standing at Alexandra Dock (ex HBR). Vessels in background are in dry docks*

(12) *One of Hull's infamous level crossings—now replaced by a bridge*

city had to be worked to the yards on the western side for mar-shalling and despatch and consequently there was a large amount of 'trip' working between the yards and the docks. The NER crossed every main road out of the city by one (and in some cases two) level crossings, whose gates were closed to road traffic many times a day. The H&B circled the city on an embankment and so avoided this, and after the amalgamation of 1922 it became possible to re-route NER traffic to Alexandra and King George V Docks over the high-level line. Victoria Dock still had to be supplied by the original route.

The level crossing position became more acute when in 1929 the LNE introduced a regular interval service on the four suburban routes radiating from Hull, using 'Sentinel' steam rail-cars. A train ran every half hour to Beverley and Brough and hourly to Hornsea and Withernsea. Most of the level crossings were crossed by tram tracks and the semaphore signals for the trams were controlled by the railway signalman. Operating the crossings was a skilled job calling for split-second timing. From experience the signalman knew just when to close the gates so that he could pull off the distant signal for a train as the driver sighted it; it was an experience to ride into Hull and watch the signals clearing before the train.

With the increase in road traffic in the 1950s it was decided that at long last something should be done about abolishing the worst level crossings. The crossing at Hessle Road was replaced by a road bridge and at the same time it was decided to provide an electric signal box and to alter the layout so that the H&B high-level line could be reached direct from the extensive mar-shalling yards to the west of Dairycoates. This was completed in 1962 and a start was then made on abolishing Anlaby Road crossing. Two other crossings which have disappeared were at Newington (also on Anlaby Road) and at Waterworks (Spring Bank West), brought about by the replacement of the Hessle Road–Cottingham South Junction line by an east to north curve at Victoria Crossing.

ENTER THE H&B

The Hull & Barnsley Railway was formed in an attempt to break the NER's monopoly. Various schemes for lines from Hull to the West Riding had been proposed over the years, but it was not until 1879 that definite steps were taken; at a meeting held in the NER Station Hotel, a scheme was finally hammered out for the construction of the railway, together with a dock at Hull. The title of the company thus formed was the Hull, Barnsley & West Riding Junction Railway & Dock Co. (amended to Hull & Barnsley Railway in 1905), and it received tremendous support from the Corporation and citizens of Hull.

Opposition naturally came from the NER and the Hull Dock Company, but an Act of 26 August 1880 authorized seventeen different lines, many of which were simply spurs connecting with the Midland, West Riding & Grimsby Joint, Lancashire & Yorkshire, and Manchester, Sheffield & Lincolnshire Railways in the West Riding, although there was also to be a connection with the NER at Hull – not actually built until forty-four years later. There were also powers for the dock at Hull opened on 16 July 1885. The railway was opened for freight traffic four days later and on 27 July 1885 passengers were carried for the first time, thus completing what turned out to be one of the last major independent railway projects in this country.

However, traffic did not reach the expected high level and within a very short time the company was in financial difficulties. Amalgamation with the NER or the Midland Railway was proposed but all the schemes proved abortive, raising strenuous opposition from one quarter or another. World War I brought renewed vigour, but as a prelude to the grouping of 1923, amalgamation with the NER took place on 1 April 1922.

In the Hull area, the embankment on which the H&B line encircled the city ran roughly parallel to the Victoria Dock branch of the NER. The western arm of the arc terminated at Neptune Street goods station and the eastern end at Alexandra Dock. A spur from Beverley Road Junction ran southwards to serve the passenger terminus at Cannon Street, some ½ mile short of the proposed terminus nearer the centre of the city at Charlotte Street.

In 1924 the connection between the H&B and the NER at Spring Bank was finally installed but only as an economy measure : it allowed H&B passenger trains to run into Paragon station, permitting Cannon Street to be closed. Passenger services between Hull and Cudworth continued until 1 January 1932;

from that date a local service between Hull and South Howden was provided but this succumbed on 1 August 1955. Through mineral-train workings ceased in November 1958 and finally, in April 1959, all traffic between Little Weighton and Wrangbrook Junction ceased and the line was closed. Of H & B rolling stock all that remain are a few preserved wagons and coaches: the last H&B locomotive was withdrawn in 1956. But most of the lines in the Hull area remain open, although due to the replacement of the level crossing over Hessle Road the H&B line south of that point has been lifted and the trains diverted on to the former NER line via a new connection.

OF STATIONS AND SHEDS

Thanks to the bravery of the staff in dealing with incendiary bombs, Paragon terminus was not badly damaged, and emerged in 1945 fully operational, although surrounded on almost every side by the shells of bombed and burned buildings. (One casualty was the interesting little railway collection established on the station by the City Museum, and the Transport Museum tucked away on the old High Street near the River Hull also suffered severely.)

Hull Paragon, which at one time was also referred to as Paragon Street, once had a total of fourteen platforms, of which Nos 1–9 were for normal traffic; No. 10 was a short platform, used in the 1930s largely for trains worked by 'Sentinel' steam railcars and for fish traffic; Nos 11, 12, 13 and 14 were excursion platforms. The station as it stands today dates from 1903–5 when extensive alterations and additions took place, although a recent addition is a fine new office block straddling the forecourt.

When the track and signalling layout was modified to suit the new station, the opportunity was taken to introduce the Westinghouse electro-pneumatic system in Park Street and Paragon boxes – the two signal boxes controlling the entrance to the station. This system remained in use from 3 July 1905 until replaced by colour-light signalling on 24 April 1938.

Park Street box and the staff employed therein were responsible for a head-on collision between a departing Scarborough train and one arriving from Withernsea on 14 February 1927. In their anxiety not to delay the Withernsea train the staff in the box restored a signal to danger behind the Scarborough train and then mistakenly changed a crossover in front of it so that it was diverted from an outgoing to an incoming line – on which the Withernsea train was approaching. The crew of the Scarborough train did not notice the locomotive pass over the crossover but soon afterwards the driver, Sam Atkinson, had a feeling that something was wrong and that he was out of position amongst the seven running lines. He had just verified this, shut off steam and applied the brakes when he saw the Withernsea train approaching. In the ensuing collision eight passengers were killed and four subsequently died in hospital; twenty-four suffered serious injury. Both engines – No. 96 of Class D22 (NER Class F) and 1628 of Class D17/1 (NER Class M) – were so badly damaged that they were broken up for scrap.

In conjunction with the station alterations, the engine shed on the north side of the station was demolished and replaced by a new shed at Botanic Gardens, but this has since been rebuilt as a diesel railcar depot. The main locomotive shed was at Dairycoates, which was established primarily for engines working freight trains, although on a number of turns the Hull engine worked a passenger train to Sheffield or Doncaster and returned on a freight or mineral train.

The first shed at Dairycoates appears to have been opened in 1863 after Mr Fletcher had reported 'a great want of engine shed room at Hull and that the engines suffered in consequence from exposure to the weather'. Many extensions were made, culminating in a new shed and coaling plant in 1915–16; six roundhouses and one straight shed could accommodate almost all the 150 engines at Dairycoates when the LNE took over in 1923. At this same period a further 198 engines were stationed at the other sheds in Hull: Botanic Gardens (47), Springhead (122), and Alexandra Dock (29). The two latter sheds housed ninety-one and six former Hull & Barnsley engines respectively. Dairycoates was one of the first sheds in the country to have a mechanical coaling plant and all water supplied to locomotives was specially treated by a water-softening and pumping plant at Hessle. The shed was closed in September 1970.

Springhead shed was the headquarters of the Hull & Barnsley Railway locomotive department and until 1923 carried out major repairs and overhauls to its own locomotives. Thereafter major overhauls were transferred to Darlington, but the old erecting shop continued to be used for repairs until British Railways days – although in the 1930s, when trade was slack, it was frequently used for storing surplus engines. It was sad to enter the building and find rows of once-busy engines standing cold and lifeless through no fault of their own. The shed was closed on 1 December 1958.

Another H&B shed was situated on Alexandra Dock to house the tank engines employed thereon. The ramshackle building the LNE inherited was demolished in 1928 but engines still continue to stand there, although the site has now been demoted from a Motive Power Depot to a Signing-On Point! It was once the home of the quaint 0–4–0 T engines with Kitson valve gear, for which the H&B paid £1,120 each. One of these small engines came to an unusual end after it was withdrawn by the NER: the boiler was removed and the frames, wheels, cylinders and valve gear were presented to Hull Technical College for demonstrating the principles of steam distribution.

CROSSROADS AT MARKET WEIGHTON

At the start of 1846 the East Riding was encompassed by lines completed, or well under way, but the huge rich agricultural area bounded by Hull–Bridlington–Scarborough–Malton–York–Church Fenton–Selby–Hull was still unserved. A line from Beverley to York was being surveyed by the Hull & Selby Railway when Hudson took a lease on that company in 1845, and on the agreement for the lease being drawn up the Y&NM agreed to proceed. At the time the Y&NM monopoly was being threatened by the proposed York, Hull, East & West Yorkshire Railway, and to forestall any invasion the Y&NM decided to apply also for powers to build a line from Selby to Market Weighton, as well as a branch to Hornsea and another to Victoria Dock at Hull. Both the York–Beverley and the Selby–Market Weighton schemes were authorized on 18 June 1846, by separate Acts. In the event the York–Beverley line was completed only as far as Market Weighton: it opened on 4 October 1847. The Selby–Market Weighton line followed on 1 August 1848.

The double line from York to Market Weighton, and the single line from Selby to Market Weighton, cost £380,000 and £156,000 respectively, and to the total of £536,000 had to be added £18,000 spent because 'in order to get rid of opposition in obtaining these powers, it was necessary to make agreements to purchase certain Canals, the authority for doing which was obtained in the following session. One of these Canals, the Pocklington Canal, which barely pays its working expenses, has in consequence been purchased at a cost of £18,000.' Also purchased under an Act of 1847 were the Market Weighton Canal and the Leven Canal; powers were granted for the purchase of Sir Edward Vavasour's Canal (also known as the Holme Canal) but this was not actually taken over.

Powers to divert the extension between Market Weighton and Beverley by a different route were granted on 13 July 1849, but the previous day the Committee of Investigation had presented the shareholders of the Y & N M with a discouraging report. So the powers lapsed and it was left to the N E R to plan and build the line, eventually opening it on 1 May 1865.

Twenty years later completion of part of the Scarborough Bridlington & West Riding Junction Railway between Driffield and Market Weighton placed Market Weighton at the intersection of the Bridlington–Selby and Hull–York services. The S B & W R J evolved from the Scarborough & East Riding Railway, which planned a line from the Hull & Barnsley Railway (then incomplete) near Howden to Scarborough. This scheme faltered through lack of support and opposition by the N E R. Instead the company, under its new title, applied for powers for two lines – 16½ miles from Cayton to Nafferton, and 13¼ miles from Driffield to Market Weighton. Both ends of each line were to connect with the N E R. Powers were granted on 6 August 1885 but only the latter was built.

Freight services commenced on 18 April 1890 and passenger services on 1 May 1890, both worked by the N E R, which took full control in 1913. The line was double throughout and in view of the increased traffic expected the N E R agreed to double its Selby–Market Weighton line: this was completed on 1 July 1890, just in time for the summer traffic from the West Riding to Bridlington, Filey and Scarborough.

In 1893 the S B & W R J again attempted to obtain its own line south of Market Weighton but its plans for a line to join the Hull & Barnsley at Newport and the North Eastern at Staddlethorpe were rejected by Parliament.

The route to Market Weighton and York left the Bridlington branch at Beverley North Junction, half a mile north of the station. Market Weighton station was one of the first to have the handsome Y&NM overall roof removed (*c.* 1948): the original engine shed still stands outside the north wall of the station although no engine has been shedded there since 1917.

The lines to Selby and York diverged immediately west of the station. The first station on the York line was Londesborough, closed in 1964, which was renamed from Shipton (Y&NM) in 1867. Londesborough Park, nearby, was the home of George Hudson when he was at the height of his fame, and from his private station half a mile north-east of the public station he constructed a tree-lined drive over the two miles to the house. The drive can still be seen. Pocklington, with its famous school, was the busiest station (still covered by an overall roof) on this section, which was chosen by the North Eastern Region for an experimental installation of Central Traffic Control (CTC), but later it was decided to seek closure instead. It is interesting to note that 115 years previously – at a Y&NM half-yearly meeting held on 6 September 1849 – a shareholder remarked that York–Market Weighton was 'a beautifully made line but, unfortunately, without passengers to travel on it'. The line between Beverley and York, through Market Weighton, was closed to all traffic on 29 November 1965 and has since been lifted.

A number of stations in this area once carried the suffix 'Gate' in their names; the 'Gate' indicated that the trains stopped where the railway crossed the road, possibly before there was an actual station on the site.

THE COASTAL BRANCHES

Until recently there were three routes from Hull to the coast – to Bridlington, Filey and Scarborough, to Withernsea, and to Hornsea. The Bridlington branch was originally a Hull & Selby venture, although the Act was obtained only the day prior to the take-over by the Y&NM – 30 June 1845. The Y&NM had obtained an Act on the same day for a line southwards to Bridlington from its York–Scarborough branch at Seamer. Since completion of the various sections, the line has been regarded as the Hull & Scarborough branch.

When opened on 6 October 1846, the Bridlington branch left the Hull & Selby line at Dairycoates and turned northwards towards Cottingham, but eighteen months later the southern half of this section was closed to regular passenger traffic and trains diverted to Paragon station. The original route remained in use for goods, and eventually it provided a useful link for West Riding to Bridlington trains not needing to call at Paragon station, where a reversal would have been necessary. Its popularity declined after the opening of the SB&WRJ line between Market Weighton and Driffield, which provided a more direct route, but in the 1960s the Selby-Driffield line fell into disfavour and the excursions and Saturday Only trains reverted to the Hull line. This led to the closure of the Selby to Driffield route on 2 August 1965. At Hull the trains from the West Riding to Bridlington now use the Cricket Ground curve opened on 24 May 1965.

Beverley, an old market town with a Minster dating from the thirteenth century, still provides some residential traffic to and from Hull, and in addition to the Scarborough trains, which all stop, a reduced local service to Hull is provided by diesel railcars. As already mentioned, the York line diverged half a mile north of the station which, incidentally, retains its overall roof. Arram, the first station towards Bridlington, was to have been the starting point of a stillborn branch to Hornsea for which the Y&NM obtained powers in 1846. Driffield, the next important station on the branch, has lost its overall roof and now looks cold and bare. As well as being junction for Market Weighton, from 1853 until 1950 it was the terminus for passenger traffic of the little Malton & Driffield Railway, an independently built line which climbed the north-western side of the Wolds with gradients between 1 in 64 and 1 in 104, before passing through the almost mile-long Burdale tunnel; its 1846 Act also included powers for a branch from Driffield to Frodingham Bridge but this was not constructed.

The opening date was 19 May 1853, the same as that for the line from Pilmoor to Malton, but because the local population was sparse passenger traffic never was heavy, although the service was a blessing to those who farmed on the Wolds. Until the advent of the motor car the railway was their only means of reaching the markets at Malton and Driffield, and this was particularly true during the winter months when the hilly roads became blocked with snowdrifts many feet deep. Almost invariably the trains managed to keep running, albeit sometimes with great difficulty, and even after the line had closed to normal passenger traffic in 1950 it was occasionally used to provide transport for stranded villagers. The freight service was withdrawn in October 1958 and since then the track has been dismantled. At one time it carried a large amount of stone from the gigantic quarries at Burdale and Wharram, and in 1925 Wharram traffic alone amounted to 104,808 tons of chalk in 7,885 wagons, whilst the normal station freight traffic amounted to 2,447 tons despatched in 424 wagons. Now, forty years later, Wharram station remains, but without any track, trains or traffic.

Returning to the Bridlington–Scarborough line, the extensive carriage sidings at the approach to Bridlington gave a clue to the resort's dependence on catering for holidaymakers. At the peak of popularity of day excursions Bridlington station handled between twenty and thirty trains, some of which terminated there whilst others went on to Scarborough. The carriage sidings became so full that some coaches had to be stabled at adjacent wayside stations, and the small three-road engine shed and yard were packed to capacity with strangers from GNR, GCR, MR, and L&Y sheds. Summer Saturdays were also busy times, with trains to and from all parts of Lancashire and Yorkshire for the holidaymakers who were staying by the sea for a week or a fortnight.

Bridlington station is a hotch-potch of different styles of design, ranging from Y&NM of 1846 to BR of 1961. The original station comprised up and down platforms under the usual Y&NM overall roof (removed 1961), but successive additions and alterations have changed the up platform into an additional down platform, and new up platforms have been added on the east side of the station: there are also two bay platforms for excursion traffic. The goods yard is reached across one of the approach roads, necessitating a flagman when a train is shunting in the yard as there are no gates. One of the sidings in the goods yard is a remnant of the branch to Bridlington harbour. This ran behind the houses in Windsor Crescent and although opened in 1851 it was derelict by 1866, albeit the rails were not lifted until 1917. The land was sold in 1925, but it is still easy to trace the line's course.

Leaving Bridlington the Scarborough line climbs at 1 in 92 for five miles, and before Flamborough is reached passengers get a fine view of Flamborough Head and Bridlington Bay : unfortunately views over the sea from trains are not very common in the North East. From the summit a mile south of Speeton the line drops almost all the way to Filey and it was on this stretch that an empty coaching-stock train ran out of control in 1956. The crew had been in a hurry to get away from Bridlington and in their haste the fireman's failure to couple up the vacuum brake pipe between engine and train was not noticed by either the driver or the guard. When the driver came to apply the brakes to take the turn ino Filey Holiday Camp station he found that they had little effect and he was unable to get the train under control before it hit the buffer stops. The engine, Class K3 2–6–0 No. 61846, came to rest standing on the station platform : the crew jumped from the footplate just before the engine struck the buffers and were unhurt.

Opened in 1947 to serve the Butlin's camp, Filey Holiday Camp station is approached by double-track connections from both the Hull and Scarborough directions. There is a small modern signal box at each corner of the triangle and these, together with the station itself, have to be manned by relief staff each Saturday the station is open. Filey itself handled substantial holiday traffic and still retains most of its original roof. The two remaining stations on the branch, Gristhorpe (closed 1959) and Cayton (closed 1952), call for little comment except for the fact that for many years the latter had a female stationmaster.

The Seamer–Filey section was opened on 5 October 1846, the day prior to the opening of the Bridlington–Hull line; the intervening section between Filey and Bridlington was not opened until 20 October 1847 due to the extensive earthworks necessary between Speeton and Hunmanby.

The Hull & Holderness Railway, formed to build a branch to Withernsea, was one of the few truly independent lines in the North East. It had its own locomotives and coaches, whereas most of the so-called independent lines persuaded the NER to work their trains for them, on various terms. The Act was obtained on 8 July 1853 and when the line was opened to the public on 28 June 1854 the Hull & Holderness trains shared the Y & N M Victoria station; however the Y & N M trains were those on the unproductive service round the city to Manor House Street, and after these were withdrawn in November 1854 the H&H had the station to itself for the next ten years, although from 1 January 1860 the line was worked by the NER. Parliamentary authority for amalgamation was given on 7 July 1862.

On 30 January 1863 it was decided to run the trains into Paragon station via a curve authorized by the NER (Beverley Branch) Act of 1862 : this connection had been authorized by the original H&H Act but the powers had been allowed to lapse. Although running into Paragon station was planned to start on 1 July 1863 the Board of Trade refused to sanction the curve 'as the signals are incomplete. Three sets of Saxby Patent Junction signals to be obtained.' It was mid-1864 before through running commenced. The branch was single track throughout when opened, but it was all doubled in the early years of this century except for the sections between Hedon and Rye Hill, and Ottringham and Winestead. The latter station was closed to passengers on 1 July 1904 but remained open as a freight siding until 1956. Other closed stations on the branch include Hedon Racecourse, of which traces have long since disappeared, and Hedon Speedway Halt, opened as recently as 1948 but now derelict.

It was hoped that the post-war introduction of diesel railcars would enable the branch to remain open, but in spite of the use of conductor-guards and the withdrawal of staff at intermediate stations the service still showed a loss and passenger services were withdrawn on 19 October 1964.

The Hull & Hornsea also commenced life as an independent company but its line was worked by the NER from the outset and its independence was short-lived. An Act was obtained on 30 June 1862 and the line was ready for opening on 28 March 1864 : it was easy to build, the difference in height at Hull and at Hornsea amounting to only 16 ft, although at one point the line did climb to the dizzy height of 66 ft above sea level !

The Hull & Hornsea was formally taken over by the NER under an Act of 16 July 1866, but prior to that date the trains had commenced running through to Paragon station. Originally they had terminated at Wilmington station, built in the 'V' of the junction at the point where the Hornsea branch left the Victoria Dock branch of the NER. It was planned to extend them to Paragon from 1 June 1864 and, in fact, W. W. Tomlinson quotes that date, but the Board of Trade refused to sanction the use of the junction at Wilmington for passenger traffic until 15 June and the through working commenced on 1 July.

In 1910–12 the whole layout at Wilmington was rearranged in order to dispense with a level crossing. This involved a new swing bridge over the River Hull, and the closure of Sculcoates and the original Wilmington stations. In their place a new Wilmington was opened midway between the two.

Two other stations on the Hornsea branch call for special mention: Wassand (Goxhill until 1904) was one of the last remaining Market Day Only stations in the North East: from its opening in 1865 to its closure in 1953 it was open only one day a week, and then for but one train in each direction. Nearer Hull there were three stations in a mile and a half – Skirlaugh, Ellerby and Burton Constable: as an economy measure Ellerby was closed in 1902 but twenty years later it was decided to change the name of Burton Constable to Ellerby in order to avoid confusion with Constable Burton on the Wensleydale branch.

In 1960 similar economy measures to those on the Withernsea branch were introduced, with guards issuing tickets to passengers joining at intermediate stations; this failed to save the line and it was closed to passenger traffic at the same time as the Withernsea branch, 19 October 1964.

The Hornsea branch was double throughout and at one time both branches carried a steady flow of residential traffic all the year round. In summer a spell of fine weather, particularly at a weekend, made the thoughts of the citizens of Hull turn to the seaside, and Hornsea and Withernsea, being the nearest resorts, were very popular. To cater for this extra trains were run, often at very short notice, frequently packed to capacity and worked by any suitable engine available – passenger or goods.

LIGHT RAILWAYS AND BUSES

The Light Railway Act of 1896 gave a chance to supply railway travel to parts of the country where the traffic potential was not large enough to support a full-sized line with all its intricate rules, regulations and block system equipment. In 1898 the NER was interested in a number of such schemes, and the three to be mentioned here were the Flamborough & Bridlington, the Bridlington & North Frodingham and the North Holderness Light Railways, none of which was actually built. The Flamborough & Bridlington scheme just faded away but something – though not a railway – did materialize from the other two schemes.

The Bridlington & North Frodingham was planned to be of 4 ft 8½ in. gauge, leaving the Bridlington to Hull line at Carnaby and running for 9¾ miles to North Frodingham, where a joint station with the North Holderness Light Railway was authorized. The North Holderness line was also to be standard gauge and was planned to run from North Frodingham, via Brandesburton, Leven and Tickton, to Beverley – a distance of 12½ miles – terminating on the east side of the NER station.

The NER appears to have been fully prepared to go ahead and on 31 July 1902 the Traffic Committee inspected plans. Six months later, however, the same Committee passed a resolution stating that the scheme was to be deferred 'pending the establishment of a Motor Car service'. On 2 April 1903 the Committee decided to accept the offer made by Stirlings Motor Carriages Ltd to supply by 15 June 1903 three motor omnibuses for the Beverley–North Frodingham service at £898 each, and according to the *Hull Daily Mail* the first two vehicles reached Beverley from Edinburgh on 31 August 1903 – some eleven weeks behind schedule. They were of 24 h.p., painted red and white, and accommodated fourteen passengers and light luggage.

Because of the delay in delivery of the buses the NER became the second railway company to introduce them: it was beaten by a short head by the Great Western Railway which introduced its Helston to The Lizard service on 17 August 1903. The NER was not able to start until 7 September 1903. Instead of being extended to Bridlington to cover the route authorized by the Bridlington & North Frodingham LRO, the service was extended to Driffield and, again quoting the *Hull Daily Mail* (2 December 1903),

At a steady gait the NER Company's motorbus swept down the incline and round the corner at the River Head, and so completed her first journey inaugurating the service between

Beverley and Driffield via Brandesburton and other villages. She was half an hour behind time but several false starts had kept the three or four score folks on the tiptoe of expectation. The delay was due to bad roads, the snow, frozen hard and lumpy, making a poor running track. Five passengers dismounted – three farm servants, a woman and a child, and a porter jumped on the top of the car to hand down the solitary piece of luggage. It was a heavy package and he called for assistance, but it was then discovered that its contents were motor spirit – the fuel which makes the engine go – and they relinquished their task amid laughter.

Mr E. L. Davis, chief passenger agent of the NER, told the Departmental Committee on Motorcars in June 1904 that 'although these vehicles – which have been running since September – have been much used by the public, he was not prepared to affirm that they answered commercially, for they had broken down a good deal owing to the bad roads, and the public had lost a lot of confidence in the service'. The NER timetable for the summer of 1906 showed only four buses from Beverley to Brandesburton – at 10.30 a.m. (extended to Driffield on Thursdays only), 1.45 p.m., 4.35 p.m. (Saturdays only when required), and 6.0 p.m. (extended to Beeford). In the opposite direction the first 'up' service started from Beeford at 7.55 a.m., 11.45 a.m. ex-Brandesburton (Saturdays only when required), 11.52 a.m. ex-Brandesburton (Thursdays excepted), 4.25 p.m. ex-Brandesburton, 5.35 p.m. ex-Brandesburton (Saturdays only when required), and 5.10 p.m. Driffield–Beverley (Thursdays only, arr. 7.54 p.m.). The service continued to be run by the NER, but after the formation of the LNE it was taken over by the Newington Motor & Engineering Company and eventually passed to the East Yorkshire Motor Services.

Although the full story has not been uncovered it seems that the NER had second thoughts about constructing a light railway – probably because of the troubles experienced with the motor buses – for in 1919 a diagram for a proposed 2 ft 0 in. gauge tank locomotive was prepared at Darlington works. An approach was also made to the late Henry Greenly, and he submitted designs for a type of locomotive suitable for working the line.

What is believed to have been one of the last buses used on the Brandesburton service – a 36–40 h.p. Leyland with registration number DN 6058 – was for a number of years employed by the district engineer at Hull for carrying men and materials. It was scrapped about 1933. Finally, mention must be made of the motor tours introduced at Bridlington in 1905 : these ran in the summer only and they were operated by Durkopp, Saurer and Fiat char-à-bancs.

A light railway in the East Riding which did reach fruition was the Derwent Valley, planned to serve the rich agricultural area to the south-east of York and for most of its length built parallel to the River Derwent but about one to two miles west of it. The DVL terminus at York (Layerthorpe) is reached via the NER Foss Islands branch, and at the other end of the line the Derwent Valley station was adjacent to Cliff Common station on the Selby – Market Weighton line. The line was financed by local landowners and opened to the public on 21 July 1913.

Traffic was originally worked by locomotives hired from the NER but after World War I, in an attempt to cut expenses, the company purchased two Ford buses mounted on rail wheels for the passenger traffic and a 'Sentinel' steam locomotive for the goods. The passenger service was withdrawn on 1 September 1926 and the two buses were sold to the County Donegal Committee, where the bodies were lowered to allow access from ground level and the gauge altered to 3 ft 0 in. There they continued to work until they were scrapped in 1934. The 'Sentinel' locomotive was also sold shortly afterwards to a private company in Darlington. Since then the company continued to hire locomotive power, first from the North Eastern Area of the LNE and later from the North Eastern Region of BR, until in 1969 it was decided to purchase two surplus 204 h.p. diesel shunters from British Rail. These were formerly BR 2245 and 2298.

The line was not nationalized in 1948 and it continues to run and make a profit from its agricultural, timber and oil traffic. It was also of strategic value during World War II when, so it is said, its grass-grown track made it difficult to locate from the air and consequently it was extremely valuable for storage purposes. In January 1965 the six miles of route between Wheldrake and Cliff Common were closed, together with the intermediate stations of Cottingwith, Thorganby, Skipwith & North Duffield, and the DVL station at Cliff Common, all of which had remained open for goods after the passenger trains were withdrawn in 1926. The line has since been cut back to Dunnington, leaving open for traffic a route mileage of only 4¼ miles!

Industrial railway systems with their own locomotives are few and far between in the East Riding, being mostly confined to the Hull area. However, an interesting line was that which ran from Howden (NE) station to the airship sheds about a mile away. The massive hangars were built during World War I and after being used for building the airship R100 they were demolished in the 1930s. Supplies were conveyed over a private branch laid for some distance on the roadside grass verge. It appears that locomotives were used on the branch, although at one time the motive power was one horse!

Hull has suffered more severely than any other North Eastern centre. Three of its rail outlets have gone – those to Hornsea, Withernsea, and York (via Beverley) but Hull still retains excellent outlets to Doncaster and Leeds, and a tenuous link with Bridlington and Scarborough. It is in Hull itself where the greatest changes are to be seen. The old docks in the centre and to the west of the city are too small to handle large ships and traffic is being concentrated on the western docks – the Alexandra and the King George. This has caused many of the sidings and yards to become redundant, and the concentration of cross-city freight traffic on the former Hull & Barnsley line has deprived the citizens of Hull of one of their favourite grumbles – the delay at the level crossings!

The decline in facilities has led to the downgrading of the city as far as rail services are concerned. For long Hull has been the headquarters of a District, with its own echelon of officers and staff, but it is now an outstation of alien Doncaster of Great North persuasion!

Perhaps the greatest changes have taken place in the field of motive power. At the Grouping of 1923 the NER had 348 steam locomotives stationed at Hull (16 per cent of its stock) whereas the traffic is now handled by about twenty-four diesel shunters and a fleet of railcars.

SCARBOROUGH TO SALTBURN AND MIDDLESBROUGH

(13) *Ravenscar, prior to construction of passing loop and additional platform (now demolished)*

(14) *Middlesbrough–Scarborough train on Newholm Beck viaduct (now demolished). Sandsend in distance*

VIADUCTS—I

(15) *Belah viaduct—between Barras and Kirkby Stephen. Now demolished*

(16) *Durham viaduct*

CHAPTER IV

The North Riding of Yorkshire

THE WHITBY & PICKERING RAILWAY

High on the bleak Yorkshire Moors stands the functional Ballistic Missile Early Warning Station at Fylingdales – surely a sign of the times in which we live. Less than a mile away runs the preserved railway from Whitby to Pickering, an outmoded form of transport to many people but one which continued to serve the inhabitants of this sparsely-populated area for more than a century and a quarter. Except for the incursion of the Stockton & Darlington Railway at the northern extremity of the county, this was the first passenger-carrying railway in the North Riding of Yorkshire, although for its first eleven years it was worked by horses and not by locomotives. The line has long been a favourite subject for railway historians, largely no doubt because of the original method of working traffic up and down the well-known incline between Beck Hole and Goathland. As long ago as 1836 – the year the line was opened – the *Scenery of the Whitby and Pickering Railway* was published, with its charming engravings, and G. W. J. Potter's *A History of the Whitby and Pickering Railway* was a worthy successor seventy years later.

At the turn of the eighteenth century Whitby was a prosperous seaport. The inhabitants contributed 7 per cent of the capital required for the pioneer Stockton & Darlington Railway and it is only natural that on the success of that line thoughts should have turned to a railway to serve their own town. Prolonged discussion took place regarding the direction the line should take: should it go north-westwards to join the Stockton & Darlington near Yarm, or south-westwards to serve the country market towns of Pickering and Malton? At that time the second scheme had no prospects of joining up with any other railway.

Early in 1832, after six years of wrangling, it was decided to call upon George Stephenson for his opinion, given in a report dated 5 July 1832. The great George favoured a line from Whitby to Pickering and his advice was so quickly acted upon that an Act was given the Royal Assent on 6 May 1833. The line was opened from Whitby to Grosmont in June 1835, and throughout to Pickering on 26 May 1836. Incidentally, an odd feature of the Act was that Section 114 empowered the company to use locomotives, whereas Section 134 expressly forbade the use of such machines.

Whitby is situated at the mouth of the River Esk, which hereabouts flows along a valley some 120 ft deep, and finding a suitable route for the railway was difficult. However, the problem was overcome by building the line along the floor of the valley, first on one bank of the river and then the other, until Grosmont was reached. Here, by means of a short tunnel, the track could get out of the Esk Valley and set course for the south, although within the next four miles it had to climb some 350 ft to reach the plateau at Goathland. As no course for a gradual ascent could be found, recourse had to be taken to a rope-worked incline.

The incline, just short of a mile in length, climbed at an average gradient of 1 in 15 and the time taken by an ascending coach was between four and five minutes.

This is how the railway's treasurer, Thomas Clark, described the first train to go up:

> On the signal being given three carriages loaded with passengers glided up the steep ascent with a pleasing, rapid, and easy pace; and both on going and returning many were heard to declare that the ascending and descending of the incline so far from being in any way disagreeable, was certainly as pleasant as any other part of the day's journey. The other carriages followed in succession, and the band during the time played several enlivening airs.

The coaches were drawn up at the end of a rope, which passed round a horizontal pulley at the summit. To the other end of the rope was attached a large water tank on wheels which, in its descent, hauled up the coaches. At the foot of the incline the water was allowed to drain out of the tank and the next set of descending coaches hauled the empty tank back to the summit. This method was later superseded by a stationary steam-worked winding engine. In July 1861 powers were obtained to build a new line, with a more gradual ascent which could be surmounted by steam locomotives. However, before this was opened, on 1 July 1865, a number of accidents occurred on the incline, culminating in one which killed two passengers and injured thirteen when the rope broke and the carriages rushed down out of control.

Although through working from Whitby to Pickering by locomotives did not commence until the deviation was ready, they had worked traffic between Whitby and the foot of the incline, and between Pickering and the top of the incline, since 1847. The replacement of the original horses was due to the takeover of the Whitby & Pickering Railway by the York & North Midland Railway from 30 June 1845. This preceded by eight days the opening of the Y&NM line from York to Scarborough, with a branch from Rillington to Pickering. To allow locomotives to work between the foot of the incline and Whitby the short tunnel at Grosmont had to be replaced by one of larger diameter, constructed alongside. The original tunnel is still there, with a footpath to some cottages passing through it. At Goathland the incline too is used as a footpath.

A few years after the track on the incline had been dismantled it was relaid by the NER at the expense of Messrs Manning Wardle, the Leeds firm of locomotive builders, who in 1872 wished to try out some locomotives designed for a steeply-graded Fell-worked line between Caxoeira and Nova Friburgo in Brazil.

The line at the foot of the incline remained in place even after the incline was abandoned, and in 1908 it was decided to reopen it to passenger traffic from Whitby. A service for holidaymakers ran during July, August and September of each year until 1914, when it was cut short late in September because of the outbreak of World War I, never to reopen. A fortnightly freight service was provided along part of it to serve some isolated cottages, and this was not discontinued until 1951, when a road was made to the hamlet of Esk Valley.

Before leaving the area mention must be made of the ironworks which were built at Beck Hole and Grosmont: the former began production in June 1860, but due to a number of misfortunes the blast furnaces closed down in less than eighteen months. The first mishap was when one of the two furnaces cracked and allowed the molten iron to pour out; the final blow was the collapse of the roof of the mine which yielded the iron ore. Despite the efforts of 180 employees to rescue the company, the whole concern was put up for auction in September 1861. At the same time more successful ironworks were under construction at Grosmont; these are believed to have opened in 1863 and lasted until 1891. Iron ore for the blast furnaces was won from the hillsides in the vicinity of the works and the area was also a large supplier of stone, most of which was transported to Whitby by rail and then forwarded by sea to its destination.

After taking over the Whitby & Pickering Railway in 1845 George Hudson (in the form of the Y&NM) decided that one way to obtain more passengers was to develop Whitby both for residential and holiday purposes. He formed the Whitby Building Company with the object of developing the area known as West Cliff, but the scheme did not prosper and when Hudson fell from grace work was stopped. The assets eventually passed to the NER, which in 1857 advertised for sale the Royal Hotel and 400 acres of building land. The response was slow and it took many years to dispose of all the land.

Considering its size Whitby was well served with railways: from 1885 it had four outlets – to Malton, Stockton, Saltburn (later Middlesbrough) and Scarborough – and it was obvious that eventually economies would have to be made. First to go was the coast route to Loftus in 1958 but the greatest blow came in 1965 : on 8 March the main outlet was closed when Whitby–Malton trains were withdrawn together with those from Scarborough, leaving only the Whitby–Grosmont section of the Whitby & Pickering line in use by trains to Middlesbrough via Battersby.

NORTHWARDS FROM WHITBY

The Whitby, Redcar & Middlesbrough Union Railway was formed in 1866 but it ran into financial difficulties and finally had to ask the NER to complete its line. The NER agreed to this in 1875, but found that the work done was of poor quality, and that a portion of the route along the cliffs between Sandsend and

Kettleness had actually fallen into the sea. A new route was surveyed between these two stations when the NER took over and this involved the construction of two tunnels to bypass the original course along the cliff edge. However, between the northern portal of Sandsend tunnel (1652 yd) and the southern end of Kettleness tunnel (308 yd) the line was allowed to remain on a sheltered shelf on the cliffs. Fortunately scenes of the line under construction at this point were photographed by the indefatigable Frank Sutcliffe of Whitby, whose photographs once warranted a programme of their own on television!

The five picturesque viaducts on the line were all of similar construction with tubular metal columns, as mentioned in T. E. Harrison's report quoted in Chapter I, but these have all been demolished since the line was closed in 1958. The largest of the viaducts was, of course, that at Staithes, well-known because of the wind-gauge affixed to it. In latter years, at least, the bell signal to stop traffic was heard ringing when no wind was blowing and, conversely, when a howling gale tore in from the North Sea the bell remained silent. It is said that on one wild and stormy night the driver of a train proceeding south rang up Staithes from Grinkle, the station north of the bridge. He asked if the bell was ringing and when told it was not he said, 'It b— well should be.' As he did not fancy loitering on the viaduct in the full fury of the gale he travelled across so fast that he was unable to stop the train in the station and had to set back into the platform.

Reconstruction was due for completion by July 1881 but took until December 1883. However, proof that it was being pushed on with all speed comes from, of all places, Trinity House. It appears that after dark large bonfires were lit along the line so that the men had sufficient light to continue working. Unfortunately the fires on the cliffs between Sandsend and Kettleness were taken for the lights of Whitby by the Master of the brigantine *Colina* who, when turning (as he thought) into the River Esk, found himself ashore. Correspondence followed between Trinity House and the N E R, which finally agreed to request the contractors to screen all lights on the cliffs.

The navvies on the contract must have been fond of game for their suppers, as the Easington Estate Company (Grinkle

station was known as Easington until April 1904) was authorized
to provide a gamekeeper to keep them in check. His wages were to
be paid by the railway and when the NER took over the Estate
Company had to resort to solicitor's letters to press the account.

At Loftus (Lofthouse until November 1874) the WR&MU made
an end-on junction with what started life as the Cleveland Railway, built to serve the rich ironstone field in the Cleveland Hills
and transport the ore across the River Tees to Messrs Bell's ironworks at Port Clarence. Although most of the ironstone mines
were to the north-west of Loftus, there were one or two to the
south, of which the most interesting was that at Grinkle Park.
The mine was set in a deep secluded valley and for many years
the ore was carried to the harbour at Port Mulgrave (seven miles
up the coast from Whitby) by a 3 ft gauge line almost three miles
long, having one tunnel ¼ mile long and another one mile long.
The latter had originally been a drift mine driven in from the
cliffs. Wagons of ore from the mine emerged from the cliffs some
50 or 60 ft above the sea shore and ran out over the stone piers
of the harbour on wooden gantries, tipping the ore directly into
the holds of the small vessels which took it to Palmer's works at
Jarrow. In 1921 the harbour line was abandoned and an incline
built up to the NER north of Staithes, but now both the incline
and the NER line have been dismantled, although there are still
plenty of traces.

Immediately north of Loftus the railway crosses a deep ravine
through which flows Kilton Beck. The track is now carried on
an embankment but in this embankment is buried Kilton
Viaduct – a structure with stone piers and wrought iron girders,
226 yd long and 150 ft high. The foundations of the viaduct
were gradually undermined by ironstone workings and in 1911
passenger traffic had to be stopped. It was decided to convert the
viaduct into an embankment by burying it in refuse from the
numerous local mines. Altogether some 720,000 tons of spoil
were required and the task was completed in 1913. While trains
were barred from the viaduct passengers were conveyed between
Loftus and Skinningrove stations by motor char-à-banc, and the
ironstone from Liverton Mines (at the south end of the viaduct)
had to be carried to Middlesbrough by way of Whitby and
Battersby.

From the northern side of the valley a line descended almost to sea level by means of a zig-zag course, with two reversing necks; this was built to serve the Loftus mines and, later, Skinningrove gasworks. The gradient was as steep as 1 in 29 in one section but the number of runaways was not great. Perhaps the most tragic happened in 1880, when former SDR 0–6–0 1220 ran out of control while descending with fourteen loaded and eight empty wagons. On the footplate at the time, in addition to the driver and fireman, were a youth who had brought the driver's tea, and a locomotive inspector with his son and a friend. After colliding with the buffers at the end of one of the reversing necks the engine ran tender-first up the bank and came to rest with the tender tilted up : the son of the locomotive inspector was trapped by the tender and before he could be freed he was scalded to death by steam from a broken gauge-glass. The zig-zag lasted until 1958, when it was closed simultaneously with the withdrawal of passenger trains beyond Loftus.

Dominating the valley on its northern escarpment are the large Skinningrove steelworks, with their pall of smoke. It is traffic to and from these works which keeps open the line to the north, but whereas the distance from the works to Brotton by road is $1\frac{1}{2}$ miles the distance by rail is $3\frac{1}{2}$ miles. This is because the line was built round Warsett Hill, right on the cliff edge, to serve more ironstone mines, all of which are now closed. From Brotton two routes were available to Middlesbrough – the old Cleveland Railway to Guisborough, where the Middlesbrough & Guisborough line was joined for the remaining distance to Middlesbrough, or the Saltburn Extension through North Skelton, which joins up with the Saltburn to Middlesbrough line about $\frac{1}{4}$ mile outside Saltburn station. The former route is now closed and all traffic to and from Skinningrove is worked over the latter.

Until 1933 passenger traffic along the coast was worked between Saltburn and Scarborough, but for the summer of that year the working was changed to Middlesbrough–Guisborough–Scarborough and this was continued until closure to through traffic on 5 May 1958. An unusual feature of this fifty-eight mile route was that for some trains five reversals were necessary – at Guisborough (twice), Whitby (twice) and Scarborough. When the Middlesbrough & Guisborough line was connected to the

Cleveland Railway at Guisborough in 1862, the station was left a terminus at the end of a short spur. All stopping trains had to run into the dead-end station and, when station work was completed, the engine propelled them back to the junction, where after reversing again they set off for Whitby. This operation continued when diesel railcars took over between Middlesbrough and Loftus in May 1958, but ceased when passenger services beyond Guisborough were withdrawn on 2 May 1960. Similarly at Whitby, trains first called at West Cliff before descending the 1 in 54 to the Town station: when station duties were finished the engine propelled back up the 1 in 54 as far as Prospect Hill Junction and, after reversing, once again set off for Scarborough. At 'the Queen of Watering places' trains had to reverse yet again to enter the station.

Whitby West Cliff station closed on 12 June 1961 and thenceforward trains to and from Scarborough reversed at Prospect Hill Junction. With the withdrawal of services between Scarborough and Whitby on 8 March 1965 this too ceased, leaving Whitby with only one outlet out of the four it once enjoyed.

UP THE ESK VALLEY

Between Battersby and Grosmont the present-day trains use a route which started off from Picton (between Northallerton and Eaglescliffe) as the North Yorkshire & Cleveland Railway, although it was taken over by the NER in 1859 before being completed throughout.

The lower section between Castleton and Grosmont was originally conceived as the Castleton branch of the Y&NM and authorized in 1846 but, owing to the downfall of George Hudson, it was not opened until 2 October 1865. On this section is situated the picturesque village of Glaisdale; today a visitor would hardly believe that at one time this was the site of an ironworks with three blast furnaces. Here again the industry had a short life, lasting only from 1866 to 1876. The slag heaps remained untouched for many years, but since about 1918 every scrap has been removed, mainly for making roads. To supply the furnaces a drift mine was opened out on the moors high above the village, and the ironstone was carried to the works on a steeply-graded rope-worked narrow-gauge railway which passed under much of the village in a tunnel, emerging on the south bank of the River Esk and crossing it on a wooden viaduct.

Further supplies of ironstone were to have been obtained from the Brotton area by means of the Cleveland Extension Mineral Railway, 10¼ miles long across bleak Lealholm Moor. Much work was done on its construction but before it was completed the ironworks closed down and work was abandoned. The earthworks remaining are still known locally as 'Paddy Waddell's line' after the contractor who was employed.

Until the section between Battersby and Picton was closed to passenger traffic on 14 June 1954, the majority of trains along the Esk valley ran between Whitby and Stockton, with an odd train reversing at Battersby to reach Middlesbrough. After the closure of the western end of the branch *all* trains had to reverse at Battersby and this ready-made route was available for Scarborough–Whitby–Middlesbrough services when the coast line was closed between West Cliff and Loftus on 5 May 1958. From that date all passenger services in the area were taken over by diesel railcars and thus the time taken in reversing at Battersby, Prospect Hill (at West Cliff until June 1961), Whitby Town, and outside Scarborough station could be kept to a minimum.

The section between Picton and Stokesley was closed completely and between Trenholme Bar and Stokesley the track was lifted: a freight service was provided between Battersby and Stokesley until 2 August 1965.

On 23 July 1930 a bridge between Glaisdale and Egton was washed away by the River Esk, swollen by heavy rain, and through traffic was suspended until May 1931, when a new bridge was opened. Only three and a half months later this suffered the same fate and the line was closed for another twelve months until a third could be built.

An interesting branch serving ironstone mines and long since closed was that to Swainby (or Whorlton), opened in March 1857 with the first portion of the NY&C line between Picton and Stokesley. The branch ran southwards for two miles from Potto and soon carried ore for the furnaces at Stockton. The rails were removed in 1904 after the branch had lain derelict for about fifteen years, but at least one set of level-crossing gates remained in place until the 1960s, although they would probably have dropped to bits if anyone had tried to move them!

RISE AND FALL OF ROSEDALE IRONSTONE

The second portion of the North Yorkshire & Cleveland Railway, from Stokesley to Ingleby, was opened on 1 February 1858 and on 6 April 1858 a further 2½ miles were added when the section to Kildale was completed. The Ingleby Mining Company then laid a private branch from its mines near Ingleby Greenhow to join the NY&C at Ingleby Junction, ¾ mile west of Ingleby station, opening it on 6 April 1858.

The next move was the purchase of the Ingleby Mining Company's line by the NY&C for £40,000 and the Act of 23 July 1858 authorizing this also sanctioned a line to Rosedale, using the course of the private line as far as the foot of the Cleveland Hills. It seems certain that these powers were obtained at the instigation of the NER, which was about to take over the NY&C completely. The extension involved the construction of a gigantic incline and the laying of eleven miles of track across barren moorland, with no chance of any traffic except from the mines at the terminus. Could it be that the decision to build to Rosedale was influenced by the fact that one of the lessees of the royalty to work the ironstone was George Leeman, M.P., deputy chairman of the NER?

The crest of the Cleveland Hills was reached by the famous Ingleby Incline, sixty-five chains long and mostly at gradients of 1 in 5 and 1 in 6. As the normal flow of loaded wagons was down the incline it was built on the self-acting principle, with a brakeman in the drum-house at the summit controlling the speed of the descending (and therefore also the ascending) wagons. In June 1869 traffic on the incline had to be suspended because the heat generated by the braking system set fire to the drum-house, which was completely destroyed! Except for a short length of single line at the foot of the incline, the track was double to a point just above the half-way mark, and from there to the summit had three rails, the centre one common to both ascending and descending wagons.

Specimen loads of ore from Rosedale were taken to Pickering by road and forwarded by rail to various ironworks in County Durham some years before the railway reached Rosedale on 27 March 1861. Five words in the official returns of ironstone production for the year 1860 clearly show the impatience with which the mine-owners and workmen must have watched as the line crept slowly towards them across the wild moorland in 1859 and 1860: 'Much raised: not any sold.' Once the line was in operation the ironstone began to flow rapidly, and production jumped from 79,786 tons (valued at £11,967 18s) in the remaining nine months of 1861 to 219,123 tons (valued at £32,768) in 1862, and to 297,580 tons (valued at £66,950) in 1864.

In 1865 new mines were opened on the east side of the valley and a branch to serve them was constructed from Blakey Junction and opened on 18 August 1865. Production from both the East and West mines totalled only 230,382 tons in 1866, but because of the increased demand the value rose to £93,490. There certainly was 'gold in them thar hills'. Maximum production seems to have been reached in 1873 when 560,668 tons fetched £168,200, but a slump was soon to follow and in 1880 only 6,079 tons were raised.

Over the years the mines' fortunes fluctuated considerably, partly due to the rise and fall in demand and partly because of their own difficulties. The 1914–18 war prolonged their life for a while but the General Strike of 1926 dealt a blow from which they never recovered. Due to the foresight of the NER (or of George Leeman himself?) the Act for the construction of the Rosedale branch also included powers for its abandonment 'if and when the Minerals in the District served by the said Branch Railway shall, in the opinion of the Company, be worked out or exhausted, or become insufficient to yield a Profit to the Company . . . and it shall be lawful for the Company to take up, pull down, and dispose of the Rails, Buildings, and Works of the Railway so abandoned'. No doubt the directors of the LNE discovered with glee that they need not go to Parliament for an Act! The line was closed on 29 September 1928 and sold for scrap, and the last locomotive was lowered down the incline in June 1929.

For many years the Rosedale service was worked by the sturdy long-boilered 0–6–0 engines which originated on the Stockton & Darlington Railway, but latterly three Worsdell Class P engines were used, one being a spare. As the whole line was single track some safety measures had to be adopted and a metal ring was provided for each of the three sections, West Rosedale Mines to Blakey Junction, East Rosedale Mines to Blakey Junction, and Blakey Junction to Incline Top. The first driver away from the shed in a morning took with him only the ring for the section on which he was going to run beyond Blakey Junction. The second driver carried the ring for the West Rosedale–Blakey Junction section and that for the section beyond Blakey Junction over which he was to run; he then left the West Rosedale–Blakey Junction ring in the Staff Cabin at the Junction. When work was completed the first driver back at Blakey Junction left his ring there and when the second engine arrived the driver collected both the Blakey Junction–West Rosedale ring and the one left by the other driver. Another unusual feature of the working over this remote line was that the brake vans did not carry tail lamps – only the normal two sidelamps.

Because of the preparation involved the engines stationed at the small stone shed at West Rosedale paid only very infrequent visits to the works for overhaul. To go there necessitated the centre pair of driving wheels being taken out at the shed, and the engine being towed to the top of the incline and then lowered down, finally being towed from the incline foot to Darlington or Gateshead Works.

To work the traffic away from the foot of the incline, engines were provided from a shed at Battersby; this was built in 1877 but a new shed was erected in 1889, only to be closed on 30 November 1895. Before World War I the building was used as a miniature rifle range, and later it was advertised as 'To Let', but after years of standing empty and derelict it was demolished in 1966.

The course of the railway is still visible almost throughout, and it makes an admirable path for walkers.

YORK TO SCARBOROUGH

Scarborough is delightfully situated in the recess of a bay, whence it rises in the form of an amphitheatre to the summit of a cliff or scar. Its name, signifying a fortified rock, is of Saxon derivation; and there is reason to suppose that it was also a Roman settlement. It ranks amongst the most ancient boroughs which send members to Parliament.

The first mention of a railway to serve Scarborough appears to have been in 1833, when a line was proposed from the Leeds & Selby Railway near Sherburn (in Elmet), through Tadcaster, York and Malton to the coast. This did not materialize, and the next definite step was a public meeting held in Scarborough Town Hall on 19 October 1839, addressed by George Hudson and George Stephenson. Although the directors of the York & North Midland Railway approved of the scheme it was shelved until the line from Darlington to Newcastle was well under way. Eventually they turned again to the question of a railway to Scarborough, and at a meeting held on 17 November 1843 it was decided to apply to Parliament for the necessary powers. Within a few days the plans (which must have been ready and waiting) were bound and by 30 November they were deposited with the interested parties.

The Act was passed on 4 July 1844 and on 7 July 1845 the line was opened with the usual elaborate festivities, commencing with a public breakfast at York. On arrival at Scarborough 'the company proceeded to an elegant luncheon which had been laid out in the temporary station', and this was followed by a procession round the town before entraining again for York, where the day concluded with a dinner in the Town Hall attended by 700 gentlemen. Because for most of the forty-two miles the course lay over level ground, with the Howardian Hills (to the west of Malton) as the only obstacle, construction was speedy. It was originally planned to go through these hills by means of a tunnel 1,430 yd long, reaching the banks of the River Derwent east of Kirkham Abbey station; to save expense, however, the line was built further west along the river bank, at a cost of $1\frac{3}{4}$ miles additional mileage and a 40 m.p.h. speed restriction for $3\frac{3}{4}$ miles as the route twists and turns with the meandering river.

Castle Howard station has by far the most imposing buildings : they had to serve the famous residence of the same name some $2\frac{1}{2}$ miles to the north. Queen Victoria alighted here one day in August 1850 when on her way to open the Central station at Newcastle and the Royal Border bridge at Berwick. In honour of the visit a certain A. G. Tyson wrote an epic of 231 verses, some of which dealt with the railway :

Vulcan! thou lord of forging skill
Now warrant well thine arts,
And bid the rails, and bolts and springs
Act well their destin'd parts.

The gorgeous engine strong and free
Puffs out and fumes amain,
 So loathe to stand that scarce can she
Her swelling steam restrain.

Then steadily along the curves
The locomotive starts
And quickly soon along the line
She like the lightning darts.

The station at Malton – a market town in the North Riding –
is actually in Norton, on the south bank of the River Derwent
and therefore in the East Riding. With the opening in 1853 of
the branches to Thirsk and Driffield, Malton began to grow in
importance as a railway centre and an engine shed was erected
there in the same year.

To the east of Malton the Driffield branch (dealt with in
Chapter III) went off southwards, and until September 1962 this
was used as far as Scarborough Road Junction by the trains
from Scarborough to the north via Gilling, which reversed at
Scarborough Road and then climbed over the Malton–Scarborough line and the River Derwent.

At Rillington, which has now lost its typical Y&NM all-over
roof, the branch to Pickering and Whitby turned off to the
north and ½ mile farther on can be seen the site of the short-
lived curve installed in 1865 to allow through running from
Whitby to Scarborough.

Approaching Seamer Junction the site of the dismantled line
to Pickering can be seen on the left, and then on the right the
line from Filey, Bridlington and Hull (Chapter III). Connections
between York–Scarborough and Scarborough–Hull trains are
often made at Seamer for passengers travelling to Filey or Bridlington, and although a curve for through running was once
considered the idea was abandoned.

When the North Eastern was formed in 1854 the receipts at
Scarborough amounted to a mere £65, but at the end of its life
the company was taking an average of nearly £3,000 per week.

Week ending 2 July 1854

		£	s	d
First-class passengers	38	15	6	7
Second-class passengers	103	25	1	1
Third-class passengers	63	7	13	11
Fourth-class passengers	79	9	19	2¾
	283	58	0	9¾
Paid by other companies		3	2	3
Parcels		3	16	1
		64	19	1¾

The climb to a peak in the 1920s, and the catastrophic drop only ten years later, are illustrated in the following figures:

Year	Passengers	Receipts	Parcels Horses Carriages Dogs	Total
		£	£	£
1885	222,042	37,525	5,947	43,472
1890	248,221	41,586	5,671	47,257
1895	279,575	44,574	6,739	51,313
1900	313,271	48,102	10,339	58,441
1905	328,304	47,952	9,979	57,931
1911				60,371
1921				148,461
1931				74,936

Even 1d platform tickets brought in £774 19s 7d in 1922, but this had fallen to £471 17s 10d ten years later.

'THE QUEEN OF WATERING PLACES'

Scarborough's rise from a small fishing port to a major holiday resort has been greatly helped by the railway which, under the auspices of George Hudson, reached the coast in July 1845. Not everyone welcomed the prospect, however, and a local character, George Knowles, published a pamphlet in 1840 condemning the proposed railway and saying that the town had 'no wish for a greater influx of vagrants, and those who have no money to spend. Scarborough is rising daily in the estimation of the public as a fashionable watering place on account of its natural beauty and tranquillity, and in a few years more the novelty of not having a railroad will be its greatest asset.'

But Scarborough duly began to flourish as a resort and holiday centre and countless excursions have been run to attract further passengers. In fact W. W. Tomlinson records that the first – an excursion from Newcastle – was advertised within a month of the resort getting its railway. They must have been hardy souls who ventured to travel from Newcastle to Scarborough and back in a day in 1845 – a total distance of 250 miles.

Except during the two World Wars excursions continued in plenty, although under Dr Beeching's plans the number has greatly decreased. Locomotives from distant sheds appeared, usually at busy weekends, and within living memory it was possible to see engines from six 'foreign' companies in Scarborough, with an even greater variety of coaching stock. The majority of excursions have always run at weekends, and with the many extra trains put on for holidaymakers travelling to and from their destinations, Saturdays have been by far the busiest days, requiring extra staff, coaches and locomotives, and causing inconvenience. As long as seaside hotels and boarding houses maintain their preference for Saturday to Saturday bookings then the peak day for travel – be it by rail or road – with its delays and overcrowding will continue to be Saturday.

Scarborough Central station now has nine platforms, of which Nos 3, 4 and 5 are in the original station shed. Nos. 1 and 2, now the main platforms, were used for excursions before a separate excursion station was built; Nos 6, 7 and 8 are inside the original goods shed; No. 9 is built alongside the wall of the goods shed. The clock tower was erected in 1884, Scarborough Corporation agreeing to pay for the gas needed to illuminate the clock at night if the NER would provide one suitable for illumination (at an additional cost of £15). To handle the large number of excursionists around the turn of the century the Excursion station, latterly known as Londesborough Road, was opened on 8 June 1908, together with some four miles of carriage sidings on the west side of the Whitby line on the northern outskirts of Scarborough. Locomotive stabling facilities, including a 60 ft turntable, were provided. To handle the heavy weekend traffic, passengers were detrained at the through platform at Londesborough Road (which also had a single bay platform) and then the train worked forward empty to the sidings. There was no need for the engine to block the single-line tunnel by returning

NORTH EASTERN RAILWAY

NIDDERDALE FEAST.

CHEAP EXCURSION TO THE SEA-SIDE.

On TUESDAY, Sept. 20th, 1870,

A SPECIAL TRAIN will leave PATELEY BRIDGE, and
Stations as under, for

SCARBRO

FARE THERE AND BACK.

COVERED CARRIAGES.

3s.

LEAVE	A.M.
Pateley Bridge -	6 0
Dacre Banks - - - -	6 8
Darley - - - - -	6 12
Birstwith - - - -	6 17
Hampsthwaite - - -	6 21
Ripley - - - - -	6 30
Starbeck - - - - -	6 40
Knaresbro' - - - -	6 50

Children under Twelve Years of Age, Half-fare.

The Return Train will leave Scarbro' at 5.30 p.m. same day.

NO LUGGAGE ALLOWED.

☞ The Tickets are only available for Scarbro' in going, and for the Stations at
which they were issued on return.

As only a limited number of Carriages can be allotted to this Train, the following Regulations
will be strictly observed, in order, as far as possible, to secure the comfort of the public, and to
avoid delay :—The number of Tickets supplied for issue will only be equal to the amount of Carriage accommodation, and no persons except holders of Tickets for this Train will be permitted to
travel by it, *and any person attempting to travel without a Ticket will be charged the full ordinary
fare both ways. The Tickets are at the Stations ready for issue;* and persons who intend to
travel by this Train must apply early enough to enable the Station Clerks to procure any
additional Tickets that may be required.

YORK, August, 1870.   **W. O'BRIEN, General Manager.**

EDWARD BAINES AND SONS, GENERAL PRINTERS, LEEDS.

Excursion to Scarborough 20/9/1870. Note provision of 'covered carriages'

6—ROGB * *

to the shed : relief staff were provided and the footplate crews were allowed to book off duty for some hours; they could often be seen relaxing on the sands in their dungarees.

Londesborough Road had an exceptionally large covered circulating area where returning excursionists could be formed into separate queues. At departure time, as soon as the train arrived at the platform the passengers concerned were allowed through the barrier; they could be loaded and away in a few minutes.

By using both the Excursion and Central stations it was possible to load and work out some ten trains an hour over the peak period between 7 and 10 p.m. The most essential work was carried out unobtrusively by the pilot engines, manned by local crews, which propelled the sets of coaches from the carriage sidings into the platforms at Central station. Because of their long familiarity with the cramped layout they could bring the sets of up to thirteen bogie coaches into the station at a rare turn of speed, slowing down at the last moment to allow the buffers of the leading vehicle to kiss those at the end of the bay platform. The pilot engine then uncoupled and departed for the carriage sidings to fetch another set and the train engine backed on in readiness for departure.

The carriage sidings adjoined the engine shed and an obvious economy, both in engine power and in signalling movements, was to have the train engine back the coaches up to Central station. This was tried on a number of occasions over the years and the result was always the same – late departures and general confusion. Trains being backed into the station conflicted with those departing and the propelling movement had to be carried out smartly in the three or four minutes between the clearance of one train and the setting of the road for the next. Scarborough men were able to accomplish this, but when the train engine was used, the driver, who visited Scarborough perhaps only once or twice a year, was wary of backing a long train into a dead-end platform and as he crawled into the station he delayed the next departure and this effect snowballed. On one occasion in 1937 or 1938, when a large number of evening excursions were run, trains from York, only forty-two miles away, were taking four hours on the journey, stopping at almost every signal on the way because of the congestion at Scarborough.

Construction of Londesborough Road station brought the demolition of the original Y&NM locomotive shed at Scarborough, but the nearby Locomotive Cottages still survive, some distance from the later locomotive sheds, which closed in May 1963. Londesborough Road station itself is now closed, having last been used in August 1963, and ironically for a time it was used to store bus chassis awaiting bodies from a local bodybuilding concern: it has since been demolished. The carriage sidings have also gone – lifted in 1965 – and the land (now derelict) may be used for housing.

Those who know Scarborough will appreciate that it is an extremely difficult station to work. The through platform at Londesborough Road would hold fourteen bogie vehicles and the bay platform eleven, but it was at Central station that the greatest difficulties arose. Only No. 1 platform would take thirteen-coach trains, the others being limited to between six and ten vehicles: consequently it was necessary to know the size of the train before it was allocated a platform. Confusion sometimes resulted if a train arrived with an extra vehicle tacked on the rear: the signalman routed it into its appropriate platform perhaps a minute or two prior to a booked departure from the adjacent platform. When the arriving train came to a stand the last vehicle was foul of the departure line and a pilot engine had to be hurriedly obtained either to remove the extra vehicle or to draw the set out until the other train had left.

Perhaps the busiest period ever experienced at Scarborough was in the summer of 1939: on August Bank Holiday Saturday, for instance, 102 arrivals and 106 departures were scheduled between 5.7 a.m. and 11.45 p.m., many of them long-distance Saturdays-only trains to and from London, Newcastle, Birmingham, Stoke-on-Trent, Edinburgh, Manchester, Leicester, etc. It was impossible to fit in any excursions, so these ran in force on the Sunday, half-day trips coming from York, Sheffield, Wakefield, Scholes, Bolton-on-Dearne, Bradford, Leeds, Barnby Dun, Doncaster, Burton-on-Trent, Manchester, South Shields, Hartlepool and Newcastle.

An additional attraction introduced in the 1930s were the evening excursions. These arrived at Scarborough from Leeds, Hull, York, Shipley and Wakefield between 6.0 p.m. and 7.30 p.m. and departed between 10.15 and 11.25 p.m. For two or three shillings it was possible to spend an evening by the sea; sometimes in good weather four or five trains had to be run from Leeds instead of the one booked.

Until 1934 much inconvenience was caused by the trains on the Whitby line. Because of their size – normally up to seven bogies – they used the short platforms on the south side of the station, whereas the line to Whitby branched off on the north side. This meant that all trains to and from Whitby had to cross the main flow of traffic on the York and Hull lines and also the trains of empty stock to and from the various carriage sidings. But this was not all! The Whitby line could only be reached directly from the Seamer direction, and consequently all trains bound for the branch had to reverse to gain the route through Falsgrave tunnel: this also meant that the engine had to run round its train because the regulations insisted that the train should be drawn and not propelled out of Central station. An additional complication arose when another train was standing in the through platform at Londesborough Road, the usual route for the running-round movement: the density of traffic did not allow for the engine to run round via the main lines and consequently the Whitby train just had to wait until a path was clear.

In 1933 the popularity of holiday Runabout Tickets and other cheap fare facilities, together with the alteration of the coast line service to run between Scarborough and Middlesbrough instead of Scarborough and Saltburn, brought an unprecedented flood of passengers. Working became chaotic. The Class A6 4–6–2 T engines – for long known as the 'Whitby Willies' because of their NE class-letter W – were inadequate, and the more powerful Class A5 and A8 engines were hurriedly requisitioned from other services. Late in the season the engineer withdrew restrictions on the use of Class J39 0–6–0 engines, and they put in some sterling work until a bad derailment near Whitby caused the immediate re-imposition of the ban.

Things were so bad that after the summer a committee was set up to see what improvements could be carried out before the start of the 1934 season. This resulted in a master stroke. Platform No. 1 at Scarborough was extended and at its western end a separate face was built (No. 1A). This did not restrict the use of platform 1, which was still the longest, but now the trains could be propelled out of 1A to a point opposite Londesborough Road station, where the engine had previously run round. Then the driver only had to reverse his engine and he could set off for Whitby. Similarly trains from Whitby could be propelled into the new platform; in addition this new method of working obviated the conflicting movements formerly necessary.

The only objection came from the passengers. To reach the new platform meant a walk of at least 300 yd from the ticket barriers and to allow for stragglers the working departure time was always three minutes later than that given in the public timetable. Platform 1A was last used in 1964.

Emphasis has necessarily been placed on the summer working. In the winter there is a small amount of residential traffic, augmented at times by seaside landladies making shopping forays to Leeds. Even with the modern diesel railcars and locomotives the 75-minute non-stop timing between Leeds and Scarborough, which was in force during the summers 1900–14 and 1922–9, has never been equalled. It was on this run that the NER introduced a breakfast-car in 1902, leavinng Scarborough at 8.30 a.m. and returning as a tea-car at 5.5 p.m.

It was between York and Scarborough that the policy of closing strings of wayside stations at one stroke was introduced, with the idea of eliminating stopping trains and speeding up traffic generally. From 22 September 1930, therefore, twelve intermediate stations, excluding Malton and Seamer, were closed to passengers. Since then, however, special trains and excursions have stopped at these places to pick up passengers going to some event, such as the illuminations at Blackpool, and until recently they were still served by a daily pick-up goods train.

The North Eastern was one of the earliest railways to purchase petrol-engined road vehicles, and for many years before the Great War numerous tours to surrounding beauty spots were worked by char-à-bancs from Scarborough station forecourt. Some of these vehicles – mainly built by Durkopp or Saurer – had interchangeable bodies so that they could be used for goods in the winter and passengers in the summer. Some seventy years since their introduction, tours are still run from the station yard, now worked by United Automobile Services – a BTC-owned company.

The NER was also in the forefront with internal-combustion-engined railcars and two of these, using electrical transmission, were put in service between Scarborough and Filey as long ago as 1904. Within a few years they were unable to handle the traffic available and were replaced by steam autocars (the NER term for a push-and-pull unit). Now the wheel has turned full circle and once again the service between Scarborough and Filey is maintained by internal-combustion-engined railcars.

SCARBOROUGH TO WHITBY

The Scarborough & Whitby Railway was opened on 16 July 1885, although as early as 1848 a railway along the coast had been suggested. It was not until the late 1860s that definite steps were taken and a company formed. The first sod was cut on 3 June 1872 but after work had gone on for some time the company ran short of money and in 1878–9 it was touch-and-go whether the whole scheme should be abandoned. Fortunately, W. H. Hammond of Raven Hall (now an hotel) came to the rescue with both energy and capital and the line was duly completed.

The original plan was to have an entirely independent line, with the Scarborough terminus at Gallows Close and the Whitby terminus near Whitby Abbey, on the south side of the River Esk. At Scarborough the station would have been separated from the NER by a ridge of land carrying the main road out of the town, and at Whitby by the river. However, at a late stage in the construction it was decided to join up with the NER at both ends: at Scarborough this was accomplished by constructing a 260-yd tunnel under Falsgrave Road, and at Whitby by building the 915-ft long brick viaduct over the River Esk. The idea was undoubtedly that the NER could be approached to work the line; this it did from the outset, for 50 per cent of the gross receipts. In 1898 the NER decided to purchase the Scarborough & Whitby outright and issued stock to the value of £261,633 – for a line which had cost £649,813!

During its independent existence the Scarborough & Whitby Railway frequently complained to the NER that its line was not being fully used, and its advertisements carried the exhortation 'Passengers are particularly requested to ask for tickets by the COAST ROUTE, and TO SEE THAT THEY GET THEM.'

In its *Official Guide* the company claimed that

> The Scarborough and Whitby line has opened out the country and made it accessible in all its virgin loveliness. The line runs through pleasant undulating pasture lands at either end, winds in and out amongst the gorse and heatherclad hills, dips into wooded dales, skirts the edges of a wild moor, climbs the highest cliff on the Yorkshire coast, runs round one of the bonniest bays in the Kingdom, and over a portion of its course is perched on the brow of a cliff against which the waves ceaselessly break.

In addition to its scenery the line was noted for its gradients : the summit at Ravenscar (Peak until 1 October 1897) was reached by a long climb at 1 in 41 from the south and 1 in 39 from the north. Mention of the station at Peak recalls that early in 1895 the NER threatened that unless the S&W built a house for the stationmaster trains would no longer call at Peak. As no house was built, this threat was put into effect from 6 March 1895. Agreement on the matter was not reached for a year and the station did not reopen until 1 April 1896.

In LNE days the various types of 'Sentinel' steam railcars were put through their paces on this line : each succeeding type of car would be run from York, via Malton and Pickering, to Whitby, returning to York via Scarborough. The first to be tested was two-cylinder car No. 21 – later named *Valliant* – in April 1927, and the five twelve-cylinder cars built in 1930–2 were, in fact, specially designed for the hilly coast route between Scarborough and Middlesbrough. The Armstrong Whitworth diesel-electric railcar *Tyneside Venturer* was also tried out on the round trip from York and subsequently it too worked between Middlesbrough and Scarborough, but during the winter only; in summer it was stationed at Scarborough and worked a scenic excursion to Whitby via Pickering, returning along the coast. This working was re-introduced in 1959 using normal BR diesel railcars, but it was short-lived.

Both before and after World War II steam-hauled scenic

excursions were run from the West Riding, taking the circular route used for testing the railcars. These trains normally loaded to eight bogie coaches and required two locomotives : occasionally three engines were used between Whitby and Prospect Hill – one heading the train and two banking, although the two bankers became the two train engines when direction was reversed at Prospect Hill. The crescendo of sound as the two engines blasted away up Ravenscar bank with full regulator was one never to be forgotten.

Only once has a diesel locomotive worked one of these scenic excursions and then the most noticeable feature was less the silence while the bank was climbed than the lush vegetation and the absence of fires started by the steam locomotives. In steam days the heather and bracken were constantly being set alight and never established themselves but now, with the disappearance of steam, they have taken hold and altered the appearance of the lineside.

Around the turn of the century efforts were being made to develop Ravenscar into a holiday resort and Peak Estate Ltd acquired 750 acres of land on which to build houses and shops. A block of four shops was built just outside the station and a wide road was laid to the main road but, unfortunately, the scheme came to nothing. The road, usually full of potholes, remains as a monument to yet another unfinished dream.

Scalby station was closed completely on 2 March 1953 although until 1964 certain trains stopped during the summer to serve the occupants of the camping coaches; Hayburn Wyke and Fyling Hall were converted to unstaffed halts on 23 March 1955 and 5 May 1958 respectively. The final blow came on 6 March 1965 when, after a long and bitter fight against British Railways' decision to close the line, the last trains ran, leaving the inhabitants to face what the TUCC described as 'serious hardship'.

PILMOOR–MALTON AND GILLING–PICKERING

The truly rural branch between Pilmoor and Malton at one time played an important part in the lives of the rural communities it served in the course of its twenty-four miles. For many years it was their only means of communication with the outside world; but they deserted it for the bus and the private car. The section between Gilling and Malton was closed to local passenger traffic at the end of 1930, after a life of seventy-seven years, its early demise being undoubtedly due to the bus service running parallel to it almost all the way.

The line was opened throughout on 19 May 1853 by the York, Newcastle & Berwick Railway and for many years it formed part of the recognized route from Scarborough and Malton to the north. In fact until 1 May 1952 the fare from Scarborough to Darlington was calculated on the mileage via Gilling, although from 1 January 1931 all passengers (except on summer Saturdays) had to travel via York.

During the summer the line was used on Saturdays only by trains between Scarborough and Newcastle, Edinburgh and Glasgow: it was occasionally possible to see mighty 'Pacific' locomotives ambling along this single-line branch on which the maximum permitted speed was 20 m.p.h. between Pilmoor and Gilling, and 30 m.p.h. from Gilling to Malton. In addition two special trains were run to and from Gilling at the beginning and end of every term, for boys attending the Roman Catholic College at Ampleforth.

At Malton there was no direct connection with the York–Scarborough line, and trains bound for Scarborough had to be hauled by a pilot engine from Scarborough Road Junction to Malton station, with the train engine remaining in the rear. When Malton station was reached the train was the right way round for setting off for Scarborough. Freight traffic was handled between Malton and Gilling in connection with the following branch until 10 August 1964.

On leaving Gilling for Pickering the first two miles were covered over what appeared to be double track. Actually there were two single lines as the Gilling–Malton route ran alongside until trains for Pickering swung away northwards to Helmsley. This branch was worked in conjunction with the Pilmoor–Malton service and shared the same metals between Gilling and Sunbeck Junction, where trains from the Pickering direction usually took the curve to Bishophouse Junction and continued along the east coast route to York.

The line was built in stages and it was opened from Gilling

to Helmsley on 9 October 1871, on to Kirby Moorside on 1 January 1874, and finally to Pickering on 1 April 1875. It was originally planned to join the Malton–Whitby line north of Pickering by means of a junction leading in the direction of Whitby, thus missing Pickering, the market town and natural centre of Ryedale; fortunately this idea was dropped. The final train from York to Pickering ran on 31 January 1953, the night of the great storm when much of eastern England was flooded by the sea, but many people braved the elements to pay their last respects. This closure also affected the Sunbeck Junction–Gilling section of the Pilmoor–Malton line dealt with above.

SEAMER–PICKERING

The single-line branch between Seamer and Pickering was not opened until 1 May 1882 to serve the villages along the northern perimeter of the wide Derwent valley, but these were an easy target for bus competition. The buses passed through the centre of almost every village on the route whereas the station was all of $\frac{1}{2}$ mile away! Consequently passenger and goods traffic was withdrawn from 5 June 1950, except for freight (mainly stone) from Thornton Dale – reputed to be Yorkshire's prettiest village – to Pickering. This too succumbed in 1964, when it was closed and lifted.

About the most exciting happening on this branch was when a train ran through the gates at one of the numerous level crossings; then in 1942 a stray barrage-balloon got its trailing cable entangled in the telegraph wires and brought traffic to a standstill.

NUNTHORPE–BATTERSBY

The North Yorkshire & Cleveland Act of 2 July 1855 authorized the construction of a branch from Ingleby to join the Middlesbrough & Guisborough Railway at Ormesby. Before this the two companies had disputed who should build the line, and the NY&C was awarded the right by an independent arbitrator. The connection with the Middlesbrough & Guisborough was eventually made at Nunthorpe and this line, $5\frac{1}{4}$ miles long, is better known as the Battersby–Nunthorpe branch. It was opened for freight traffic on 1 June 1864 by the NER, which by that time, of course, had control of both the NY&C and the Middlesbrough & Guisborough. The branch proved an invaluable link in the transport of Rosedale ironstone to Tees-side; in fact apparently it was not at first capable of carrying a passenger service as well – this facility was delayed until 1 April 1868. Numerous mines and quarries were also directly served, particularly in the Great Ayton area.

Since the closure of the coast route between Whitby and Loftus in 1958 all Tees-side to Scarborough passenger traffic used this line, with a reversal at Battersby. A curve east of the station, to allow through running without a reversal, was authorized in 1866 but was never built. The one and only intermediate station at Great Ayton was converted to an unstaffed halt from 1 January 1962.

A MISCELLANY

The second railway to be built in the North Riding is believed to have been a short line at Kepwick, six miles north-east of Thirsk, which was constructed for carrying limestone from quarries above the village to kilns near Leake Church (adjacent to the Thirsk–Stockton road), and opened in 1833. Little is known about it, but the lower section was worked by horses, whereas the upper section to the quarries was an incline of some sort, presumably self-acting. It closed down about 1890 but there are still numerous remains and the course can easily be traced throughout its three miles.

Another line on which work was actually started was a light railway from Sinnington (between Pickering and Kirby Moorside) to Rosedale Abbey. A Light Railway Order under the title Lastingham & Rosedale Light Railway was obtained on 31 July 1900, and the first sod was turned at Rosedale on 14 June 1902. Support for the venture was not very great and, after one or two extensions of time, it fizzled out.

In the south-west corner of the North Riding was the Sand Hutton Light Railway which started life in 1910 as a 15 in. gauge private miniature railway in the grounds of Sand Hutton Hall, near York. In May 1920 a Light Railway Order was obtained and extensions were constructed outside the grounds of the Hall, mainly to serve the estate farms. An unusual feature for a line of this size was that it was authorized to enter into agreements with the NER for its construction, management or working, with powers to lease itself to the NER, subject to the consent of the Minister of Transport.

Shortly afterwards a quantity of surplus 18 in. gauge War Department railway equipment was purchased : the existing line was then altered to 18 in. and all new extensions built to this gauge.

Passengers were carried from 4 October 1924, but facilities were withdrawn in July 1930, although goods traffic continued until 1932 when the line was closed completely. Goods consisted mainly of agricultural produce, which could be tipped directly into NER wagons at Warthill, and a brickworks turning out up to 20,000 bricks a day was also served.

The locomotive used on the railway in its original form was a Bassett Lowke 4-4-2 named *Synolda* in honour of the first wife of the owner, Major Sir Robert Walker, Bt, and after conversion to 18 in. gauge four Hunslet engines were used – No. 2, No. 3, No. 4, and *Esme* – named after the owner's second wife. An extension to Scrayingham – across the River Derwent and therefore in the East Riding – was planned but never materialized. It is at Scrayingham that the Railway King – George Hudson – is buried.

Two major events remain to be recorded. The first is the reopening to public passenger traffic on 22 April 1973 of the now preserved stretch of line between Grosmont and Pickering, part of the Whitby & Pickering Railway of 1836. It is operated by the North Yorkshire Moors Railway. The line was formally opened by the Duchess of Kent on 1 May 1973 when a special train headed by two steam locomotives traversed the whole length from Grosmont to Pickering.

The second concerns the relaying of the line southwards from Carlin How (Skinningrove) to Boulby (north of Staithes) where a potash mine has been sunk. The mine is not yet in production and thus, although the railway is complete, there is no service over it as yet.

CHAPTER V

Lines to the North

THE GREAT NORTH OF ENGLAND RAILWAY

Trains now travel over the east coast main line from Darlington to York at speeds in excess of 100 m.p.h. along exactly the route opened in 1841 by the Great North of England Railway, surely one of the easiest in the country as far as gradients and curves are concerned. For most of its forty-four miles it is almost level and straight and there are now four tracks from York to Northallerton, a distance of thirty miles.

The GNE was based on the ideas of Joseph Pease, a leading figure in the development of the Stockton & Darlington Railway, who envisaged a railway connecting Tyneside with the proposed York & North Midland Railway which was planned to run southwards from York. In 1835 a start was made in surveying the northern half of the line, between Gateshead and Croft ($2\frac{1}{2}$ miles south of Darlington) and it was soon realized that this would be far more difficult to construct than the section southwards across the Plain of York. Consequently it was decided to concentrate on obtaining powers for the northern section first, leaving the application for powers for the southern section to the following session of Parliament. The one-year difference in construction time would be cancelled out by the one-year delay to the southern half, and thus the whole line from the Tyne to York would be ready for opening simultaneously.

At this time the North Midland Railway was also casting envious eyes on an outlet from Leeds to the north, but by completing the survey in fourteen days and preparing the deposited plans in another fourteen the GNE easily led the field. Its original scheme was for a line southwards to a point near Ripon, there forking to Wetherby, Tadcaster and Leeds on the one hand, and via Easingwold to York on the other. But the supporters in York for a direct line to Newcastle saw that traffic via York was likely to become secondary to traffic via Leeds, and persuaded the GNE Committee to change its mind, so that when the bill was deposited it sought powers for a line from Croft to York only. This, the second Act obtained by the GNE, received the Royal Assent on 12 July 1837; the first Act, incorporating the company and authorizing the line between Croft and the Tyne, was granted a year earlier and will be dealt with in Chapter VIII, although it can be mentioned here that the whole of the proposed line was estimated to cost £1,000,000, made up as follows :

	£	s	d
Gateshead to Hurworth Lane, Croft (34 miles 34 chains)	659,851	0	0
Hurworth Lane to York (41 miles 16 chains)	326,374	0	0
Junction with Y&NM at York, and Thirsk branch	13,775	0	0
	1,000,000	0	0

This figure excluded locomotives and rolling stock but included two lines, with sufficient land for four. Although covered by the first Act, the section between Darlington and Croft had to be considered as part of the line from Darlington to York, on which the company decided to concentrate in accordance with the wishes expressed at a General Meeting held in August 1837.

The first sod was cut near Croft on 25 November 1837 and within a few weeks some of the most important construction contracts had been let; a tender amounting to £14,481 had been accepted for building a bridge over the Tees immediately south of Croft, which is in use to this day. Engineering works of any magnitude were required at only three other points : a bridge over the River Ouse approaching York; an embankment at Northallerton necessitating the tipping of 252,641 cubic yards of soil; and a cutting at Dalton, where 388,742 cubic yards had to be excavated. Work on the bridge at Croft progressed slowly and labour troubles there are referred to frequently in the Minutes : on 9 October 1838, for instance, it was reported that 'the Contractors are now proceeding with more spirit on the Tees Bridge. If more complaints are received the Engineer is authorized to employ more men at the Contractor's expense.'

The following month these men were on strike for higher wages but in December the engineer was able to report that work was progressing, with twenty-eight masons.

In 1839 the Croft branch of the s&d was purchased for £20,000 so that the gne could incorporate it in the main line; about half of it at the northern end was used. The southern end of the branch was left on its original course to serve the coal depot at Croft and remained in use until April 1964.

In spite of the directors' eagerness to get the line opened there were numerous delays, culminating in the resignation of the engineer, Thomas Storey, whereupon George Stephenson was asked to take charge. He sent his son, Robert, to report. It was intended to open the line on 25 November 1840 but it was not ready, and shortly afterwards the directors issued 'a peremptory order to open the line for coal trade, if not General Traffic, on 4 January 1841'. They did manage to open for mineral traffic on this date but passenger traffic did not commence until 30 March 1841. The new station at York which the gne was to share with the y&nm was opened on 4 January 1841 although, of course, not used by gne trains until they began carrying passengers almost three months later. Needless to say both occasions were made an excuse for festivities!

On the opening day of the gne the stations were Shipton, Tollerton, Alne, Raskelf, Sessay, Thirsk, Northallerton, Cowton and Croft. The junction stations at Dalton (Eryholme from 1901) and Pilmoor were opened later to serve the Richmond and Boroughbridge branches respectively, and Danby Wiske followed in 1885. Shipton was renamed Beningbrough in 1898 and Croft had Spa added in 1896. Eryholme closed to passenger traffic on 1 October 1911, there being no more changes until in 1958 Beningbrough, Alne, Raskelf, Pilmoor, Sessay, Otterington, Danby Wiske and Cowton disappeared from the timetable, while Croft Spa, although open until March 1969 was latterly served by Richmond branch trains only.

Before the line was opened the gne directors authorized recruitment of the following staff :

1 superintendent (£400 p.a.)	1 foreman of carriages
1 storekeeper	1 head of merchandise
1 head of locomotive power	1 coal manager (£75 p.a.)
1 resident engineer	1 check clerk

1 inspector
1 agent at York
2 ticket clerks (£70 p.a.)
11 clerks in charge (Note 1)
1 parcel clerk
5 clerks in offices
11 sub-inspectors (policemen)
(£46 p.a. plus clothing and lodging)

6 conductors (4s per day plus clothing)
6 guards (3s 8d per day plus clothing)
2 policemen (Note 2)
10 porters (at Darlington)
1 storeporter (at Darlington)
12 porters on the line
13 coal agents

Note 1 : Clerks in charge : Thirsk, £80 p.a.; first-class stations, £70 p.a.; second-class stations, £52 p.a.
Note 2 : Policemen 18s per week without lodging : 16s per week with lodging.

Two other interesting decisions taken in 1840 concerned the locomotive superintendent and the ticket system to be used. Mr James Cudworth was appointed 'to undertake the management of the Locomotive Department at £120 p.a. previous to the opening of the line, to be increased to £150 as soon as the line shall be opened, later to be increased to £200 should his service be satisfactory'. In March 1840 the superintendent recommended that the company should use the

Ticket System as now in full operation on the Manchester & Leeds Railway as eminently superior to every other in simplicity, economy and facility of management. He lays before the Board the printed circulars of Mr Edmonson and proposes that he be empowered to make the necessary arrangements with Mr Edmonson on the terms therein mentioned for the purpose of adapting his system to this railway.

Minor happenings of 1841 included a report from the head of the locomotive department that the merchandise engines were too long for the turntables by 5 in.! On the day the line was opened to passengers, while a merchandise train was stopped at Alne some drunken labourers attempted to throw the engine off the line. They were arrested the following day and fined amounts up to £10 each. One, James Buston, was arrested for travelling without a ticket and fined £10 or a week in prison.

Except for various widenings the GNE between York and Darlington is much the same as when it opened in 1841, although nowadays all the trains are diesel-hauled and many

THE IRONSTONE AREA

(17) *Ingleby incline on Rosedale Branch. Dismantled 1929*

(18) *Kilton viaduct being converted to an embankment by tipping spoil from adjacent ironstone mines. Liverton mines in background and note zig-zag line (with reversing neck under viaduct) to reach Skinningrove. Line across embankment relaid 1972.*

STATION EXTERIORS

(19) *Scarborough (1845, with clock tower added 1884)*

(20) *Hornsea (1864, closed 1964)*

of the passenger trains reach speeds of 100 m.p.h. In the final days of the NER there was a proposal to electrify the main line and also the Northallerton–Stockton–Ferryhill section, thus joining up with the electrified Newport–Shildon mineral line. Detailed investigations into the types of locomotives necessary were carried out and, in fact, one express passenger engine was built; but the grouping of 1923 put an end to the scheme, which would have made the NER main line the best in the country.

Between Alne and Thirsk the NER installed automatic semaphore signals in 1903–4 but because of extensive teething troubles they were not brought into use until 4 June 1905. Thereafter they gave twenty-eight years' good service and were only replaced in 1933 under a main line widening scheme. The signals were to an American design noted by officers of the NER who visited the New World to study railroad operation. Within a few months of their return to England a contract was signed with the Hall Automatic Signal Co. of New York for the installation between Alne and Thirsk. The contract price was 22,000 dollars – equivalent to £4,583 6s 8d at that time – which included a quantity of spare parts. The signals normally stood at danger and if the line ahead was clear they moved into the 'off' position when an approaching train occupied a track circuit. This movement was actuated by compressed carbon dioxide gas stored in cylinders at the foot of each signal, but the arm returned to danger by gravity.

The automatic semaphores were replaced by colour light signals when the main line was widened in 1930–3 under the Development (Loans, Guarantees and Grants) Act of 1929. Prior to this date the NER had carried out various widening schemes and at the grouping there were four tracks between Eryholme and Cowton; Wiske Moor and Northallerton; Otterington and Thirsk; and Beningbrough and Alne. However, as all these schemes excluded the stations mentioned, the only station situated on a four-track section was Tollerton, which fell between Alne and Beningbrough.

The 1930 scheme involved the extension of the Alne–Beningbrough section southwards to Skelton Bridge on both sides of the line, and northwards to Pilmoor on the down side only, leaving the Alne and Easingwold bay at Alne untouched. This necessitated new station buildings at Beningbrough, Alne (down side only), and Raskelf (down side only). Further north a new down slow line was constructed from Otterington to join the down Longlands loop avoiding line at Northallerton and a new up loop was provided together with an up slow line to Otterington, enabling trains from the Eaglescliffe direction to join the up main line without a single fouling movement.

As a wartime measure new up and down slow lines were installed between Thirsk and Pilmoor in 1942 and at the same time a new link was put in between Skelton Yard and the down slow at Skelton Bridge. Finally, in 1959, a new up slow line was put in from Pilmoor to Alne. Now the whole line between York and Darlington is controlled by colour light signals, with only six intermediate signal boxes in the forty-four miles – at Skelton, Tollerton, Pilmoor, Thirsk, Northallerton and Eryholme.

NOTABLE ACCIDENTS

Considering the millions of trains that have travelled over the main line in the 133 years it has been open the number of serious accidents has been small. Mishaps, yes : hardly a week goes by but there isn't a wagon or two derailed somewhere between York and Darlington.

Near Thirsk on 2 November 1892 there was the famous Manor House collision, caused by a signalman falling asleep during the night and accepting a train when he already had one in his section. A contributory factor was that the signalman had been active all day instead of resting : he had been searching for a doctor to attend his sick child and when he returned he found the child dead. Although he was not fit for duty no relief was forthcoming. The train the signalman forgot was a Middlesbrough to Starbeck goods and its rear was run into by the second part of an up Scotch express.

The engine of the passenger train was Fletcher Class 901 2-4-0 No. 178 and it was severely damaged, although both the driver and fireman escaped with their lives; eight passengers were killed and thirty-nine injured.

Less than two years later – on 4 October 1894 – a similar rear-end collision occurred just north of Northallerton and this time no passengers were killed. Again it was an up night Scotch express and the engine, No. 1622 of Class M1, took charge at Newcastle. On the way south the driver experienced trouble with his Westinghouse brake and at Darlington he asked for a pilot engine: No. 905, another Fletcher 2–4–0 of Class 901, was coupled on the front. The driver of the pilot engine considered that as he was only assisting he was not responsible for looking out for the signals; but as the driver of No. 1622 assumed the pilot to be in charge, they both continued oblivious of the signals they were passing at danger. Eventually they collided with the rear of a Darlington–York mineral train.

It was at this period that Pullman cars were being used in the East Coast Joint Stock, and the car *India* was completely destroyed in the Manor House collision: consequently the NER had to pay the Pullman Car Co. £1,700. Car *Iona* was damaged in the Northallerton collision, although it was not beyond repair.

The worst accident, without doubt, was that at the south end of Darlington station on 27 June 1928, when twenty-five passengers were killed and forty-five seriously injured. Class B16 4–6–0 No. 2369 was shunting some vehicles of a parcels train it was working south when the driver over-ran a signal and stopped foul of the main line, on which was an excursion returning from Scarborough to Newcastle, headed by Class C7 4–4–2 No. 2164. The excursion was not booked to stop at Darlington and consequently was travelling at about 45 m.p.h. when it struck the engine of the parcels train, which was pushed back some 60 yd. Some of the passenger train vehicles were badly telescoped but fortunately the wreckage did not catch fire, as has happened in numerous collisions.

In 1870 a boiler explosion took place at Northallerton; the engine, which was built by Stephenson's in 1847, was recorded as having an elliptical boiler 3 ft 8 in. x 3 ft 5 in. On 28 March 1877 the boiler of 0–6–0 No. 510 exploded at Alne and a large piece of boiler plate was found 539 ft away!

On 5 May 1950 the driver of Class A1 4–6–2 No. 60153 was surprised to see that the track in front of him was buckled. At the speed he was travelling it was impossible to stop before reaching the buckled track and the engine was derailed and thrown into the side of a shallow cutting. The buckling was due to the heat of the sun and the inability of the track to expand at the fishplates.

THE LEEDS & THIRSK

The second important line to the north was the Leeds & Thirsk – later the Leeds Northern Railway – for which the prospectus was issued in May 1844. Shortly before this the GNE had been considering an approach to Harrogate from its main line at Pilmoor, via Boroughbridge and Knaresborough, with a branch to Ripon, and also proposed was a Y&NM-supported line from Bolton Percy to Harrogate. The general feeling in Harrogate and district was that the latter would spoil the chances of a more suitable route from Leeds and the inhabitants managed to get it rejected. Meanwhile the Provisional Committee of the Leeds & Thirsk decided to press on, and in 1845 deposited a bill, at the same time as the GNE deposited one for the line from Pilmoor, which was now planned to be extended to Leeds. While the two bills were under discussion George Hudson took a lease of the GNE and he immediately had that company's scheme withdrawn, leaving a clear field for the Leeds & Thirsk, which obtained its Act on 21 July 1845. In addition to its main line, the company was authorized to make two spurs to connect with the Leeds & Bradford Railway at Bramley; a further connection with the Leeds & Bradford at Holbeck; a curve to connect with the GNE at Thirsk; and two short branches at Starbeck leading to Harrogate and Knaresborough. On the same day the Y&NM Act for a line from Church Fenton to Harrogate, via Wetherby, also received the Royal Assent.

When the first sod of the Leeds & Thirsk was cut on 20 October 1845 the company was already contemplating extending its line to join the Stockton & Hartlepool Railway at Billingham, and application to Parliament for the necessary powers was made in the session 1845–6. The route applied for was direct from the Leeds to Thirsk line at Melmerby, passing under the GNE at Northallerton and on the west side of Yarm by means of a long viaduct. But under pressure from George Hudson it was agreed that the section between Melmerby and Northallerton should be withdrawn and that the Leeds & Thirsk trains would use the GNE line between Thirsk and Northallerton. This, the second Leeds & Thirsk Act, was passed on 16 July 1846 and, in addition to the extension, the company was authorized to make junctions with the Stockton & Hartlepool, the Stockton & Darlington and the Clarence Railway, at Billingham, Eaglescliffe and Stockton respectively. On the same day permission was given to divert one of the proposed spurs to the Leeds & Bradford Railway (known as the St Helen's Mill or New Laith's branch) and also to extend the proposed Knaresborough branch across the River Nidd 'into and through the town of Knaresborough'.

In the following year (9 July 1847) deviations at Thirsk and in the Crimple Valley were authorized, and in 1848 (22 July) three further Acts gave the company powers to extend from Melmerby to Northallerton, with a connection to the YN&B, and from Harrogate to Pateley Bridge, and to alter the proposed junction with the S&D at Eaglescliffe. It should be pointed out, however, that the Pateley Bridge branch was not built under this Act.

While all the Parliamentary business was progressing satisfactorily, sections of the line were being completed; the first to be opened was that between Ripon and Thirsk over which mineral traffic commenced on 5 January 1848. The formal opening took place on 31 May 1848 and the line was opened for general traffic the following day. Next came the section between Weeton and Wormald Green (which included Starbeck) on 1 September 1848, and Wormald Green to Ripon twelve days later. Completion southwards to Leeds was delayed by the enormous amount of work entailed in constructing Bramhope Tunnel, 3,761 yd long. Trouble was caused by the inrush of large quantities of water and it was estimated that 1,563 million gallons were pumped out. A number of men employed on this task were killed in various accidents, and a memorial in the form of a replica of the northern portal stands above their grave in Otley churchyard. Eventually, on 9 July 1849, the line was opened throughout, three trains being used to carry some 2,000 shareholders from Leeds to Thirsk and back.

The multiplicity of services between Leeds and Harrogate, and the termini used at Leeds between 1849 and the present day would require at least a chapter to explain in detail. For instance the Leeds & Thirsk trains originally terminated at a temporary station in Wellington Street; from there they soon moved to Central station, and shortly afterwards to the Midland

Railway Wellington station, where they remained until the joint NE–LNW New station was opened in 1869. In 1897 an L&Y service between Liverpool and Harrogate commenced: this brought about the use of Central station again, where a reversal was necessary. Between 1897 and 1901 NER locomotives were in charge of the trains between Leeds and Harrogate, but from 1901 until the service became a wartime casualty in 1915 L&Y locomotives worked through.

Midland Railway trains between St Pancras and Harrogate commenced in 1902, worked by Midland engines throughout. Reversal was again necessary, this time at Wellington station, and thus it became possible to catch a train to Harrogate from any of the three Leeds termini. The MR service ceased in 1928.

When train services were being restored after World War I some of the King's Cross–Harrogate trains were diverted from their original route via Askern, Knottingley, Church Fenton and Tadcaster into Leeds Central where, of course, they had to reverse. After some uncertainty this became the accepted route to and from the south, although the long-established 1.40 p.m. from King's Cross continued to use the Church Fenton route until 1947.

A swing back to Leeds Central for local services took place in June 1954, when the first BR diesel railcar units were introduced between Bradford (Exchange) and Harrogate (extended to Knaresborough on Sundays), and in 1962 these were joined by an improved pattern of railcar, working Liverpool (Exchange) and Manchester (Victoria) to Harrogate.

HARROGATE

Harrogate, a busy town of some 40,000 inhabitants, owes much of its nineteenth-century development to its mineral springs, found around the end of the sixteenth century. It became so fashionable to 'take the waters' at Harrogate that numerous large hotels and hydros were built, quite out of proportion to the size of the town. To cater for the visitors through trains from London were introduced by the Great Northern and the Midland railways and in LNE days some of the services from King's Cross were provided by Pullman trains. The first of these, originally known as the *Harrogate Pullman*, began running between King's Cross and Newcastle, via Leeds and Harrogate, in July 1923. Two years later it was extended to Edinburgh, but in September 1925 it was re-routed via Church Fenton, omitting the call at Leeds but still serving Harrogate. From 1 May 1928 it reverted to the Leeds route and at the same time it was re-named the *Queen of Scots*.

In September 1925 the *West Riding Pullman* commenced running between King's Cross and Leeds, although the up working started from Harrogate; in May 1928 it was extended to Harrogate and Newcastle. From September 1935 the train, re-named the *Yorkshire Pullman,* terminated at Harrogate, so that it did not clash with the streamlined *Silver Jubilee* service introduced on the same day between Newcastle and London via York. Similarly the introduction in September 1937 of another LNE streamlined service – the *West Riding Limited* – led to the re-routing of the up *Yorkshire Pullman* via York, which continued until Pullman services were withdrawn at the start of World War II.

The *Queen of Scots* and the *Yorkshire Pullman* were both re-instated after the war, but the former ceased running in 1964 because of lack of patronage north of Harrogate. However, be-tween King's Cross and Harrogate it was replaced by the *White Rose* – a Pullman service run in approximately the same times as its predecessor.

Whereas the Pullman trains of the pre-1939 era carried mainly visitors to Harrogate, today they are chiefly used by business men. The 1914-18 war was the first blow to Harrogate's spa trade, and World War II sealed its fate. With its wealth of hotels it became a major evacuation centre for Government departments and Ministries moved from London: more than twenty hotels were requisitioned for offices. Since the war those able to reopen have catered extensively for conferences and con-ventions; delegates are often brought by specially chartered trains from London and elsewhere.

For many years Harrogate has been popular as a dormitory town for Leeds, Bradford and York business men, but today they do not travel by train: the services to Bradford (Forster Square) were withdrawn in February 1957 and the York ser-vices are currently threatened.

The first railway to reach Harrogate was actually the Y&NM

branch from Church Fenton and Wetherby, opened to Brunswick station just six weeks before the Leeds & Thirsk reached
Starbeck. This line is dealt with in Chapter II, but as a portion of
it was used in 1862 to gain access to the new central station in
Harrogate it will be referred to again here.

The Leeds & Thirsk was barred from direct entry to Harrogate by Almscliff bank and took the far easier route via the
Crimple and Stonefall valleys to Starbeck, at the price of not
having a station in Harrogate proper. Harrogate's main affinity
was with Leeds, but the journey thence from the Y&NM Brunswick station in the centre of Harrogate was long and roundabout. The shorter Leeds & Thirsk route involved travelling to
Starbeck to join the trains.

The two routes to the south crossed at Crimple, on the
southern outskirts of Harrogate, with the Y&NM being carried
over the valley on Crimple Viaduct and the Leeds & Thirsk on
the floor of the valley. With the formation of the NER in 1854
some form of unification became a possibility; on 8 August 1859
an Act was obtained sanctioning the construction of three connecting lines and a new centrally situated station :

1. From the original Leeds & Thirsk line a mile north-east of
    Pannal station to connect with the former Y&NM branch
    at the southern end of Crimple Viaduct.
2. From the line leading to Brunswick station, through the
    centre of Harrogate, to connect with the Leeds & Thirsk
    a mile north-west of Starbeck.
3. From a point a mile north-east of the new Harrogate
    station (Dragon Junction) to join the L&T at Starbeck.

The new station was built on line 2, and together with the three
new lines it was opened on 1 August 1862.

The final link was a short connecting curve at Starbeck between the Leeds Northern line and the Knaresborough branch,
authorized in 1863 and probably installed in the following year;
it is known to have been disconnected at the eastern end by the
turn of the century.

And what of the position today? Most of the lines opened in
1862 are still in use, but the Leeds & Thirsk line from Pannal
Junction to Starbeck has been closed and lifted. Regular passenger trains continued to use the route until L N E days although

mostly they were LMS trains from Leeds Wellington station. They entered Harrogate station from the north at 2.42 and 4.50 p.m. and as there was no need to detach and turn the engine they could work forward again on their return trip to Leeds at 3.5 and 5.10 p.m. The route was closed to goods traffic in May 1951 and part of the site is now the permanent base of the Royal Yorkshire Show.

THE LEEDS & THIRSK (LEEDS NORTHERN) CONTINUED

It has already been mentioned that to obtain the Act of 1846 the company agreed to amend its requirements to a line from Northallerton to Stockton instead of from Melmerby to Stockton, and to use GNE metals between Thirsk and Northallerton. But subsequently there were second thoughts about this matter: in its 1848 bill the company applied once again for the Melmerby–Northallerton section and was successful. Consequently when its trains from Leeds to Stockton commenced on 2 June 1852 they did not run via Thirsk, and in fact could not do so because there was then no connection between the Leeds Northern and the GNE at Northallerton. Not until 1 January 1856, when the connecting curve had been installed, did it become possible to travel over the Leeds–Thirsk–Northallerton–Stockton route. From that date until 1901, the Melmerby–Northallerton line was treated as an unimportant branch; in 1901, however, it was doubled and henceforward was the more important route of the two. The Melmerby–Thirsk line was then allowed to decline until it was finally closed in 1959. To allow trains using the improved route to call at Northallerton station a connecting spur had to be made from the former Leeds Northern line at Cordio Junction to the GNE line at Northallerton South Junction; they could then use the 1856 curve to rejoin the Leeds Northern line at Low Gates. At the same time a single-line connection was provided for traffic from the down main line to the Leeds Northern line to the north-east, thus obviating trains crossing the path of those on the up main line; a similar connection for up trains was not built until thirty years later.

Early in World War II two temporary platforms were constructed on the low-level ex-Leeds Northern line, on the site of the Melmerby branch platforms which had become redundant after the 1901 alterations. These platforms were part of a scheme to provide an alternative main-line route through North-allerton in case the high-level lines suffered bomb damage. Two tracks were laid from the Leeds Northern line to join the main line north of the station, but as they crossed the Northallerton–Hawes branch at only a slightly lower level a novel method of working was adopted : the Hawes branch was carried over the emergency line on bogies, which could be moved away should the emergency line be required. The Northallerton–Hawes service could still have been worked by using the north side of the Castle Hills triangle, which would have simply entailed the reversal of all trains to and from the branch.

At the turn of the century the NER initiated plans to make Northallerton an important centre for freight traffic. A large marshalling yard was to be built in the V between the main line and the Leeds Northern line south of Northallerton, with access and exit curves to both lines, but although extensive powers were granted by the NER Acts of 1901 and 1903 the scheme was dropped. Consequently although Northallerton did possess a small locomotive depot, mainly for serving the Wensleydale branch, it did not develop as a railway centre and it remains a typical North Riding market town. It is, however, the adminis-trative centre of the North Riding.

North of Harrogate the Leeds Northern was closed to passenger traffic as far as Northallerton from 6 March 1967, although by this time only Ripon and Melmerby were still open. Newby Wiske was closed in September 1939 as a wartime measure, never to re-open; Pickhill was closed in September 1959, Sinderby in Janu-ary 1962, and Nidd Bridge and Wormald Green in June 1962. Goods traffic continued to reach Ripon from the south until 6 October 1969.

The long-established service between Leeds and West Hartle-pool had been reduced to a single down train and the one-time popular joint NE–LNW service between Newcastle and Liverpool, via Sunderland, Stockton and Harrogate, had dwindled to one train from the Tyne to the Mersey, although other trains on this service ran via Leeds, Harrogate and Nor-thallerton, thence over the main line via Darlington. The Pull-man services north of Harrogate ceased with the disappearance of the *Queen of Scots* in 1964, already mentioned.

During World War II the Leeds Northern route proved invaluable for freight traffic from the north-east coast to the Midlands and Lancashire as it could travel to Leeds without occupying the main line; in addition, if it was routed via Wetherby, it could reach the yards at Neville Hill without passing through the bottle-neck at Holbeck. Now every scrap of freight traffic has disappeared between Leeds and Northallerton, but there is still a large amount between Eaglescliffe and Northallerton as this provides the main outlet to the south from the dense industrial area on Tees-side.

BRANCH LINES

The North Eastern was fortunate in having some delightful country branches – delightful for anyone not in a hurry, but considered anachronisms in this motor car and bus age. Those which ran along the Yorkshire dales were some of the best.

First came the branch to Richmond – the gateway to Swaledale, but although various schemes were mooted for its extension along the dale nothing ever materialized. Powers for the branch were applied for by the Great North of England Railway in 1844 and the Act, passed on 21 July 1845, authorized a line 9¾ miles long from Dalton (later Eryholme) to terminate at 'Back of Friars' at Richmond, on the opposite side of the River Swale to the ancient town which is famous in history and song.

The terminus at Richmond dates back to the opening of the line on 10 September 1846, and it is a picturesque example of Victorian railway architecture adapted to fit in with the local buildings.

It was on this double-line branch that Vincent Raven, the C M E of the North Eastern Railway, carried out tests with his final design of electrically operated fog signalling apparatus. He had patented a mechanical system in 1895 and this, with slight modifications, continued in use on the main line until October 1933. The electrical system installed on the Richmond branch was brought into use in August 1911 and, in addition to indicating in the engine cab the position of the distant and home signals, it could be used to show the driver which route was set up at diverging junctions. The current for the apparatus was picked up on the engine by a wire brush which came into contact with a ramp in the four-foot at the respective signals.

The three intermediate stations on the branch and the terminus were closed on 3 March 1969 although one – Moulton – was converted to an unstaffed halt on 1 October 1956. The junction station at Eryholme was closed in 1911.

Near Richmond the famous (or infamous) Catterick Camp was built during World War I, and to serve this sprawling establishment a four mile single-line branch was constructed, leaving the Richmond branch at Catterick Bridge. In the 1914–18 war troop trains were run to and from the terminus of the military line and on one occasion a set of coaches laden with soldiers ran away, were derailed and wrecked. Between the wars the Catterick Camp line was operated as a siding, but the large influx of troops from 1939 onwards necessitated an unadvertised passenger service, which was worked by the LNE. Finally the service comprised three trains from Darlington to Catterick Camp in the early hours of Monday mornings, provided to enable soldiers returning from week-end leave to reach their units in time for duty.

In 1846 the GNE obtained powers for three branches, Pilmoor–Boroughbridge, Northallerton–Bedale, and Dalton–Malton, but within a matter of weeks the company was taken over by the Newcastle & Darlington Junction Railway which thereupon changed its name to the York & Newcastle Railway (from 27 July 1846).

The first branch to be completed was that to Boroughbridge, a distance of six miles : this had started life in 1843 as a proposed line from Pilmoor to Harrogate, with a branch to Ripon. The inhabitants of Harrogate were, of course, far more interested in a line to Leeds, and eventually the GNE offered to extend to Leeds in competition with the Leeds & Thirsk Railway. The bill for the Pilmoor–Harrogate section had actually reached the Committee stage in Parliament when, as described earlier in this chapter, George Hudson obtained a lease on the GNE and had the measure withdrawn. The powers were then pruned to the line from Pilmoor to Boroughbridge and this was opened on 17 June 1847. To provide a connection with main-line trains the isolated station at Pilmoor was erected.

In 1847 the Y&NM obtained Parliamentary sanction to a line from its Church Fenton–Harrogate branch near Pannal to join the GNE line at Boroughbridge, but because of the financial economies necessary on the downfall of George Hudson construction was abandoned.

The scheme was resurrected in 1865 as part of a plan for a through route from Leeds to Scarborough, with new lines between Leeds and Wetherby, and Knaresborough and Boroughbridge, together with a link across the main line at Pilmoor between the Boroughbridge and Malton lines, and also a curve at Malton to allow through running on to the York–Scarborough line. Existing lines to be utilized were Wetherby-Knaresborough, Boroughbridge–Pilmoor–Malton, and Malton–Scarborough. The Act was passed on 23 July 1866 but here again economy brought about second thoughts, and as far as we are concerned in this chapter only the Knaresborough–Boroughbridge section was eventually built. Work on the link at Pilmoor was well advanced and a bridge across the main line lasted until the widening scheme completed in 1933. The embankment west of the main line acquired a gantry of signals although there was no track and no trains : they were erected for testing the eyesight of drivers.

The seven miles of track between Boroughbridge and Knaresborough were eventually opened on 1 April 1875 and as it was impossible to project the Pilmoor–Boroughbridge line westwards a new station was necessary at Boroughbridge. The original branch was operated by an engine stationed at Boroughbridge but when the extension to Knaresborough was opened the whole line was worked as a branch from Knaresborough to Pilmoor by an engine stationed at Starbeck. The line was single throughout and it served a purely agricultural area.

The 1875 station at Boroughbridge remained in use until passenger trains on the branch ceased from 25 September 1950, while the older station continued in use for goods until 1964. After the withdrawal of the passenger trains the branch was cut at the Pilmoor end and until 1957 the goods service operated as far as Brafferton from the Knaresborough end.

It was on this branch that the LNE introduced a novel form of signalling in 1936, whereby the ordinary semaphores were dispensed with and various types of movable and immovable boards provided instead. The fixed boards comprised a location marker board with black-and-white diagonal stripes and a section-limit board with red-and-white stripes; the movable ones were a station board pivoted on a vertical axis, and a gate caution board, pivoted on a horizontal axis. To signal danger, the two latter boards were placed facing at right angles to the line; in the clear position they were revolved through 90 degrees to present only their edge to an approaching train. After dark only the station board exhibited a light, and that only when in the clear position. The other signals were illuminated by a special headlamp carried on the engine.

The Northallerton–Bedale line was the first part of a branch which eventually stretched thirty-four miles to Hawes, at the head of beautiful Wensleydale. Authorized by the GNE Act of 26 June 1846, it was actually opened by the York, Newcastle & Berwick in 1848. The 11¾ miles on to Leyburn were built under the Bedale & Leyburn Act of 4 August 1853, with capital largely provided by local landowners. This section was opened to freight traffic on 24 November 1855 and to passengers on 19 May 1856.

Invasion of the large area of the North Riding unsupplied with railways was constantly threatened, the plans most dangerous to the NER perhaps being those of the Northern Counties Union Railway of 1846, which hoped to build lines from Thirsk to Clifton (south of Penrith) and Bishop Auckland to Tebay: the northern portion was, of course, eventually built by the South Durham & Lancashire Union Railway. In the Wensleydale area, however, the possibility of invasion continued to haunt the NER, which from 1 January 1858 took over the small Bedale & Leyburn Railway to forestall any attempts at infiltration: this takeover was ratified by the Act of 8 August 1859.

In 1865, by the Hawes & Melmerby Act, powers were obtained to build a line from Hawes to Wensley, with a connection from Finghall to the ex-Leeds Northern line at Melmerby; this scheme was postponed for economy reasons and it was eventually replaced by a cheaper plan to connect Hawes and Leyburn, a distance of sixteen miles. This was duly authorized on 4 July 1870, opened to goods traffic on 1 June 1878 and to passengers four months later.

The main traffic over the single-line Wensleydale branch was milk and stone – the former from the rich pasturelands in the valley and the latter from the hills lining each side. To travel the length of the line was a fascinating experience. Sitting in the branch train at Northallerton awaiting departure time one could see a procession of expresses and goods trains on the main line, whilst the little Class O 0-4-4 T stood at the head of the Hawes train with its Westinghouse brake pump busily panting away. As the train progressed up the dale the soft lush countryside gradually gave way to the hard moorland with its stone walls and rushing streams, until one finally arrived at the grey little town of Hawes, where the station was actually joint North Eastern and Midland property.

And what entrancing names some of the wayside stations had: Leeming Bar (where the Great North Road was crossed), Jervaulx, Finghall Lane, and Constable Burton. West of Leyburn was Aysgarth with its famous falls.

Passenger services along the length of the dale were withdrawn on 26 April 1954 and ten years later the goods service was withdrawn from the western end of the line, which is now open only to Redmire.

Returning to Pilmoor, the single-line branch to Malton was opened on 19 May 1853, but this was only after three Acts in three years, applied for by three companies! First came the GNE application to build from Malton to Dalton (three miles north of Pilmoor) with north and south connections to the main line; this was actually authorized on 18 June 1846. Next came the York & Newcastle Act of 9 July 1847, with powers for a line south-westwards from the above line at Husthwaite, to join the main line at Raskelf; and finally the line as built was authorized by the York, Newcastle & Berwick Act of 22 July 1848. The latter Act involved complete modification of the line west of Gilling, with connections to the main line between Raskelf and Pilmoor. Actually only the northern curve was built and the southern curve had to be re-authorized in 1865. It was finally opened between Bishophouse Junction and Sunbeck Junction on 9 October 1871.

The original passenger service between Malton and Thirsk used the north curve and the later service between Pickering and York used the south. Trains between Malton and Thirsk gradually faded away west of Gilling and the Malton–Gilling service was withdrawn from 1 January 1931. The section between Gilling and Bishophouse Junction was used until the

York trains were withdrawn on 2 February 1953, and subsequently the south curve was removed. The north curve remained in use for the summer Saturday-only trains between Scotland and Scarborough until September 1962; before the summer of 1963 the junction at Pilmoor was destroyed by the derailment of a parcels train. To get trains on the main line moving again the junction was relaid with plain track, and when the Scarborough service was due to recommence it seemed pointless to replace the junction when the trains were eventually to run via York anyway. Consequently the branch could henceforward be reached only from the Malton end. The branches themselves are dealt with in Chapter IV.

In recompense for the withdrawal of the Hawes & Melmerby line the NER agreed to build a branch from Melmerby, north of Ripon on the Leeds Northern line, to Masham. This was authorized on 13 July 1871 and opened on 9 June 1875, with one intermediate station at Tanfield. It served a purely agricultural community but it did have its moments of activity. In the early years of the century a private narrow-gauge railway was built westwards from the terminus to serve the contractors building reservoirs for Leeds and Harrogate Corporations. In World War II the lanes around Masham were used for storing ammunition for use on the Second Front and numerous special trains were run to deliver and remove this.

The passenger service was an early casualty, being withdrawn on 1 January 1931, but the goods service managed to continue until 11 November 1963.

Further south the Leeds & Thirsk planned a branch to Pateley Bridge and this was actually authorized by Parliament in 1848 but was allowed to lapse. The NER revived the idea and received powers for the branch on 21 July 1859. Opened on 1 May 1862 it played an important part in the life of the fertile dale until killed by the internal combustion engine : the passenger service was withdrawn from 2 April 1951 and the freight service followed in 1964.

Here again the higher reaches of the valley were served by a private railway needed for reservoir-building. Bradford Corporation constructed a standard-gauge line along the valley to the site of the reservoirs at Angram and Scar House, and from 11

STATION EXTERIORS

(21) *Tynemouth (1847, closed to passengers 1882)*

(22) *Newcastle Central (1850)*

STATION INTERIORS

(23) *York, looking north along Platform 4 (now platform 8)*

(24) *Typical wayside station—Piercebridge (closed 1964)*

September 1907 until 1 January 1930 there was a passenger service between Pateley Bridge and Lofthouse, worked latterly by a steam railcar purchased from the Great Western Railway. The line closed in 1936 on completion of the constructional work on the reservoirs and the line was then dismantled.

There was an end-on connection between the NER and the Bradford Corporation lines at Pateley Bridge, although through running was not operated; special instructions allowed coaches conveying special parties to be transferred between the lines.

E. L. Ahrons records how the whistle of an earlier branch engine was used on Saturday nights to announce the forthcoming departure of the branch train to the citizens of Pateley Bridge, who were drowning their sorrows in the public houses of Harrogate!

The East & West Yorkshire Junction Railway – a protégé of the York & North Midland – was authorized on 16 July 1846 to run 15¼ miles from York to join the Leeds & Thirsk at Knaresborough. In the following year the company did not see eye-to-eye with George Hudson and considered throwing in its lot with the Leeds & Thirsk, then making advances. The Hudson influence triumphed, however, and from the partial opening on 30 October 1848 the line was worked by the York, Newcastle & Berwick Railway, although later the motive power was provided by E. B. Wilson & Co., the locomotive builders of Leeds. From 1 July 1851 it was taken over by the Y&NM, a move ratified by the Act obtained in the following year. On 1 October the remaining portion of the line was opened to join the Leeds & Thirsk, thus completing a route across the River Nidd to Starbeck.

By its Act of 9 July 1847 the York & Newcastle was authorized to build a branch from Raskelf to Easingwold but this was never constructed. Forty years later the independent Easingwold Railway was formed to serve the country market town, and a standard-gauge branch was built leaving the NER main line at Alne. The branch, 2½ miles long, cost £17,000 and was opened on 27 July 1891. The Easingwold Railway possessed two engines, although when the second was obtained in 1903 the first was sold. When the locomotive was under repair, another was hired from the NER or LNE. Eventually ex-NER locomotives of Classes J71 and J72 took over the working completely, although neither class could be accommodated in the small engine shed at Easingwold. The coaching stock originally comprised two ex-NER four-wheelers and subsequently two similar vehicles of North London Railway origin. Finally an ex-Great Central six-wheeler made its appearance.

A passenger service was provided until 29 November 1948 and the last train conveying freight and parcels traffic ran on 27 December 1957. A Station Hotel adjoined the single-platform terminus at Easingwold, and never can this establishment have done as much business as it did one day in the summer of the line's final year, when two or three hundred thirsty railway enthusiasts descended on Easingwold after traversing the line in open wagons !

On the very day that this is being written British Rail is introducing its summer 1973 service, with even faster trains over the east coast main line. The famous Flying Scotsman is booked to cover the $268\frac{1}{4}$ miles between Kings Cross and Newcastle in 217 minutes passing York in 149 minutes and Darlington in 185 minutes. However, the timing of 36 minutes pass to pass between York and Darlington is little better than the 40 minutes North Eastern locomotives were regularly achieving over the same stretch of line (but in the opposite direction) sixty-five years ago! And that was from start to stop!

The closure of the Leeds Northern line, and of the branches on the east side of the main line, means that the main line is now the only link between north and south in North Eastern territory. At one time, for instance, passengers from Scarborough to the north could travel via Whitby and Middlesborough; Malton and Gilling; or Malton and York, but now only the latter remains, involving extra mileage and expense.

CHAPTER VI

East to West in Southern Durham

THE STOCKTON & DARLINGTON RAILWAY

We now cross the River Tees and for the first time enter County Durham. It perhaps helps to state at the beginning that most of the lines described in this chapter go from east to west and that here we are not concerned, for example, with any part of the south–north east coast trunk line.

The coal-producing area around Shildon and Bishop Auckland was unfortunate in having no waterway, and consequently the coal supplies for the Darlington area had to be carried in the panniers of pack-horses and asses, more than trebling the price at Darlington compared with the price at the pit-head. It was of course suggested that a canal should serve the area, and in October 1768 Robert Whitworth put forward plans for one from Winston (nine miles west of Darlington) to Stockton. This would have served only a district outside the coalfield, and the idea lapsed.

After years of fruitless discussion the subject came up again at a dinner held in Stockton in 1810, when a railway from Winston to Darlington and Stockton was suggested by Leonard Raisbeck. Almost as an afterthought a canal was suggested as an alternative, and a committee was set up to look into the proposals. The famous engineer Rennie was engaged to make a survey, and in 1813 he came out in favour of a canal, on the same course as Whitworth had recommended forty-five years earlier.

Once again the matter was allowed to rest until in May 1818 a further report on a canal was issued, this time after a survey by George Leather. This proposed canal would have bypassed Darlington and Yarm completely, a fact that spurred Richard Miles, Jonathan Backhouse and others to seek yet another opinion, this time of George Overton, a Welsh engineer who was related to the Cairns family of Yarm. Overton reported upon the feasibility of a canal or a railway, the latter at an estimated cost of £124,000, and as his line passed through Darlington and near to Yarm it found favour with the inhabitants of both towns. Naturally the citizens of Stockton preferred the scheme which left Darlington out in the cold and a struggle between the two factions developed.

The speed with which the Darlington Committee worked finally swung opinion in its favour. Overton presented his report on 29 September 1818, and to enable the scheme to be considered at the next session of Parliament the plans were hurriedly prepared and deposited by the end of the month, even though it had not been settled whether a canal should be dug or a railway built. The decision for a railway was taken on 13 November 1818 and within a week £25,000 had been subscribed. Although the Stockton Committee changed its tune and advocated a railway instead of a canal – still bypassing Darlington, however – it was fighting a losing battle, although its persistence did eventually lead to the formation of the Clarence Railway.

Unfortunately the first Stockton & Darlington Railway bill was narrowly rejected, by 106 votes to ninety-three. Application to Parliament was again made in 1820, but on the death of George III the bill was withdrawn. The Act was passed in 1821, receiving the Royal Assent on 19 April, and authorized a line from Witton Park Colliery to Stockton, together with five branches – to Yarm Bridge, Northgate Bridge (Darlington), Coundon Turnpike, Evenwood, and at Stockton.

Edward Pease of the famous Darlington Quaker family was not satisfied with Overton's survey, and he called in George Stephenson to make yet another. In spite of protests about wasting money Stephenson was authorized to go ahead and before the end of 1821 he submitted a modified route, certain sections of which were outside the limits of deviation imposed by the original Act, thus making a further application to Parliament necessary. The Act, the Royal Assent for which was given on 23 May 1823, included powers for the Croft branch (part of which is still in use in the east coast main line), and the Haggerleases branch.

After many trials and tribulations the line was opened throughout on 27 September 1825, and most readers will know

Dobbin's famous painting of the scene, with the inaugural train hauled by *Locomotion No. 1* crossing the bridge over the River Skerne at Darlington. Although Dobbin was present at the opening he was only a boy and the painting was done years later from drawings and impressions. On the opening day the first wagons were transported over the Etherley and Brusselton inclines by means of winding engines and attached to *Locomotion No. 1* at Masons' Arms level crossing at Shildon. Preceded by a man on horseback carrying a red flag, the first train on the first public steam-worked railway set off amid cheers for Stockton, which was reached in mid-afternoon. Then followed what was to become a familiar pattern at the opening of new lines, namely a banquet with numerous toasts, held in this case at the Town Hall in Stockton.

The main concern of the s &d was the carriage of coal and at that time it was never considered that passengers would be of any importance. They were carried in horse-drawn vehicles provided by contractors, but the railway company itself did not bother with them until October 1833.

In the early days, of course, there were no stations as we know them today: the horse-drawn coaches would stop almost anywhere to pick up passengers, the usual locations being adjacent to inns and public houses. Masons' Arms crossing at Shildon, and Fighting Cocks station between Darlington and Stockton, were both named after local hostelries where passengers could enjoy themselves while waiting.

Much of the route opened on that eventful day is still in use, although some of it does not now have passenger trains. The section over Brusselton and Etherley inclines has been dismantled, and even there it is still possible to find many traces of the 1825 line, including stone sleepers, bridges and embankments. By using the Darlington–Bishop Auckland railcar service it is still possible to cover the section between Albert Hill Junction (Darlington) and Shildon, and similarly, by using the regular-interval Darlington–Saltburn service it is possible to cover the section between Oak Tree Junction (east of Dinsdale) and Eaglescliffe. Between Albert Hill Junction and Oak Tree Junction and between Eaglescliffe and Bowesfield Junction, the present trains do not run on the original course. In the former section it was replaced by a line from the south end of Darlington station, which joined the original line at Oak Tree Junction, authorized under an Act of 1883 and opened on 1 July 1887. A station at Dinsdale on the new line replaced Fighting Cocks on the original route from that date but Fighting Cocks remained open as a goods depot until 9 March 1964. Between Eaglescliffe and Stockton much of the original route was abandoned when the line was moved to run adjacent to the Leeds Northern in 1852-3. Between Oak Tree Junction and Eaglescliffe was held the famous Centenary Procession of 1925, when fifty-three engines and trains, old and new, proceeded slowly along the line watched by thousands of people. The last exhibit was the veteran *Locomotion No. 1* which had worked the very first train here a century earlier. For the procession it was propelled by a petrol engine hidden in the tender, and to add to the illusion oily waste was burned in the firebox to produce smoke from the chimney.

Once the S&D had begun shipping coal at Stockton it was soon inconvenienced by the shallow channel up the River Tees and began looking for a suitable site for a wharf further down the river. Haverton Hill, on the north bank, was considered but eventually the choice was what is now Middlesbrough, on the south (or Yorkshire) bank.

Whereas Darlington (population 5,800) and Stockton (population 6,500) were both established towns, Middlesbrough at that time consisted of a few houses only. Now it has 157,000 inhabitants, and although the last of the Cleveland ironstone mines has closed it is still an important iron and steel centre – in fact the Lackenby Works of the British Steel Corporation is one of the most modern steel works in the world. The numerous industrial installations include the large Imperial Chemical Industries chemical plant at Wilton, to the east of Middlesbrough.

The Middlesbrough extension of the S&D was authorized by an Act of 23 May 1828 and it was opened on 27 December 1830, leaving the main line to Stockton at what is now Bowesfield Junction and within 100 yd crossing the River Tees into Yorkshire on a suspension bridge. The Act stipulated that the bridge should have one arch 72 ft wide and not less than 19 ft above low-water mark, and to fulfil these conditions it was decided to erect a suspension bridge to the designs of Captain Samuel Brown. Unfortunately the bridge did not prove successful, the loads carried over it having to be severely restricted, and it was replaced by a bridge with masonry piers and cast-iron girders in 1841; this had three river spans of 89 ft, and two shore spans of 31 ft, with four girders for each span as the two lines were carried independently. When it came to be replaced in 1907 the original piers and foundations were retained, and they are in use to this day.

At its western extremity the S & D consisted of four rope-worked inclines worked by stationary engines at Etherley and Brusselton, with a 1½ mile level stretch between the foot of the eastern Etherley incline and the foot of the western Brusselton incline. This stretch was worked by horses and to carry the line across the River Gaunless the first iron railway bridge was erected. The North Eastern Railway carefully preserved this historic bridge when it was replaced in 1901, and it became one of the most prized relics in the Railway Museum at York, opened in the early days of the L N E.

At the foot of the eastern Etherley incline the line crossed the Bishop Auckland–Barnard Castle road on the level, and it was here that the S & D passenger service from Shildon terminated : as mentioned earlier the company took over the passenger services in 1833, and the Shildon–St Helens to Auckland service was inaugurated on 1 December. Passengers were conveyed over the Brusselton Ridge in rope-hauled trains until 13 October 1858, when the trains were diverted to the so-called Tunnel branch, which had been opened to goods traffic two years earlier. The Tunnel branch did not in fact pass through Shildon tunnel : it forked off the Shildon–Bishop Auckland line, swung round the northern end of the Brusselton Ridge into the Gaunless Valley and then connected with the 1825 line at St Helens. For the next five years – until 1 August 1863 – a service was provided from Bishop Auckland to St Helens via a reversal at the north end of Shildon tunnel, but this was modified when a direct line from Bishop Auckland joined the Tunnel branch at Fieldon Bridge Junction in connection with the South Durham & Lancashire Union Railway.

At the western end of the S & D were two branches – to Black Boy and Haggerleases – both built to serve collieries.

Progress north of Shildon was blocked by a range of hills over 500 ft high, and although a branch to Coundon was authorized in the original Stockton & Darlington Act of 1821

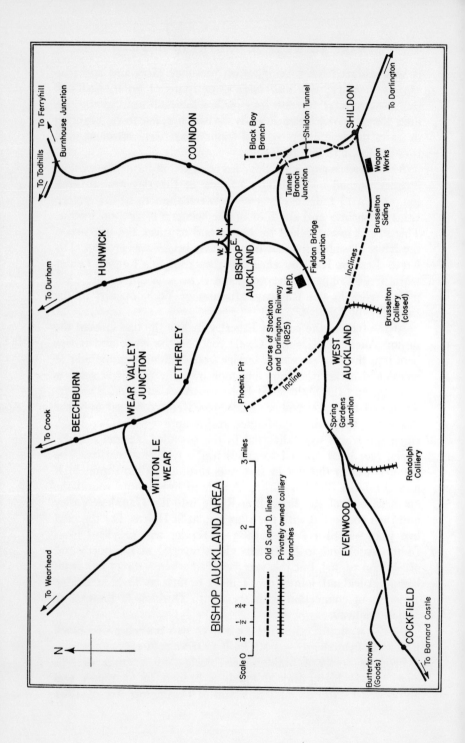

BISHOP AUCKLAND AREA

Scale 0   1/4   1/2   3/4   1   2   3 miles

Old S. and D. lines
Privately owned colliery branches

To Ferryhill
Burnhouse Junction
To Todhills
COUNDON
Black Boy Branch
Shildon Tunnel
SHILDON
To Darlington
Tunnel Branch Junction
Wagon Works
To Durham
HUNWICK
N.
E.
W.
BISHOP AUCKLAND
Fieldon Bridge Junction
Brusselton Siding
Inclines
M.PO.
Course of Stockton and Darlington Railway (1825)
WEAR VALLEY JUNCTION
ETHERLEY
Phoenix Pit
WEST AUCKLAND
Brusselton Colliery (closed)
To Crook
BEECHBURN
Incline
Spring Gardens Junction
Randolph Colliery
To Wearhead
WITTON LE WEAR
EVENWOOD
COCKFIELD
To Barnard Castle
Butterknowle (Goods)

N

(and modified in the Act of 1823) nothing was done until the success of the railway had been assured. Consequently the Black Boy branch, as it was known, was not opened until 1827. This was worked by horses at first, as the winding engine situated on the crest of the hill was not complete. It was estimated that the transport of coal to Shildon by rail instead of horse and cart saved 1s 6½d per ton.

		s	d
Leading by carts from pit to railway per ton		3	0
Expenses of man at Shut (sic) and repairs 30 tons per day			1½
Railway dues and haulage to join Black Boy intended branch, being ¼ mile at 2d per ton per mile			½
		3	2
By railway 2¾ miles at 2d per ton per mile			5½
Self-acting plane to Denburn Beck			6
Engine at Shildon Bank Top			6
Expense of getting on to the branch from the present pits, deterioration of value of road to pits etc.			2½
		1	7½ (sic)

Advantage by railway 1s 6½d

In addition to the Black Boy Colliery, Adelaide, Eldon and Deanery pits were also served by the branch and by 1842 the annual tonnage was:

Black Boy Colliery	92,641	tons
Adelaide	65,622	,,
Eldon	59,399	,,
Deanery	49,308	,,

The inconvenience of the two Black Boy inclines was largely obviated when Shildon tunnel was opened on 19 April 1842, although they continued to serve the pits connected to them.

In an attempt to obtain some of the north-to-south passenger traffic the s&d commenced a service to a temporary terminus at South Church. From 1 May 1842 a horse-bus service connected with the terminus of the Durham Junction Railway at Rainton Meadows. The bus was provided by a contractor, paid 2s 3d per mile; the horses had to be changed twice on the fifteen mile journey and if the scheduled time of two hours was exceeded by more than five minutes the contractor was liable to a fine of 5s; if the lateness exceeded ten minutes the fine rose steeply to £1 ! From Rainton Meadows, Gateshead could be reached via the Brandling Junction Railway and the Pontop & South Shields.

Shildon tunnel, variously quoted in NER records as 1,217, 1,220 and 1,225 yd long, was constructed without an Act of Parliament by Joseph Pease, Thomas Meynell and Henry Stobart, and they retained ownership until it was taken into the Wear Valley Railway, together with the Bishop Auckland & Weardale Railway, the Weardale Extension Railway, and the Wear & Derwent Railway, by an Act of 22 July 1847. The Wear Valley Railway was then leased to the S&D for 999 years from 1 October 1847. The section northwards from South Church, opened in 1843 by the Bishop Auckland & Weardale Railway, will be dealt with in Chapter IX.

On 1 October 1830 the Haggerleases branch was opened throughout from St Helens to its terminus near Butterknowle : it was renamed the Butterknowle branch in 1899. It followed the course of the River Gaunless and was built primarily to serve pits at the head of the valley; these, owned by the Rev Luke Prattman, employed 700 men and boys by 1894. Powers for the branch were obtained by the Act of 17 May 1824, replacing those granted in the original Act of 1821 for a line to Evenwood Lane. Some 400 yd short of the terminus the line crossed the river on a stone bridge built on the skew and this aroused a great deal of interest when it was built : although it was predicted that it would not stand long enough to carry traffic it did in fact remain in use until 30 September 1963, when the section west of Evenwood Colliery was closed.

Trains were worked by horses until 1856, although in 1848 the engineer was asked to report on the cost of putting a small locomotive to work. His report stated that this would be too expensive, and the idea was shelved, to be successfully resurrected in 1856. A passenger service commenced running as far as Lands in 1858 and for a short period in 1859 was extended to Haggerleases. On the opening of the adjacent line to Barnard Castle the inhabitants of the valley were served by the stations at Evenwood and Cockfield, and the service on the Haggerleases branch was reduced to market trains on Thursdays and Saturdays until it was withdrawn in 1872.

A section of the Haggerleases branch was used to form part of the Bishop Auckland–Barnard Castle line and the portion built by the South Durham & Lancashire Union Railway commenced at Spring Gardens Junction, 1¼ miles west of St Helens. This will be referred to later in this chapter.

OPENING AND CLOSING DATES, SHILDON AREA

	OPENED		CLOSED	REMARKS
	Goods	*Pass*	*Pass*	
Shildon–Witton Park	27.9.1825	–	–	Service diverted via
Shildon–St. Helens	–	1.12.1833	13.10.1858	Tunnel branch
St. Helens–Haggerleases	1.10.1830	–	–	–
St. Helens–Lands	–	13.10.1858	1.5.1872	–
St. Helens–Tunnel Junction	13.9.1856	13.10.1858	1.8.1863	Replaced by direct service
Fielden Bridge Junction–Bishop Auckland	1.2.1863	1.8.1863	18.6.1962	–
Shildon–South Church	1.1842	19.4.1842	–	Still used by Darlington–
South Church–Bishop Auckland	8.11.1843	8.11.1843	–	Bishop Auckland service
Spring Gardens Junction–Barnard Castle	1.2.1863	1.8.1863	18.6.1962	South Durham & Lancashire Union Railway

Retracing our steps from Shildon to Darlington we first pass the now-deserted Shildon marshalling yards, once the scene of great activity as coal poured eastwards, and at Simpasture Junction the old Clarence Railway route struck off to the left. At Heighington (originally known as Aycliffe Lane) there is still a portion of the cobbled platform and it was here that *Locomotion No. 1* was put on the rails after being hauled from Newcastle by horses. Approaching Darlington the Barnard Castle line came in on the right and on the opposite side was the entrance to North Road Works, opened in 1863 and closed in 1966 after a century's invaluable service. Before reaching the present North Road station the site of the locomotive scrap yard can be seen on the right, and it was hereabouts that the Depots branch left the main line to reach the coal depots adjacent to Northgate Bridge. On the opening day six wagons of coal were detached from the inaugural train and run on to the depots, which have now disappeared.

The current North Road station is the second, opened in 1842 to replace the original station of c. 1825 which stood east of the bridge over North Road (formerly A1). The building with the clock tower, between the station buildings and North Road, was the goods station. Unfortunately all traces of the original station have now disappeared – it was demolished in 1864. The North Road was at first crossed on the level, but a bridge was provided under an Act of 1855.

Shortly after crossing the stone bridge over the River Skerne – prominent in Dobbin's painting of the opening-day scene but now widened by the addition of another bridge alongside – the Croft branch goes off to the south at what was Albert Hill Junction. This was authorized under the Act of 23 May 1823 but it was not opened until 27 October 1829 : ten years later it was purchased for £20,000 by the Great North of England Railway, which thought of incorporating it in the main line from Gateshead to York. In the event, of course, the GNE built only the section from Darlington to York, but it did use part of the Croft branch through what is now Bank Top station. North of Bank Top the branch was used solely as a connection to the s&d until the Newcastle & Darlington Junction completed its line from Shincliffe and joined what was the Croft branch at Parkgate Junction.

The completion of the n&dj on 18 June 1844 brought into being the famous level crossing over the s&d a short distance north of Parkgate Junction, which has now been removed. The first NER Rule Book gives very explicit instructions for the working of this crossing, including the statement that 'the coal and mineral trains are invariably to give way to the passing of passenger trains'. Every driver had to 'sound his whistle at least $\frac{1}{2}$ mile before reaching the crossing, and continue to do so until he has got the attention of the signalman'. Speed over the crossing was then limited to 10 m.p.h. Anyone disregarding the rules had to be reported and 'the signalman to be liable to a fine of Five

Shillings in every case in which he shall omit to report any engine driver or other person not complying with these rules'.

Until 1887 all the east coast main line and the s&d cross-country trains used this level crossing, but on 1 July 1887 a new line was opened from Polam Junction (immediately south of Bank Top station) to join the former s&d line at Oak Tree Junction, east of Fighting Cocks station. This meant that much more convenient connections could be provided by diverting the Saltburn to Tebay and Penrith trains into Bank Top station at the south end. They could then rejoin their old route at Albert Hill Junction by leaving from the north end. Previously there had been no direct connection between the trains on the two lines and passengers wishing to pass from one to the other had to use the connecting shuttle service between Bank Top and North Road.

Fighting Cocks station, of which a fair proportion still remains, was closed on the opening of the new line and replaced by Dinsdale. From Oak Tree Junction the present line exactly follows the 1825 line as far as Eaglescliffe; on this stretch there is now a public station – formerly the halt for workmen at Allens West, built during World War II. It was at this point that the Yarm branch diverged to the south to serve the old market town which is actually in Yorkshire, although the railway terminated in County Durham on the north bank of the Tees. The branch was opened on 17 October 1825, three weeks after the main line, and a horse-drawn service to Yarm was provided until 1833.

When steam locomotives began to work the passenger trains in 1833, it was decided that they should call only at the station erected at the junction of the branch and the main line, and not proceed up and down the branch as the horse-drawn coaches had done. The junction station was closed on 16 June 1862 and in the following year it was decided to transfer the waiting shed and the platform to Aycliffe (later Heighington), although the clock could remain as it was 'likely to be useful to the Mineral and Goods enginemen'.

The main purpose of the Yarm branch was to convey coal to the depots established there on land owned by the Meynell family. In 1870 the cost of converting the depots to take normal wagons instead of chaldron wagons seemed uneconomic, and the coal business was transferred to the adjacent station on the Leeds

Northern line in the following year. The land on which the branch had been laid was sold in 1874 and now little trace remains, much of the course having been obliterated by road widening; however, the depot agent's house at Yarm is still inhabited and in good repair, complete with s&d house-number plaque. Remains of the depot can also be seen.

An odd feature here is that the NER continued to pay the rent for the depots (£200 per annum) to Mrs Meynell until she died in April 1903 – more than thirty years after the depots had been abandoned.

At Eaglescliffe (known as Preston Junction from 1854 to 1878) the original course of the s&d was on the east side of the Yarm–Stockton road (now A19), but the Leeds Northern, when it came along in 1852, laid its line on the west side of the road. It was obvious that for interchange purposes the two railways should run together instead of on opposite sides of the road, so it was agreed that the Leeds Northern should lay an extra two tracks alongside its own for the use of the s&d for 1,000 years at 1s per annum rental. The s&d commenced running over the new line on 25 January 1853 and from this date Eaglescliffe became an important interchange point: there had been no station there until this date. At the south end of Eaglescliffe station the two routes crossed on the level as the Leeds Northern assumed its position on the west side of the s&d, ready to continue to Stockton. When the Stockton extension of the Leeds Northern was first mooted it was suggested that it should pass below the s&d in a cutting 18 to 20 ft deep, but John Dixon of the s&d pointed out that 'as the object of railways is, or ought to be, to afford all possible facilities for the ready transfer of traffic from one district to another' the crossing of the two lines at different levels would be unwise.

When the crossing was completed regulations similar to those at the level crossing at Darlington were issued, with passenger trains taking precedence over goods and minerals and a speed limit of 10 m.p.h. The instructions in this case were signed by Thomas MacNay for the s&d and Samuel Smiles for the Leeds Northern.

Eaglescliffe station originally comprised a single island platform, with one face used by up and down s&d trains and the

other by up and down Leeds Northern trains. This meant that
two trains of one company could approach the same platform at
one time from different ends. As might be expected the Inspecting
Officer frowned upon this dangerous method of working and
insisted that although trains in one direction could run straight
into the platform, those in the other direction must pass the
station and then reverse in.

North of Eaglescliffe the lines passed through lands owned by
Marshall Fowler of Preston Hall and six months after the
opening of the new lines he complained to the Board of Trade
about the revised method of working trains at Eaglescliffe
station. Passengers were

> exposed to inconvenience and danger – the up line is so
> far from the platform that on a wet day you must get wet in
> passing between the platform and the carriages and have to
> cross two lines of railways. As for shunting back, besides the
> delay, the public opinion is decidedly against it, for if the
> coach should get off the rail you must be squeezed together by
> the engine.

A copy of the letter was forwarded to the secretary of the
s&d, who stated that his company was quite prepared to make
the changes required to enable the trains to run into the station
as suggested by Mr Fowler; a week later plans were submitted
showing how this was to be done. The memory of the s&d
officers must have been very short (either by design or by accident), but the Board of Trade was not to be caught out, and
the Inspecting Officer replied sharply that what the s&d was pro-
posing was what he had expressly forbidden only the previous
year. Fowler's complaint on the delay brought the reply that
'this is a definite amount of time which should be allowed for in
the timetable of the Company just as much as the time required
for collecting tickets or shifting the engine from front to rear of
a train in approaching a terminal station is allowed for'. It is
odd that the possibility of running the down trains of both companies into one platform, and the up trains of both companies
into the other, was not considered !

Powers to construct a curve joining the s&d and the Leeds
Northern, to allow through running from west to south and vice

versa, were obtained in the Leeds & Thirsk (Hartlepool Extension) Act of 1846 but, according to the deposited plans, this was to join the Yarm Depots branch and not to be a separate curve as actually built. Land was purchased from Leonard Raisbeck in 1853 but it is not certain when the curve was actually installed. It has been confirmed that it was most used for the passage of ironstone from Rosedale to Ferryhill iron works.

Approaching Stockton the two routes diverge: the Leeds Northern line to the present Stockton station (for many years known as North Stockton) via Hartburn Junction takes the left fork, and the line to Bowesfield Junction takes the right. The layout at Bowesfield Junction is complicated and it used to be the busiest point in the Tees-side area, with freight and passenger trains passing almost continually. The first track here was that of the s&D, which passed in 1825 on its way to the Stockton terminus; then, when the line to Middlesbrough was opened in 1830, it struck off from this point. Next came the curve connecting the s&D with the Leeds Northern line at Hartburn Junction, thus allowing through running from the Middlesbrough direction to the north, and at present used by the hourly service of diesel railcars between Newcastle and Middlesbrough. The date of opening of this curve does not seem to have been recorded, although reference to its use by mineral trains in 1861 has been found. In 1864 the Darlington Committee was reminded that the curve had not been passed for passenger traffic by the Government Inspector and it was recommended 'that the trains between North and South Stockton (later Thornaby) be discontinued at the end of this month and that in the meantime the Engineer have the works in a state sufficiently complete to insure it being passed'.

THE CLARENCE RAILWAY

In 1823 the party who favoured a canal (and later a railway) from Stockton to a point west of Darlington promoted the Tees & Weardale Railway. Bills submitted in 1824 and 1825 were both rejected. Further changes of plan meant that the proposed line would not reach Weardale at all, and its name was changed to one that honoured the Duke of Clarence, later William IV. Challenging as it did the monopoly of the s&D, the Clarence was simply asking for trouble, and wherever possible the s&d duly placed difficulties in its way. However, on 23 May 1828 the Clarence Railway Act was passed, authorizing a main line from Haverton Hill to join the s&d at Sim Pasture Farm, between the $17\frac{1}{4}$ and $17\frac{1}{2}$ mileposts from Stockton, together with three branches, with the avowed object 'to open a shorter course than heretofore between several valuable Mines of Coal and the River Tees'.

The Act made clear that the Clarence did not intend working its own traffic: privately owned wagons could be used provided they were constructed as directed by the company, and the passenger carriages were to be licensed. They had to carry the name and address of the owner, painted in white on a black ground in capital letters and figures at least 3 in. high, and details of each vehicle had to be registered with the Clerk of the Company of Proprietors. Another interesting section prohibited waggoners from carrying 'any Net, Gun, Engine or other Instrument for taking or destroying Game, under a penalty of £5'.

Further Acts for deviations and modifications were obtained in 1829, 1832, and 1833. In addition to the main line from Haverton Hill to Sim Pasture Farm the 1828 Act included powers for three branches:

1. To the Deanery, St Andrews Auckland
2. From How Hills to Broom Hill
3. From Harrogate (or Harget's) House to Stockton at Brown's Bridge

In 1829 2 and 3 were abandoned and replaced by the City of Durham branch and the Stockton branch: the former was planned to leave the main line at Stillington Moor House and terminate at Old Elvet Street in Durham City. In addition two more branches were authorized:

4. Sherburn branch, leaving the City of Durham branch at Ferryhill
5. Byers Green branch, also leaving the City of Durham branch at Ferryhill

The 1829 Act also imposed restrictions on the use of 'locomotives (or moveable steam engines) on the City of Durham branch through Mainsforth and Chilton without the permission in writing of Robert Surtees, Esq.,' and also on the Byers Green branch 'through Whitworth of the lands of Robert Eden Shafto, Esq.'.

In 1832 the City of Durham branch was abandoned north of Shincliffe and in fact was not built north of Ferryhill, whereas the Sherburn branch did not get beyond Coxhoe, although uncompleted earthworks are visible as far as Quarrington. Nor was the Deanery branch built. Thus of the seven branches mentioned only two – to Stockton and Byers Green – were completed. In 1833 the Chilton branch was authorized and this too was built, although lifted as recently as 1962.

Dates of opening of the various sections are difficult to establish precisely, no doubt because only minerals were carried at first and presumably no public announcements were made. Even the company's Minutes are vague on such matters. A portion of the line was opened in July 1833 and Tomlinson records that the first coals for landsale passed from Sim Pasture to Stockton in August 1833, severely affecting the amount sold by the rival S&D. The amount of coal shipped by the new company increased rapidly – as did the receipts.

Period		Coal Shipped (tons)	Revenue £	s	d
July–December	1833	9,060	490	–	1
January–December	1834	43,596	2,201	18	7
do	1835	57,058	3,189	11	2
do	1836	117,321	6,777	13	2
January–November	1837	180,263	11,078	9	6

The first coals were shipped at Stockton and later, from 30 January 1834, at Haverton Hill; in the same year the line was extended to Port Clarence and shipment commenced there using a single loading point.

The City of Durham branch reached Ferryhill on 16 January 1834 and in 1835 the Sherburn branch was opened as far as Coxhoe, together with part of the Chilton branch, the remainder of which was opened in 1836. Finally the Byers Green branch was opened on 31 March 1837, for mineral traffic only, of course. Passenger services commenced between Stockton and Coxhoe in January 1836, using horse-drawn coaches, but by 1839 this traffic was let to a contractor who used his own engines and coaches, paying the Clarence Railway ¼d per mile and charging the passengers up to 2d per mile. Thus the fare for the sixteen miles was 2s outside and 2s 6d inside. From Coxhoe a horse omnibus carried passengers on to Durham at 1s outside and 1s 6d inside for the five mile journey. The restriction on locomotives was repealed by the Act of 1837.

The Clarence Railway was unfortunate in being unable to reach the coalfield, any coal consigned to it having to pass over the s&d on the first stage of its journey. By levying a duty of $2\frac{1}{4}$d per ton per mile the s&d was able to impose a crippling 2s 6d surcharge on each Newcastle chaldron wagon of 53 cwt sent over the Clarence Railway, even though the distance was five miles shorter.

Consequently the financial position of the Clarence was never healthy and was not improved by the removal of the head office to London, with a new board of directors, by request of the Exchequer Loan Commissioners. By 1842 the company owed the Commissioners the sum of £149,394 and when it was unable to meet its commitments the Commissioners took charge of the line, instructing that it should be sold. Immediate action on the part of certain shareholders raised some £80,000 which staved off disaster and the company managed to continue.

At this time the Clarence Railway was engaged in a struggle with the Great North of England, Clarence & Hartlepool Junction Railway, a company which was trying to gain access to the West Durham coalfield with the object of shipping coal at Hartlepool. This will be dealt with in Chapter VIII, but it must be mentioned here that in the struggle the Clarence was backed up by the Stockton & Hartlepool Railway, with whom it worked very closely; in fact, in August 1844, it leased its line to the s&h for twenty-one years. This lease was authorized by an Act passed by Parliament on 27 June 1843; by a subsequent Act of 30 June 1852 the amalgamation of the Stockton & Hartlepool and the Hartlepool West Harbour & Dock Co. was authorized together with the purchase of the Clarence Railway. In reality this amalgamation was already an accomplished fact, having been cleverly engineered by Ralph Ward Jackson to outwit the Stockton & Darlington Railway. The joint concern eventually passed to the NER in 1865.

Immediately before World War I it was decided to electrify part of the Clarence Railway in order to move West Durham coal to the marshalling yards at Newport (near Middlesbrough) faster and more economically. The section concerned was from Simpasture Junction to Carlton, and thence via the west to south curve to join the Wellfield–Bowesfield Junction line of 1877; from Bowesfield, of course, the route lay along the s&d Middlesbrough extension of 1830. Electrification was not completed until 1 July 1915 and because of the restrictions imposed on the shipment of coal by the war the scheme had a bad start. Even after the war the traffic did not increase as much as expected, and by 1934 when extensive renewals of the overhead equipment were becoming due, it was decided to abandon the electric working and to revert to steam. On 7 January 1935 the extensive marshalling yards at Shildon were closed and on 9 July of the same year the engine shed followed suit; the ten electric locomotives were transferred to Darlington for storage and, except in one case, never ran again, although not broken up until 1950.

The time allowed from Shildon to Newport, a distance of fifteen miles, was fifty-seven minutes, over a line which favoured the eastbound loaded trains as it had $14\frac{1}{4}$ miles of falling gradients and only $\frac{3}{4}$ mile of rising gradients. The electric locomotives were for some time allowed a maximum load of 1,000 tons, but from 29 November 1922 it was raised to 1,400 tons, exclusive of brake-van and subject to a maximum of seventy wagons.

Traffic continued to use this route until 1963 when the section between Simpasture Junction and Stillington North Junction was closed. Normally Clarence Railway passenger traffic was confined to the Stockton–Coxhoe and Port Clarence services, but from 30 November 1841 to 12 March 1842 a short-lived service was worked by the s&d between Simpasture Junction and Stillington North Junction as part of a service between Darlington and Coxhoe introduced by the s&d to gain a footing in the north to south (and south to north) traffic. Passenger traffic between Stockton and Ferryhill was withdrawn from 31 March 1952, and between Billingham and Port Clarence from 11 September 1939, although a service to Haverton Hill, latterly for workmen only, continued until 3 November 1961.

THE ROUTE TO THE WEST

West of Darlington the line to Barnard Castle was authorized on 3 July 1854 and built by an independent company – the Darlington & Barnard Castle Railway. It was opened on 8 July 1856 from a junction with the s&d at Hopetown to a terminus in Barnard Castle, which until April 1965 was used as the goods station. The station's portico is now to be found in the Valley Gardens at Saltburn : it was removed thence at the expense of the Saltburn Improvement Company in 1863 and over the last 100 years it has been used as a shelter in the gardens. A few years ago it was reported unsafe and its fate was debated by the local council, but it was decided to preserve it.

Between Darlington and Barnard Castle two independent branches were built southwards – the Merrybent Railway and the Forcett Railway – both serving quarries but also taking normal goods traffic. The Merrybent received its Act on 11 June 1866 and was opened on 1 June 1870. It was soon in financial difficulties and in 1878 it came into the possession of the Darlington District Bank, from whom it was purchased by the NER in 1890, although the Act confirming this did not receive the Royal Assent until 30 July 1900. It was closed on 6 July 1950 and the track was subsequently lifted. In 1961 the formation of the line was used as the basis of one carriageway of the Darlington bypass motorway!

The Forcett Railway, closed in 1966, received its Act on 2 June 1865 and was opened in October 1866. From its inception it was worked by the NER and under the Railways Act of 1921 it subsequently became part of the LNE.

Beyond Barnard Castle the inhospitable moors and mountains of the Pennines made a bleak outlook for a railway into Westmorland, but the promise of ore traffic from the Ulverston area of Lancashire to the blast furnaces of Middlesbrough, and of coal and coke in the opposite direction, provided a spur. In the early references to the line the amount of mineral traffic likely to be carried was the sole topic; its passenger potentialities were not mentioned, no doubt because of the sparsely populated area through which the line passed.

The line was built by a subsidiary company of the s&d, the South Durham & Lancashire Union Railway, and the engineer appointed to supervise the construction, and to design the numerous viaducts, was Thomas Bouch, whose brother, William, was locomotive superintendent of the s&d. Thomas was later the designer of the ill-fated Tay Bridge, for which he received a knighthood on 27 June 1879 – six months and a day before the bridge collapsed.

The sd&lu Act was passed on 17 July 1857 after encountering very little Parliamentary opposition. It authorized a line between the s&d at Spring Gardens Junction (on the Haggerleases branch near St Helens) and the Lancaster & Carlisle Railway at Tebay, with a connection at Barnard Castle to the Darlington & Barnard Castle Railway '187 yards east from the centre of the level crossing carrying the Barnard Castle–Middleton in Teesdale highway'. Initially only the Barnard Castle–Tebay section was built and, as the existing station at Barnard Castle was not suitably placed to allow the line to be extended westwards, the Lancashire Union line had to strike off ½ mile short of the original terminus: it was at this junction that the new station was erected.

After the first sod had been cut at Kirkby Stephen on 25 August 1857 work on the thirty-five mile stretch between Barnard Castle and Tebay proceeded rapidly and uneventfully, in spite of the difficult terrain; the whole of this stretch was passed by the Inspecting Officer on his first visit. It was opened throughout for mineral traffic on 4 July 1861. The formal opening took place on 7 August of the same year, and the line was fully opened to the public on the following day. During its construction the local inhabitants complained of the behaviour of the navvies, and the Chief Constable of Westmorland and Cumberland agreed to provide a constable to curb their poaching activities, provided his wages were paid by the railway. Actually he suggested that four constables would be necessary to cover the whole of the line but the sd&lu would only agree to pay for one. His wages were £1 1s a week, plus 1s 6d a month boot allowance, and 1s a month for oil (for his lamp?). The navvies received 3s 1d to 3s 4d a day and the masons 5s a day.

Apart from its natural beauty the outstanding features of the Lancashire Union line were the graceful viaducts of Thomas Bouch, notably the all-metal structures of Belah and Deepdale, the stone-pillared Tees viaduct, and the stone Smardale viaduct.

The last named, 553 ft long and 90 ft high, still stands between Kirkby Stephen and Tebay, whilst the other three, between Barnard Castle and Kirkby Stephen, are now demolished. Tees viaduct, which remained in use until the line to Middleton in Teesdale was closed in 1965, was 732 ft long and 132 ft high; Belah viaduct – the largest and most impressive – was 1,040 ft long and 196 ft high; and Deepdale viaduct was 740 ft long and 161 ft high. Because of its exposed position and the height reached at Stainmore Summit (1,370 ft above sea level) the weather was always a great adversary; many times the line was blocked by snow for days, and sometimes weeks.

When opened, the line from Barnard Castle to Tebay was single throughout but sufficient land was purchased to take a double line if and when required. Between Belah and Kirkby Stephen, however, three of the viaducts were built wide enough for single track only: new viaducts were built alongside when this section was doubled around the turn of the century. Bowes to Stainmore Summit was doubled in 1867; Barnard Castle to Bowes in 1873; and Summit to Barras in 1874. Eventually double track extended from Barnard Castle to Kirkby Stephen West Junction and from Sandy Bank (a mile east of Ravenstonedale) to Tebay.

The remaining section of the SD&LU, between Barnard Castle and Spring Gardens Junction, was not opened to traffic until 1 August 1863 and in the intervening period all traffic between Bishop Auckland and the west had to be worked round via Shildon and Darlington. To reach Bishop Auckland the Haggerleases branch was used from Spring Gardens Junction to St Helens, then the Tunnel branch to Fieldon Bridge Junction, and finally a new length of line also opened on 1 August 1863, but authorized by an Act in the year following the SD&LU Act.

At the western end the Eden Valley Railway was authorized between Kirkby Stephen and Clifton (south of Penrith) on 21 May 1858; the first sod was cut on 4 August 1858, and the route was opened for mineral traffic on 8 April, and passenger traffic on 9 June, both 1862. At Appleby the line connected with the Midland Railway north of the station, and although another connection south of the station was planned and work commenced, it was not completed. The Eden Valley line was single throughout except for a short section of double track between

Appleby station and the junction of the connection to the Midland, and another at the extremity of the line at Eden Valley Junction, where a later connection was made with the LNW.

The SD&LU and the Eden Valley lines were worked from the outset by the S&D and that company took them over on 30 June 1862, only to be swallowed by the NER on 13 July 1863. The cost of building the two lines had been :

South Durham & Lancashire Union	£666,879	3s	9d
Eden Valley	£204,803	0s	8d

The final development in this area was the authorization of the Tees Valley Railway from Tees Valley Junction (west of Barnard Castle) to Middleton in Teesdale, opened on 12 May 1868. For many years this branch carried a fair amount of stone traffic from large quarries at the end of the line and at one time it handled lead from mines in the hills.

Sixty years ago the line over Stainmore was a busy one, with mineral trains running night and day, raising the echoes across the moors as they blasted their way up to the Summit, or rumbled slowly over the viaducts where, incidentally, only one train was allowed across at a time. The first mineral train of the day left West Auckland at 12.20 a.m., due at Summit Cabin at 2.24 a.m., and the last left at 10.30 p.m. and reached Summit at 12.58 a.m.

There were six passenger trains in each direction 'over the top', all of which started or terminated at Darlington. Barnard Castle – a lively station in those days – was also served by trains to and from Bishop Auckland, some of which were extended to Middleton in Teesdale.

With the decline in passenger traffic a start was made in closing odd stations, but the first complete service to be withdrawn was that between Kirkby Stephen and Tebay, which disappeared from 1 December 1952. The Barnard Castle–Kirkby Stephen–Penrith service managed to last a further ten years, but its trains were withdrawn from 22 January 1962. The section between Tees Valley Junction (west of Barnard Castle) and Kirkby Stephen was closed completely at that time and the track has now been lifted and the viaducts demolished. Any stone traffic remaining from the quarries in the Kirkby Stephen area now reaches Tees-side via the roundabout route of Appleby (NE)–Appleby (Midland)–Carlisle–Hexham and Newcastle.

The Bishop Auckland–Barnard Castle service was withdrawn on 12 June 1962 and the closure of the Darlington–Barnard Castle–Middleton in Teesdale line to passengers on 30 November 1964 and to goods from 5 April 1965, destroyed the last remnants of a once busy network west of Darlington.

The connections to the Lancaster & Carlisle Railway (later LNW) at Clifton, Penrith and Tebay will be dealt with in a later volume.

Much of the Stockton & Darlington Railway is now only a memory : in fact some sections were closed more than a century ago, but traces of the formation can be found all the way from Shildon to Etherley. In the same area the Haggerleases and Black Boy branches are easily distinguishable, and with the development of a new housing estate on the south bank of the River Gaunless the site of the world's first iron railway bridge is easily accessible.

North Road station at Darlington, dating from 1842, has been sadly neglected by British Railways and is now in a sorry state. Plans to turn the station into a railway museum have been discussed locally but no decision has been reached, largely because of the expense involved. There is also a scheme to have a small railway museum at Shildon, using Timothy Hackworth's cottage, later occupied by William Bouch, and the sole remaining building from Hackworth's Soho locomotive building works.

In connection with the 150th aniversary of the opening of the Stockton & Darlington Railway, to be celebrated in 1975, a full survey is being made of all S & D R remains still in existence, and it is hoped that the results of this survey will be published.

CHAPTER VII

From Tees to Wear

COLLIERY LINES

The area covered in this chapter can be divided into two parts, north and south of the Hartlepool–Castle Eden–Trimdon–Ferry-hill line. The southern half is almost wholly agricultural, with an industrial fringe near the River Tees and the coast. Northwards the scene changes completely, with numerous collieries dotted throughout the area, each served by its own railway, either connecting with the NER or running on its own right of way to Seaham Harbour or Sunderland.

As the tide of mining activity moved eastwards across County Durham the mines became larger and deeper and those along the coast at Horden, Easington and Blackhall were amongst the last to be sunk. Some of their seams extend eastwards and a miner may be at work more than a mile out under the North Sea. The small pits adjacent to the River Wear, about five miles upstream from Sunderland, were some of the first, and our interest commences in 1693, when Thomas Allan laid the first wagonway in the area.

Over the next 100 years the mines, and the wagonways serving them, developed to such an extent that on a stretch of the river near Fatfield there were ten coal-shipping staiths rail-connected to some thirty pits. The River Wear was their objective because it provided cheap transport to Sunderland and other coastal ports. However, the larger vessels which came into use as the trade developed were unable to proceed far enough up the river to reach the staiths and small boats had to ferry the coal down to Sunderland for transhipment. This was un-economic, and the mine owners were soon looking for other ways to get their coal to Sunderland or the coast. The obvious answer was a wagonway and eventually four major systems developed :

1. Hetton to Sunderland
2. Penshaw area to Seaham Harbour
3. South Hetton to Seaham Harbour
4. Fencehouses/Rainton area to Sunderland (later running part of the way over the NE Sunderland–Penshaw branch).

The Hetton Coal Co. was a pioneer in the use of steam traction and in 1820–2 obtained five locomotives from George Stephenson to work its new line from Hetton to Sunderland. Because of the hilly country this traversed, it was worked partly by stationary engines, partly by self-acting inclines, and partly by locomotives. According to a contemporary account these sections were (from Hetton) respectively :

1½ miles locomotive hauled
1½ miles stationary engine hauled
2½ miles self-acting incline
2 miles locomotive hauled
½ mile self-acting incline

This line continued in use until 9 September 1959, since when it has been demolished. One of the Stephenson engines continued in use until the present century and fortunately, when withdrawn from service, it was presented to the LNE for exhibition in the Railway Museum at York, where it remains.

The Londonderry family owned numerous small pits in the Penshaw area and their coal was carried to the nearby Wear over early wagonways. Rather than build a line to Sunderland it was decided in this case to make for the nearest point on the coast and to build a harbour there. This turned out to be Seaham Harbour, five miles south of Sunderland, on which work commenced on 27 November 1828, when the Marquis of Londonderry laid the foundation stone. Although called 'visionary and absurd' the harbour was ready for use in less than three years and on 25 July 1831 the first coal was shipped.

As the demand for coal increased, new pits stretched as far as Pittington and the harbour facilities proved inadequate. Consequently on 8 February 1853 work began on building a line from Seaham along the coast to Sunderland, where the Hendon Dock could be used for coal shipment. Construction was so rapid that on 17 January 1854 a train of twenty-four wagons of South Hetton coal was run from Seaham to Sunderland Docks, using the new line as far as Ryhope and the Durham & Sunderland thence to Hendon. This was only a temporary measure, the order being given that the connection between the two lines 'put in specially for the occasion be immediately taken out'. Eventually the Londonderry Railway laid its own tracks parallel to the D&S, and the line was opened throughout on 3 August 1854.

Another early steam-worked railway which deserves mention is the South Hetton Coal Co.'s line from South Hetton to Seaham Harbour. Timothy Hackworth supplied its first four locomotives in 1835 and when one of these was withdrawn in 1875 the frames and boiler continued in use for many years fitted with a snowplough. Eventually it was dumped at the end of a siding, from where it was rescued by the NCB (still with the remains of the snowplough attached), and it now stands on a plinth at the Philadelphia Works.

The Lambton family owned a number of pits in the Fencehouses area. The coal was originally shipped on the Wear near Penshaw and it was on this line that an early trial was made with steam traction: on 21 December 1814 a locomotive built by Phineas Crowther of the Ouseburn Foundry, Newcastle, was set to work. Designed by William and Edward Chapman, it had eight wheels to distribute the weight over the light track. It is recorded as hauling eighteen coal wagons, weighing about fifty-four tons, up a gradient of 1 in 115 at a speed of 4 m.p.h. By purchasing the Newbottle wagonway in 1822, and extending it south-westwards to join up with its own system, the Lambton wagonway obtained a direct route to the Wear at Sunderland over a line opened in 1813. In 1864 an agreement was signed with the NER whereby coal for the staiths at Sunderland could be worked over the main-line company's lines from a point near Cox Green: eventually the centre section of the one-time Newbottle wagonway fell into disuse and it has now disappeared.

The Hon. J. G. Lambton became the Earl of Durham in 1833, and the stud of locomotives built up to work the colliery lines carried the letters E D (Earl of Durham) in cut-out brass letters on the cab or tank sides. In 1876 the title was changed to Lambton Collieries, and after amalgamation with the Hetton Coal Co. in 1911, to Lambton & Hetton Collieries Ltd. Finally, on amalgamation with James Joicey & Co. Ltd in 1924 the title became Lambton, Hetton & Joicey Collieries Ltd, and this was retained until nationalization on 1 January 1947. The main shed and works of this extensive system are at Philadelphia, near Houghton-le-Spring, where major overhauls are carried out and where a few engines were built for the company's own use between 1870 and 1900.

Privately owned colliery railways have been described at some length because of the important part they have played in the story of County Durham and Northumberland. A few of them also carried passengers : this service was originally introduced for the convenience of the miners and their families, but in some cases the general public could also travel. Unfortunately, particularly for the railway enthusiast, this is no longer possible as all such trains have ceased to run. NCB locomotives working their own trains over BR lines can still be seen at various points, and the crews concerned are examined by a BR inspector. Railway company and privately owned locomotives have occasionally collided, and in one case, so it is said, the LNE presented an engine to a colliery company in settlement of a claim when the collision was the fault of the LNE driver.

Another feature of the railway scene, although not peculiar to the North East, has been the use by colliery companies of locomotives formerly owned by a main line. The demand was so great that dealers set up in business to purchase engines from the railway companies, overhaul them, and then sell them to the colliery companies. Prior to World War I, J. F. Wake of Darlington was active in this field, and Frazer of Hebburn bought several locomotives.

THE COAST ROUTE

Practically every through route of the North Eastern was built up of small lines and the coast route between Stockton and Sunderland was no exception. Before the individual companies are dealt with, here is a list of the companies and the sections for which each was responsible :

Leeds Northern	Stockton to North Shore Junction
Clarence Railway	North Shore Junction to Norton South Junction
NER	Norton South Junction to Norton East Junction

Clarence Railway	Norton East Junction to Billingham
Stockton & Hartlepool	Billingham to West Hartlepool
NER	West Hartlepool to Cemetery North Junction
Hartlepool Dock & Railway	Cemetery North Junction to Hart
NER	Hart to Seaham
Londonderry Railway	Seaham to Ryhope Grange Junction
NER	Ryhope Grange Junction to Sunderland

However, the above route did not come into use until 1905: prior to that date there was no direct line between Sunderland and West Hartlepool and the service was worked via Murton and Haswell. In fact the through Newcastle–Liverpool expresses run in conjunction with the LNWR missed West Hartlepool altogether: from Wellfield they continued south to Stockton via Hurworth Burn, Wynyard and Thorpe Thewles. In the southbound direction this involved climbing the steep Seaton Bank, and when descending the bank a compulsory stop had to be made at Ryhope. To avoid these obstacles, to give West Hartlepool a better service and to serve new collieries along the coast, the NER developed a direct route through Horden to Seaham, and there joined up with the Londonderry Railway which gave access to Sunderland.

THE LEEDS NORTHERN RAILWAY REACHES STOCKTON

Before its line to Thirsk was opened the Leeds & Thirsk had decided to extend from Melmerby to Stockton and Billingham, via Northallerton, but in deference to opposition from George Hudson it restricted this to a line from Northallerton to join the Stockton & Hartlepool at Stockton, agreeing to use the Great North of England Railway between Thirsk and Northallerton. Powers for the extension were received in the Act of 16 July 1846 and by the same Act the L&T was authorized to purchase the S&H in order to reach West Hartlepool. This deal fell through, being superseded by a more ambitious plan to reach Newcastle, using the Clarence between Stillington and Ferryhill,

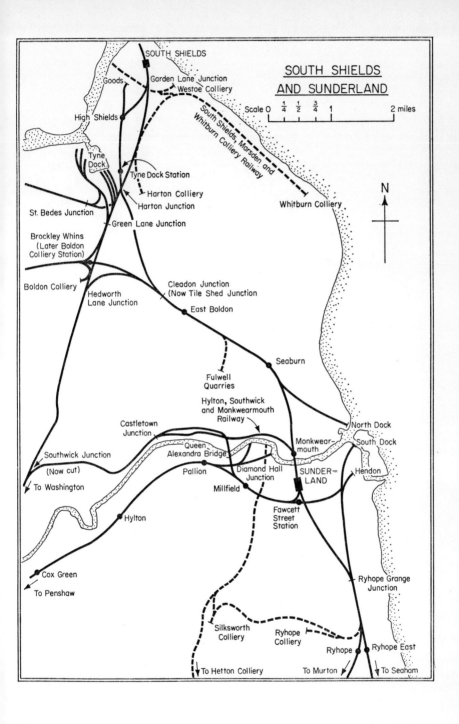

SOUTH SHIELDS
AND SUNDERLAND

Scale 0   ¼   ½   ¾   1   2 miles

SOUTH SHIELDS
Garden Lane Junction
Goods
Westoe Colliery
High Shields
South Shields, Marsden and
Whitburn Colliery Railway
Tyne
Dock
Tyne Dock Station
Harton Colliery
Harton Junction
St. Bedes Junction
Green Lane Junction
Whitburn Colliery
Brockley Whins
(Later Boldon
Colliery Station)
Boldon Colliery
Hedworth
Lane Junction
Cleadon Junction
(Now Tile Shed Junction
East Boldon
Seaburn
Fulwell
Quarries
Hylton, Southwick
and Monkwearmouth
Railway
Castletown
Junction
North Dock
Monkwear-
mouth
South Dock
Southwick Junction
Queen
Alexandra Bridge
Pallion
Diamond Hall
Junction
SUNDER-
LAND
Hendon
(Now cut)
Millfield
To Washington
Hylton
Fawcett
Street
Station
Cox Green
To Penshaw
Ryhope Grange
Junction
Silksworth
Colliery
Ryhope
Colliery
Ryhope
Ryhope East
To Hetton Colliery
To Murton
To Seaham

N

and going onwards via a new line through the Team Valley. After the rejection of this scheme the L&T had to be content with the Northallerton–Stockton extension, which was opened formally on 15 May 1852 and publicly on 2 June. By this time, of course, the Leeds & Thirsk had become the Leeds Northern Railway, considering its original title too restrictive.

The Leeds Northern joined the Stockton–Hartlepool line at what is now known as North Shore Junction, establishing its own station ½ mile south of the junction. In 1853 the West Hartlepool Harbour & Railway (as successor to the Clarence and the Stockton & Hartlepool Railways) agreed to divert its trains into the Leeds Northern station, which became known as North Stockton to distinguish it from the S&D station of 1848 on the Middlesbrough extension, which became South Stockton. The 1893 replacement of the Leeds Northern station became simply Stockton, and South Stockton became Thornaby, which it remains to this day.

In 1920 a further junction was made at North Shore when the line from Billingham Beck was opened : this had been authorized in 1913 but construction of its three miles had been delayed by the war. At Billingham Beck it joined a line from Haverton Hill, which had been opened in 1901, and this provided a new route from the south to the rapidly expanding industrial area on the north bank of the Tees between Stockton and Port Clarence, helping to relieve the busy section between the junctions at Norton and the divergence of the Port Clarence and West Hartlepool lines at Billingham.

On 1 December 1904 the NER commenced working the shuttle service between Billingham and Port Clarence with the two petrol-electric railcars which had spent the summer at Scarborough. In 1905 steam autocars were introduced, and they continued to operate the service until the 1920s; in the early days of the LNE a single engine was provided by Haverton Hill shed, from which the engine was turned out at 5.15 a.m. It shuttled backwards and forwards over the branch all day long, and did not return to the shed until 10.39 p.m. (11.14 p.m. on Saturdays). The public passenger service was withdrawn on 14 June 1954, and workmen's trains in November 1961. These all terminated at Haverton Hill, as the service to Port Clarence was withdrawn on 11 September 1939.

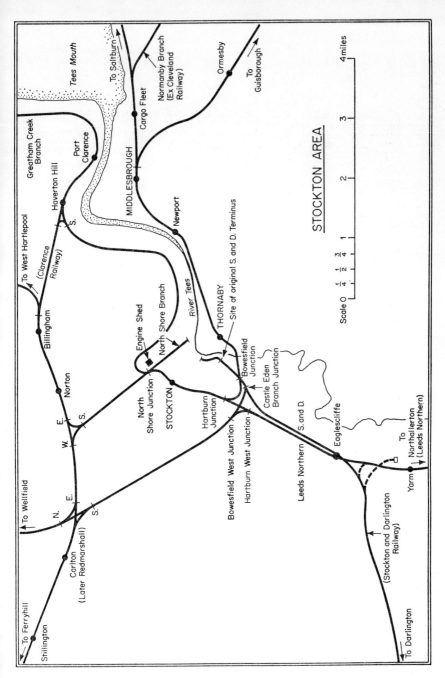

STOCKTON AREA

Scale 0 $\frac{1}{4}$ $\frac{1}{2}$ $\frac{3}{4}$ 1   2   3   4 miles

Port Clarence, although 12½ miles from Middlesbrough by rail, is only a few hundred yards away by the famous transporter bridge which straddles the river a short distance from the city centre. A private ferry plied across the river at this point until 1856, when it was taken over by Middlesbrough Town Council and the river crossing has remained a civic responsibility ever since. A bridge was considered in 1901, and by 1906 a transporter type was recommended. Work commenced in August 1910 and it was opened on 17 October 1911. The total length is 850 ft, with a span of 570 ft between the towers and a height of 225 ft. It carries 350,000 vehicles and 1½ million passengers a year.

THE STOCKTON & HARTLEPOOL RAILWAY

Of the public railways in the area between the Tees and the Wear the Clarence (Chapter VI) was first off the mark with its Act of 1828. The Stockton & Hartlepool Railway, although nominally a separate concern was, to quote W. W. Tomlinson, 'really an extension of the Clarence Railway to Hartlepool'. It was built with the object of diverting some of the coal traffic to the Victoria Dock of the Hartlepool Dock & Railway rather than relying on the tidal river at the Port Clarence staiths of the Clarence Railway. Construction commenced in May 1839, without Parliamentary sanction, and the line was opened to freight on 12 December 1840 and to passengers on 9 February 1841. To legalize the position a bill for the 'incorporation of the proprietors' was submitted and it received the Royal Assent on 30 June 1842. The advantage of having its own dock was obvious to the s&h, and on 23 May 1844 a separate company under the title of the Hartlepool West Harbour & Dock Co. was authorized to build a dock and harbour at Stranton, a bleak deserted area between Seaton Carew and Hartlepool.

The Stockton & Hartlepool struck off to the north-east from the Clarence, east of Billingham, and crossed the Cowpen Marshes around which developed a salt producing industry. The derricks used with the brine-pumping installations give the area the appearance of an oil field! Approaching West Hartlepool, the South Durham works of the British Steel Corporation are on the landward side of the line, while on the seaward side were the extensive sidings devoted to the timber traffic for which West Hartlepool was long famous.

At Norton, once a village outside Stockton but now joined to the town, an east to south curve was installed between the main line and the Stockton branch of the Clarence Railway, to allow through running between West Hartlepool and Stockton. According to the Minutes of the Clarence Railway this curve was proposed on 18 September 1840 and authorized on 26 March 1841 'to be built at the expense of the Stockton & Hartlepool Railway'. At the same time the s&h was given permission to erect a platform on the Clarence at Billingham on payment of 6d per week to the cr.

The present east to south curve was not put in until *c.* 1870 (authorized by Act of 18 May 1866) and investigation on the spot has revealed the site of a much shorter curve with a short radius. This is, no doubt, the original curve referred to in the Stockton & Hartlepool Act, over which a speed restriction of 6 m.p.h. was imposed. If the limit was exceeded the railway company was liable to a fine of £50 and the driver to one of £5. The Junction Inn, enclosed within the triangle of lines, was scheduled to be converted into Norton station house within one year of the passing of the s&h Incorporation Act, and it is believed that this is one of the buildings still remaining, now in use as a cottage.

THE HARTLEPOOL WEST HARBOUR & DOCK COMPANY

The Hartlepool West Harbour & Dock Co. opened its dock on 1 June 1847, when the population of the area was less than 300. Diversion of traffic away from Port Clarence led to friction between the Clarence and the Stockton & Hartlepool, and at one time it looked as if the Clarence might fall into the hands of the Stockton & Darlington. Then perpetual lease of the Clarence was obtained by Ralph Ward Jackson on behalf of the s&h from 1 January 1851, and on 30 June 1852 Parliament authorized 'the amalgamation of the Stockton & Hartlepool Railway and the Hartlepool West Harbour & Dock Co., and also the lease or purchase of the Clarence Railway by the s&h or the amalgamated company'. This amalgamation took place from 17 May

1853 when the new concern took the name West Hartlepool Harbour & Railway Co. It managed to remain independent until 1865 and in those twelve years it proved to be a prickly thorn in the side of the NER and S&D, with its battle for the Cleveland ironstone and the abortive attempt to link up with the LNW.

The power behind the West Hartlepool company was Ralph Ward Jackson who, in a number of respects, behaved as George Hudson had done a decade earlier. His great desire for the welfare of the company led to acts which were not strictly within the letter of the law, and although by these acts the prosperity of the company was enhanced he was censured for purchasing collieries and ships with money obtained for true railway purposes. However, he laid the foundations for the present town of West Hartlepool, with its population of more than 70,000 : a far cry from the figure of less than 300 at the time the first dock was opened! West Hartlepool has grown to be four times the size of its much older neighbour, Hartlepool. (See end of Chapter.)

As might be expected a motley collection of locomotives was handed over to the NER when the West Hartlepool company finally capitulated in 1865. Some were 0-6-0 tender engines with the cylinders placed on either side of the smokebox. These were built by Fossick & Hackworth of Stockton, the Hackworth in the firm being Thomas, brother of the more famous Timothy of Shildon fame. When E. L. Ahrons discovered an engine of similar design at Swindon he described the cylinders, in the now-classic phrase, as being like 'cats up a tree'.

The present West Hartlepool station dates from 1880 (with some additions and alterations in 1904), and it is situated between two sharp curves over which speed is restricted to 20 m.p.h. An interesting alteration has recently taken place for economy reasons. To reach the up through platform with parcels electric lifts were used for many years, but when these became due for renewal it was decided instead to handle up and down trains at the down platform : the cost of track and signalling alterations was less than that of new lifts. This, of course, is a reversion to a method of working favoured by the S&D. In fact Etherley and Crook were worked in this fashion until they closed in 1965.

THE HARTLEPOOL DOCK & RAILWAY

Following the Clarence came the Hartlepool Dock & Railway, which was planned to convert the small fishing port of Hartlepool into an important port for the shipment of coal. The company's first Act (obtained on 1 June 1832) authorized in addition to the dock the construction of a railway from Hartlepool to Moorsley (near Houghton-le-Spring), a distance of fourteen miles, together with branches from Shotton to Pittington (4¼ miles – known as the Littletown branch), Shadforth to Thornley (½ mile), and Castle Eden to Cassop (4¼ miles). Two years later – on 16 June 1834 – the City of Durham branch was authorized, leaving the Pittington branch at Ludworth and terminating at Gilesgate, in Durham.

In the event the main line stopped short at Haswell (opened 23 November 1835), and the Littletown branch terminated abruptly between Thornley and Ludworth; the Thornley branch did reach the colliery of that name on 1 January 1835. Of the Cassop branch, approximately one mile from the junction at Heads Hope was opened on 18 March 1839, but the rest (although partially constructed) was abandoned, as was the remainder of the Littletown branch and the whole of the proposed City of Durham extension.

Out of Hartlepool the H D & R had the long Hesleden bank to climb and this, with a gradient of 1 in 34 in parts, was originally rope-worked. In 1874 a new line was laid on an easier gradient (1 in 50), with one track on either side of the embankment which carried the original line. This involved an unusual modification to the minor road leading to Monk Hesleden, which had been carried through the embankment by a low bridge. Two bridges were built, each spanning one of the new tracks, with the roadway between the bridges carried across the top of the original embankment. Both bridges are still in use and it is possible to inspect the original road through the old embankment.

The route between Hartlepool and West Hartlepool has undergone various changes during the years: it now skirts the dock area whereas at one time it went through it. In North Eastern days a frequent service of steam autocars was provided between the two towns; the LNE replaced these by 'Sentinel' steam railcars. Although closed to the public from 16 June 1947 a service for schoolchildren continued to run until 23 March 1964. The locomotive depot at Hartlepool closed in 1939; the three separate sheds housed mainly freight engines, which were then transferred to West Hartlepool shed: until that time the latter had concentrated on the passenger train workings. West Hartlepool had a straight shed and a roundhouse; it was closed with the withdrawal of the last steam locomotives in 1967 and demolished three years later.

THE GREAT NORTH OF ENGLAND, CLARENCE & HARTLEPOOL JUNCTION RAILWAY

(*Wingate–Ferryhill*)

At Wingate the HD&R connected eventually with a short railway with a long name – the Great North of England, Clarence & Hartlepool Junction Railway, which was conceived in an attempt to prevent mineral traffic from West Durham being funnelled to Tees-side via the S&D or the Clarence. The company obtained its Act on 3 July 1837, and by constructing an $8\frac{1}{2}$ mile line from the Wingate branch of the Hartlepool company to a point $1\frac{1}{2}$ miles north of Ferryhill, it could connect the three railways mentioned in the ponderous title. The first portion, from Wingate to the foot of Kelloe bank, was opened on 18 March 1839. Kelloe bank was originally an incline worked by a stationary engine but latterly locomotives have been used and for a number of years some of the NER Class L 0–6–0 Ts were stationed at Ferryhill shed for banking duties. The gradient profiles show the steepest section as 1 in 37 and between Ferryhill and the summit, $1\frac{1}{4}$ miles west of Trimdon, the line climbs a total of 237 ft.

The company's Act specifically gave powers to make 'a good and substantial bridge of brick, stone, iron or wood over the Great North of England Railway, of not less than 52 ft span and 16 ft 6 in. high'. At this time the GNE line was not built; in fact, it was not until June 1844 that its successor, the Newcastle & Darlington Junction, opened between Darlington and Rainton Crossing. The Clarence branch from Ferryhill to Coxhoe was already in existence – trains had been using it for five years – but whoever drew up the Junction Railway bill forgot to seek powers to cross the Coxhoe branch to reach the Byers Green branch. For some years the Clarence placed difficulties in the way of the Junction company, even after the latter had obtained Parliamentary sanction to cross the branch. This of course delayed still further the completion of the essential link with the west. Passenger services appear to have commenced between Hartlepool and Ferryhill in October 1846 and were withdrawn on 9 June 1952.

As part of his plan to gain control of the east-coast ports, George Hudson arranged for the York, Newcastle & Berwick to take a lease on the Hartlepool Dock & Railway Co. and the Junction company, and this was ratified by the Act of 22 July 1848. The Junction lease was transferred eventually to the NER and remained thus until the grouping of 1 January 1923, when the Great North of England, Clarence & Hartlepool Junction Railway finally passed out of existence.

THE DURHAM & SUNDERLAND RAILWAY
AND SUNDERLAND

On the same day as the passing of the Hartlepool Dock & Railway's City of Durham Extension bill (16 June 1834), the Durham Junction Railway was authorized, followed on 13 August 1834 by the Durham & Sunderland Railway bill. Both these railways were intended to connect with the Hartlepool company, the first to form a link in a through route to the Tyne at Gateshead, and the second to give access to Sunderland. It has already been mentioned that the Hartlepool company did not reach further than Haswell and therefore the Durham Junction, which had hoped to connect with the Hartlepool line at Moorsley, was terminated at Rainton Meadows, leaving a gap of about four miles. The Durham & Sunderland was more successful, building from the terminus at South Dock (Sunderland) to Haswell, a distance of 9¾ miles, in time for a formal opening on 30 August 1836; coal had passed down the line as early as 5 July 1836. Although the D&S and the Hartlepool line both terminated at Haswell there was initially no connection between them as they were on different levels and almost at right-angles to one another.

The Durham & Sunderland Act merely authorized a line between the two towns, with the branch from Murton to Haswell, not specifying where the Durham terminus was to be sited. The deposited plans show that it was to have been at the head of Gilesgate – an area previously chosen for the proposed Hartlepool Dock & Railway terminus, and later actually used for one by the Newcastle & Darlington Junction Railway. Gilesgate's suitability was due, of course, to its being on a neck of land in the bend of the River Wear, the land sloping sharply down to the river on all sides except the east. To have proceeded beyond Gilesgate would have necessitated an inclined plane of some description.

By a further Act of 30 June 1837 the D&S was empowered to alter the western end of its line, beyond Broomside, and diverted it southwards to Shincliffe instead of Durham, whence it was opened on 28 June 1839. The same Act also authorized the Whitwell and Quarrington branch (planned to join up with the Sherburn branch of the Clarence Railway), and an extension of the main line westwards to Brandon. Shincliffe was closed in 1893 and replaced by a new terminus at Durham Elvet.

The Durham & Sunderland was not interested in such modern inventions as the steam locomotive, pinning its faith on steam stationary winding engines because, no doubt, of the hilly country its line had to traverse. Some years after the opening of the line the NER was concerned about the delay to passenger trains; a survey carried out in December 1855 found that the 4.15 p.m. Sunderland to Hartlepool train was an average of 52 minutes late each day. It was explained that 'the passenger trains were considered secondary to the mineral trains and the delays in consequence were inevitable'. It was suggested that the trains between Sunderland and Hartlepool could be worked throughout by locomotives if a connection was put in at Haswell, and two sidings to avoid the bank-heads constructed at Seaton and Murton. A new station was also recommended for Sunderland.

The original D&S terminus at Sunderland was situated on the Town Moor, near the mouth of the River Wear and adjacent to the docks. The site, latterly obscured by a goods yard, was a little to the west of the South Dock locomotive shed. The second station, known as Hendon and built as a result of the report mentioned above, was some 880 yd to the south. It was opened on 1 May 1858, and the local press carried some pungent criticism of the old station :

> The old building has never been much admired for its architecture, nor for its convenience and accommodation, but it was erected by plain men, with plain notions, who liked better to pocket money than to expend it in beautifying their property.

A short distance farther south was the Londonderry station, but this was closed from 1 October 1868 when its trains commenced using the NER Hendon station. The two routes ran adjacent to one another, and parallel to the coast, for the first $2\frac{1}{2}$ miles; at Ryhope the D&S route turned inland and met one of the most serious obstacles, Seaton bank, which offered gradients of 1 in 44 and 1 in 60 for $2\frac{1}{2}$ miles. Before the link between Hart and Seaham was put in, the secondary route Northallerton–Eaglescliffe–Stockton–Haswell–Ryhope–Sunderland was used for through trains between Liverpool and Newcastle. On 19 August 1889 a driver descending the bank was unable to reduce speed sufficiently to enable one of these (the 2 p.m. from Liverpool) to pass safely round the curve at the foot and the whole train was derailed, injuring 101 passengers. The accident led to the issue of an instruction that every passenger train descending the bank must come to a momentary halt in Ryhope station, thus ensuring that the driver retained control during the descent. The instruction appears to have lapsed in 1960. The route was often used when diversions were necessary because of engineering works on the coast line, and an assistant engine had to be provided for the ascent of Seaton bank.

At Murton the D&S turned westwards, through Hetton and Pittington, to reach Sherburn House from where, as mentioned earlier, it originally continued to Shincliffe. Beyond Murton the other leg of the D&S continued to climb, through South Hetton, to Haswell, where it reached the summit 462 ft above sea level – having climbed from 92 ft at Hendon.

By two separate Acts, both dated 27 July 1846, the Newcastle & Darlington Junction was authorized to purchase the D&S and to make a branch from it at Hendon to join what was then the east-coast main line at Penshaw. When passenger traffic over this line commenced on 1 June 1853 it used a new terminus at Fawcett Street, a mile west of the D & S station, to which passengers bound for Hartlepool had to make their own way.

Both Fawcett Street and Hendon stations remained in use until 1879, when a new central station was opened a short distance north of Fawcett Street. A new connection from Ryhope Grange enabled trains from Durham and Hartlepool to reach it, and another curve diverted into it the trains which formerly terminated at Fawcett Street from the Penshaw direction. A new bridge across the Wear also enabled trains to be extended from Monkwearmouth into the new station; most of the layout completed then has remained in use. The station consisted of two island platforms with an arched overall roof : this was badly damaged by bombing in World War II and was replaced by umbrella type awnings. The station was rebuilt and modernized in 1965, using only one island platform for passengers.

It is not absolutely clear when the Durham & Sunderland was converted from rope to locomotive working but an accident report issued in 1858 confirms that the western section was still rope-worked at that date; the changeover must have taken place not long afterwards. A Sunderland to Durham (Elvet) service was provided until 1 January 1931, when it was cut back to Pittington, although 'miners' gala' traffic continued to use Elvet station. In spite of economies and the introduction of attractive cheap fares the section between Sunderland and Pittington failed to pay its way and it too was closed on 5 January 1953. From 1931, therefore, the route from Sunderland to Durham was via Penshaw and even this was closed to passengers on 5 May 1964. The passenger service between Sunderland and West Hartlepool, via Haswell, was withdrawn on 9 June 1952.

NER DEVELOPMENTS

In the 1870s the NER was engaged in filling up gaps within its area and in 1872 a line was authorized between Bowesfield Junction (Stockton) and Wellfield, where connection was to be made with the West Hartlepool–Haswell–Sunderland line. The new line neatly bisected the railway-starved area bounded by Stockton, West Hartlepool, Ferryhill and Stillington, and it was opened in two sections. The first was from Bowesfield Junction to Carlton (later Redmarshall) South Junction, and the curve thence to Carlton West to give access to the former Clarence Railway, opened on 1 May 1877. This section was later to form part of the electrified route between Shildon and Newport, over which electrically-hauled mineral trains commenced running in 1915; it has never carried a regular passenger service.

The remaining section, from Carlton South Junction to Wellfield, together with the east to north curve at Carlton, followed on 1 March 1880; this carried a passenger service until 2 November 1931, serving the stations of Thorpe Thewles, Wynyard and Hurworth Burn. At one time it was planned to raise the status of the route to a secondary main line and for this purpose a curve was installed in 1901 to connect with the Leeds Northern route between Eaglescliffe and Stockton, but according to the *Railway Magazine* it was closed the following year. Use of this route would have entailed missing both Stockton and West Hartlepool; the Corporation and the Chamber of Trade of Stockton complained to the NER, which after using the route for a short time for express goods traffic decided to abandon it.

In 1871 the independent Hylton, Southwick & Monkwearmouth Railway was formed with the object of developing industry on the north bank of the Wear west of Sunderland. This short line connected with the NER at both ends when it was opened on 1 July 1876, but the connection at its western end to the Tyne Dock–Consett line at Southwick Junction was removed many years ago. The line was worked by the North Eastern from the outset but it was not a financial success and was purchased by the NE in 1883 for £130,000.

Road and rail crossings of the Wear in the vicinity of Sunderland were poor and in 1900 the NER and Sunderland Corporation jointly obtained an Act to build a double-deck road and rail bridge across the river at the western edge of the town. The railway, on the top deck, provided a connection between Diamond Hall Junction, on the Sunderland–Penshaw branch, and Castletown Junction, on the Hylton, Southwick & Monkwearmouth line.

When completed in June 1909 the Queen Alexandra Bridge possessed the heaviest single span in Great Britain, the centre span weighing some 2,600 tons – more than three times as heavy as the centre span of the Forth Bridge. Altogether the bridge contained about 8,500 tons of steel. It took four and a half years to build and cost approximately £450,000, of which Sunderland Corporation contributed £146,000. It proved a white elephant for the North Eastern, as within twelve years the line over it was closed. It is still open for road traffic on the lower deck.

The origins of the Londonderry Railway have already been mentioned, and for many years it continued on its uneventful way, providing a purely local service for coal and passengers between Seaham and Sunderland. At Sunderland its passenger trains used the North Eastern station at Hendon from 1868, moving to the new central station in 1879, but at the opposite end of the line it provided a single-platform terminus of its own, at Seaham. On special occasions the Londonderry trains ran beyond Sunderland: for instance, on the occasion of Boldon Races at Easter 1898, four LR trains were extended to South Shields and one to High Shields; in addition, one set of LR coaches was worked through to South Shields by a North Eastern engine.

The services were worked by an interesting collection of engines. For passenger trains there were some pretty 2–4–0 Ts, dating back to 1856, and a single 0–4–4 T built at Seaham in 1895: this was eventually sold by the NE and found its way to the Isle of Wight, only to return to Tyneside to end its working days. For the mineral services there were 0–6–0 tender engines dating back to 1855.

For many years the gap in direct rail communication between Hartlepool and Sunderland was a source of annoyance and various schemes were proposed, including in 1871 a plan for an independent line from Sunderland, through West Hartlepool, to Middlesbrough. This was partly in response to the proposed line between Wellfield and Bowesfield, which bypassed West Hartlepool completely. An alternative plan was for a line from Sunderland to Newport, passing under the Tees, but both schemes fell through when the NER bill was passed.

The final move came on 31 July 1893 when the NER obtained an Act to build a line nine miles long from a junction with the Hartlepool–Sunderland line at Hart to join the Seaham & Sunderland Railway at Dalton-le-Dale, near Seaham. Also sanctioned in the Act was the conversion of the Londonderry Railway for passengers and an agreement with the Marquess of Londonderry to this effect. Eventually the Marquess agreed to sell his line to the NER and this was ratified in the Act of 30 July 1900; the company commencing working it on 6 October 1900. In the meantime the NER was making progress with the line south of Seaham in spite of the number of valleys (or 'denes' as they are called locally) which had to be bridged.

The NER did not take over the Londonderry Railway's stock of coal wagons or its colliery lines; these, together with Seaham Harbour, went to a new company called the Seaham Harbour Dock Co. This still exists and now handles coal shipments for the NCB, being excluded from the nationalization of the coal industry in 1947 because it was a transport concern.

Lord Londonderry's private station, Hall Dene, used by the family when they resided at Seaham Hall, was also excluded from the 1900 sale: the Marquess retained the power 'to stop other than express trains within reasonable limits'. Between 1900 and 1923 Hall Dene was used only four times, and in 1924 the LNE approached Lord Londonderry's agent with a request that the privilege should be extinguished. This was agreed, on condition that Seaham Colliery station would be renamed Seaham, and that Marlborough Street station (the old Londonderry station) would be renamed Seaham Harbour; the changes duly took place from 1 March 1925. Hall Dene station is still in existence at a minor level crossing north of Seaham station.

Two public houses – the Bath Hotel at Hendon and the Station Hotel at Seaham – were also, not surprisingly, excluded from the sale to the NER. The latter hotel had an entrance direct from the station platform and this proved convenient when patrons had indulged too liberally: it was a simple matter to bundle them out of the hotel, into the last train, and off to Sunderland! The Londonderry station at Seaham remained in use as a terminus for a local service from Sunderland, but it was closed on 11 September 1939 as a wartime measure, never to reopen. It was demolished in 1971.

On 1 April 1905 the new line between Seaham and Hart was opened and trains began running between West Hartlepool and Sunderland without having to toil up Hesleden bank in one direction and Seaton bank in the other. Not all the main trains were transferred to the coast route; the afternoon train from Newcastle to Liverpool continued to use the old way via Wellfield for some years longer.

The Seaham Harbour Dock Co. retained a few engines to carry on its traffic, and over the years it purchased an interesting selection. It had, for instance, some vertical-boilered engines which were in use until recently, and a small tank built by Lewin, the exact age of which is doubtful. However, it is approximately 100 years old!

After many years as separate townships Hartlepool and West Hartlepool joined forces in 1967, but references in this chapter have been left unchanged to avoid confusion. The last coal staiths at the port, at Victoria Dock, were demolished at the end of 1972.

At Sunderland the famous Lambton Staiths closed in 1967, bringing to an end the shipment of coal from this site on the Wear, which had been used for over a century. Between Hartlepool and Sunderland, at Seaham Harbour, coal is still shipped but on a small scale, and it is no longer possible to see the former North Eastern locomotives MARS and MILO endlessly shunting wagons of coal on to the staiths.

At Haswell, where the track has now been lifted, it is still possible to see the site of the connection between the north end of the Hartlepool Dock & Railway and the south end of the Durham & Sunderland Railway but it is difficult to realize that this location, at the north end of this former pit village, was once an interchange point for passengers from Stockton and Hartlepool to Sunderland, South Shields and Gateshead.

The Great North of England, Clarence & Hartlepool Junction Railway is still open between Coxhoe Junction and Kelloe Bank Foot, but eastwards from that point it has been lifted. In the Wingate area, where the line was crossed by the later Bowesfield Junction to Wellfield line, reclamation of small coal used to form the embankment has led to part of the early line being obliterated.

CHAPTER VIII

Central Durham

THE MAIN LINE OLD AND NEW

The railway position north of Darlington is complicated by the fact that north of Ferryhill are the present east-coast main line and the so-called 'old main line', although unfortunately the latter title is now falling into disuse. The original main line of 1844 ran from Ferryhill to Gateshead via Shincliffe, Leamside, Penshaw, Washington and Pelaw : at first trains between Washington and Pelaw travelled via Brockley Whins, but from 1850 a more direct route via Usworth was used. To provide an alternative route between Ferryhill and Gateshead two new sections of line were built, from Tursdale Junction (north of Ferryhill) to Relly Mill (south of Durham), where the Bishop Auckland branch was joined, and from Newton Hall Junction (north of Durham) to Gateshead – and it is this route which is the main line of today. Another complication is that the present line has five separate sections, while the 'old main line' has six! Their eleven authorizing Acts are spread over the years 1823 to 1865.

Although the main flow of passengers and general freight has for a long time been north and south through the area, the flow of mineral traffic has always been west to east and the main line was crossed by numerous NER and colliery lines heading for the east coast. As mentioned in Chapter V, the first scheme for a line between York and the Tyne was that of the Great North of England Railway, and its Act for the section between Redheugh Quay at Gateshead and Croft was obtained on 4 July 1836. After opening from Darlington to York the GNE found it financially inadvisable to continue with the northern section, and on 5 October 1841 agreed to relinquish the powers to Robert Davies, James Richardson and John Hotham, all of York, who acted on behalf of the embryo Newcastle & Darlington Junction

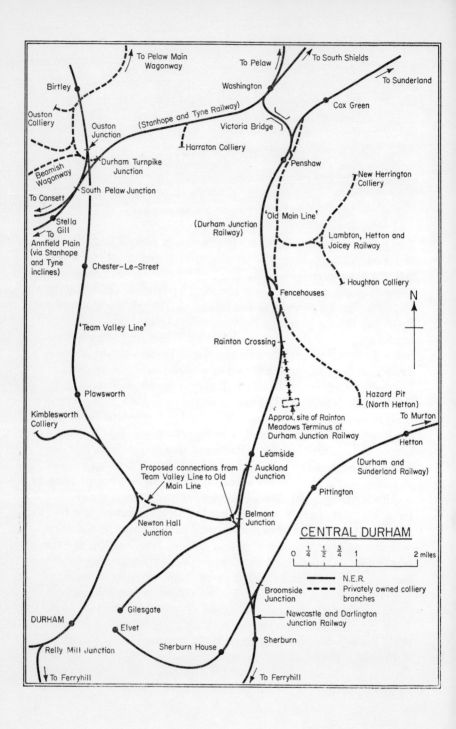

To Pelaw Main Wagonway

Birtley

To Pelaw

To South Shields

To Sunderland

Washington

Cox Green

Ouston Colliery

Ouston Junction

(Stanhope and Tyne Railway)

Victoria Bridge

Durham Turnpike Junction

Harraton Colliery

Penshaw

New Herrington Colliery

Beamish Wagonway

South Pelaw Junction

To Consett

'Old Main Line'

Stella Gill

To Annfield Plain (via Stanhope and Tyne inclines)

(Durham Junction Railway)

Lambton, Hetton and Joicey Railway

Chester-Le-Street

Houghton Colliery

Fencehouses

N

'Team Valley Line'

Rainton Crossing

Plawsworth

Hazard Pit (North Hetton)

Kimblesworth Colliery

Approx. site of Rainton Meadows Terminus of Durham Junction Railway

To Murton

Hetton

Leamside

(Durham and Sunderland Railway)

Auckland Junction

Proposed connections from Team Valley Line to Old Main Line

Pittington

Belmont Junction

Newton Hall Junction

CENTRAL DURHAM

0   ¼   ½   ¾   1   2 miles

Broomside Junction

———— N.E.R.

- - - - Privately owned colliery branches

DURHAM

Gilesgate

Elvet

Newcastle and Darlington Junction Railway

Relly Mill Junction

Sherburn House

Sherburn

To Ferryhill

To Ferryhill

Railway. The N&DJ agreed to apply for powers to complete the line and pay all the costs, and the deal included such items as blocks, rails, and chairs 'at trade price on the day of take over', together with £7,000 for the land. The N&DJ was incorporated on 18 June 1842 and in the following year, on 11 April, the northern part of the GNE was transferred to the company by Act of Parliament. Work went ahead so rapidly that the line was ready for opening throughout on 15 April 1844, the last section to be completed being that between Belmont Junction (where the Durham branch diverged from the main line) to join the Durham Junction line at Rainton Crossing.

Old Main Line

Section	Company	Act	Opened	Remarks
Darlington (Bank Top) to Parkgate Junction	S & D	23.5.1823	27.10.1829	Part of Croft branch. Purchased by GNE
Parkgate Junction to Shincliffe	GNE	4.7.1836	19.6.1844	Taken over by N & D J under Act of 11.4.1843
Shincliffe to Rainton Crossing	N & D J	18.6.1842	19.6.1844	
Rainton Crossing to Washington	D J	16.6.1834	24.8.1838	Goods opening: passengers 9.3.1840
Washington–Pelaw	N & D J	21.7.1845	1.9.1849	Goods opening: passengers 1.10.1850 From 19.6.1844 until this cut-off opened trains ran via Brockley Whins
Pelaw–Gateshead	B J	21.7.1835 7.6.1836	5.9.1839	

Team Valley Line

Darlington (Bank Top) to Parkgate Junction	S & D	23.5.1823	27.10.1829	Part of Croft branch. Purchased by GNE
Parkgate Junction to Tursdale Junction	GNE	4.7.1836	19.6.1844	Taken over by N & D J under Act of 11.4.1843
Tursdale Junction– Relly Mill Junction	NER	19.6.1865	15.1.1872	East coast through trains
			1.3.1872	General traffic
Relly Mill Junction– Newton Hall Junction	N & D J	27.7.1846 30.6.1848	1.4.1857	Part of Leamside– Bishop Auckland branch
Newton Hall Junction–Gateshead	NER	17.7.1862	2.3.1868	Goods and mineral traffic
			1.12.1868	Passenger traffic

Some while before the work was finished, the N&DJ realized that it would not be able to get any rolling stock in time, presumably because of the current large demand on the manufacturers; the GNE directors, at a meeting held exactly a week after the incorporation of the N&DJ, were asked on what terms they would supply some. The GNE agreed to provide the whole of the locomotive power, carriages, horse boxes, carriage trucks, and wagons required for through traffic, exclusive of ballast and mineral wagons, but *not* to find the guards, porters, lampmen,

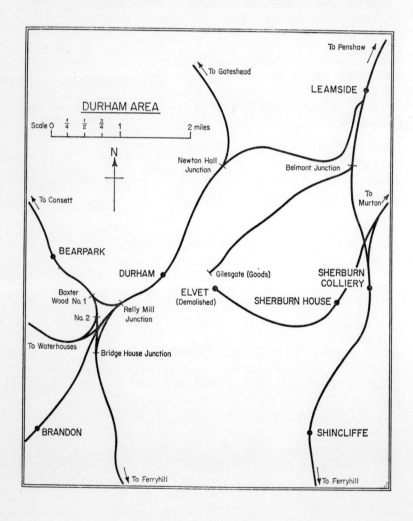

greasers and engine couplers. As on the GNE and the Y&NM, goods trains were to run at about 15 m.p.h. and mineral trains at 10 m.p.h., exclusive of stoppages. The N&DJ was to keep the way in good repair and to provide water cranes and an engine shed 'with bench and smith's fire'. Locomotives for mineral traffic were to be charged at 1s 0d per mile and for passenger and merchandise traffic at 1s 6d; ballast engines £3 per day. After some haggling the GNE agreed to accept 1s 3d per mile for the passenger engines, with the option to withdraw from the agreement after three years, with six months' notice on either side.

Within days of opening its line the N&DJ complained to the GNE about 'the irregularity of trains on their line due to the ineffective state of the engines supplied by the GNE', but the GNE countered that

> as this was said only three days after the opening of the N&DJ they had not informed themselves more accurately as to the cause of the irregularities, which were due to the inexperience of the N&DJ servants and the defective arrangements of that company as to the working of the traffic.

At the end of August 1844 the GNE received a letter terminating the agreement and this was followed by a cheque for £1,247 19s 7d in settlement of the charges for motive power. The N&DJ intended working traffic itself from 1 January 1845, but apparently had not paid its debts in full and before its engines were ready had to go to the GNE cap-in-hand to ask 'would the GNE continue if the balance of payment, improperly withheld, be paid forthwith'. Obviously the N&DJ faced the prospect of having a railway with no engines to work the trains! Fortunately the GNE agreed to continue supplying locomotives 'but if the balance of payment be not made before 1 January 1845 the charge to be 2s 0d per mile'.

The Belmont Junction–Rainton Crossing section was the last link in the chain stretching from London to the Tyne: although a special train carrying the directors ran from York to Gateshead on 24 May 1844, the line was not opened to the public until 19 June 1844. On the previous day a special train had made history when it ran through from London (Euston Square) to Gateshead, accomplishing the journey in 9 h 21 m, including stops totalling 70 m. A reversal at Brockley Whins was eliminated when the wooden viaduct built specially to allow through running was opened on 19 August 1844. At the time of opening, the N&DJ did not actually own the line beyond Washington, but had a station at Gateshead, reached via the Pontop & South Shields and Brandling Junction Railways : although only authorized by the Act of 23 May 1844 the station was illustrated by an engraving in a Gateshead newspaper four weeks later.

The Durham Junction Railway was authorized by an Act passed on 16 June 1834, prior to the incorporation of the GNE. Though it became an important link in the chain of railways forming the main line, the original idea was merely to divert to the Tyne, coal from the pits in the Houghton-le-Spring area, and also from those served by the Hartlepool Railway. As it happened, the Durham Junction never reached either. It progressed no farther south than Rainton Meadows, two miles short of its objective at Moorsley, while the Houghton-le-Spring branch, authorized by an Act of 1837, was never constructed.

The Durham Junction's biggest claim to fame was the magnificent stone viaduct over the River Wear between Penshaw and Washington : this was known as the Victoria Bridge because the last stone was laid on the day of Queen Victoria's coronation, 28 June 1838. The bridge was built under the direction of that famous North Eastern engineer T. E. Harrison, the work taking a little over two years. It has four main arches, those at each end being of 100 ft span and the centre two 144 ft and 160 ft; the total length was 811 ft and the height above high-water mark was 135 ft.

The route opened for mineral traffic on 24 August 1838 and for passengers on 9 March 1840. In 1843 George Hudson took the Durham Junction into his net as part of his plan for an integrated east-coast route : the price asked was £100,000, but as the company was in debt and being pressed for money, Hudson's offer of £88,500 was accepted, although it meant the loss of between £11 and £12 per share. The sale was ratified by the Act of 23 May 1844, which also empowered the ambitious project of bridging the Tyne.

At Washington the Durham Junction connected with the Stanhope & Tyne Railroad, whose metals were used as far as Brockley Whins (renamed Boldon Colliery in 1926). At Brockley Whins the Brandling Junction line was joined, and the passenger service between Rainton Meadows and Gateshead took this route from its inception on 9 March 1840. In fact the s&t owned more than 50 per cent of the shares of the Durham Junction and also worked the line; it would be interesting to know what happened to the Durham Junction services between the dissolution of the s & t in February 1841 and the incorporation of the Pontop & South Shields by the Act of 23 May 1842.

The inconvenience of the reversal at Brockley Whins, and the congestion caused by Durham Junction and p&ss trains sharing the line between Washington and Brockley Whins, led to application to Parliament for powers to build a direct curve and to widen the line between Washington and Brockley Whins, and these were authorized under the Act of 23 May 1844. The curve was on an awkward site intersected by the River Don and was, as already said, constructed on a wooden viaduct. This remained standing until 1940.

The through route between Darlington and Gateshead was not completed easily : the s&d felt aggrieved that part, at least, of its line had not been used, and before a through connection was ready a short-lived service was provided from Darlington (North Road) to the Clarence Railway terminus at Coxhoe; this necessitated two reversals, the first to join the cr at Simpasture and the second at Stillington. From Coxhoe it was only 3½ miles by road to the Durham & Sunderland terminus at Shincliffe and seven miles to the Durham Junction station at Rainton Meadows. This service ran from 30 November 1841 to 12 February 1842. In a second attempt to secure some of the northbound traffic the s&d commenced on 5 May 1842 a service via Shildon Tunnel and its current terminus at South Church. Between South Church and Rainton Meadows passengers were conveyed by horse bus (see Chapter VI).

Access to Gateshead from the south via the Team valley was recognized as a possibility, and the Leeds & Thirsk was casting an eye in this direction when it obtained its Act to extend as far north as Hartlepool. The danger of invasion was realized by the York & Newcastle (as it was then), and in July 1846 it announced its own intention to promote a bill for a line taking the new route. By the time a decision had been reached the York & Newcastle had become the York, Newcastle & Berwick, which was granted on 30 June 1848 an Act authorizing construction.

The proposed route was southwards from Gateshead and through the Team valley to Newton Hall, where a branch to Durham and Bishop Auckland struck off southwards, while the main section turned eastwards for about a mile before turning south to join the main line near Belmont Junction. The downfall of George Hudson in 1849 caused the YN&B to postpone the work. When the powers were revived by the NER in 1862 the line authorized was only between Gateshead and the Bishop Auckland branch north of Durham, and although the section eastwards from Newton Hall had been constructed as part of the Bishop Auckland branch there were no curves included to allow through running from the north onto the old main line via Shincliffe. Consequently the new line could only be used as an alternative route to Durham and the south via Bishop Auckland, and to start with there were only four stopping trains in each direction between Newcastle and Durham.

As a complement to the Team valley line it had been intended to provide an extension from Relly Mill southwards to join 'the old main line' two miles north of Ferryhill. This section was opposed by various landowners and it was dropped temporarily, only to appear in the bill for 1865, passed on 19 June. The northern section between Gateshead and Newton Hall was opened on 1 December 1868, and when the southern section was opened to east-coast trains on 15 January 1872 it completed the east-coast main line between York and Newcastle as we know it today.

Both sections involved heavy engineering works, including a viaduct at Chester-le-Street ⅜ mile long and 90 ft high, another over the Wear at Croxdale and another at Langley Moor. To separate main line and branch traffic, additional tracks were laid between Durham and Newton Hall (where the Team Valley and Leamside lines diverged) and between Ferryhill and Tursdale Junction (where Team Valley Extension and 'old main line' diverge). The two-track section south of Durham, as far as Relly Mill, had to be shared between main-line trains and those to and from Bishop Auckland, although the passenger service on the latter branch was withdrawn in 1964.

Anyone who has travelled over the east-coast main line will know the long, high viaduct which straddles the ancient City of Durham. Although used now by all main-line trains this is one section which was not built as part of the main line – it originally formed part of the Leamside–Bishop Auckland branch.

The first attempt to reach Bishop Auckland from the north-east was made by the N&DJ which, on 27 July 1846, obtained an Act to construct a branch from its main line just north of Sherburn (renamed Sherburn Colliery in 1874), running westwards close to the Durham & Sunderland as far as Shincliffe, and then continuing along the Wear Valley to Bishop Auckland. According to W. W. Tomlinson, the proposed line was an extension (beyond Houghal) of the D&S; but plans in the British Railways Board Archives at York showed the Bishop Auckland line to have been completely separate, from its junction with the 'old main line' at Sherburn, crossing on its way the D&S west of Shincliffe, with a proposed triangular junction giving access to a branch terminus at Durham Elvet. Nor does the Act refer to the use of any part of the D&S: it describes the line as commencing at Pittington.

But before the line could be started the N&DJ became the York & Newcastle, and later the York, Newcastle & Berwick. This company's Act for the Team Valley line, passed on 30 June 1848, included details of a new route for the Bishop Auckland branch: it entailed leaving the Team Valley line at Newton Hall where, it will be remembered, it was to have turned eastwards to join the 'old main line' south of Leamside; the branch was then to pass through Durham to Relly Mill and along the northern side of the Wear valley on much the course we know today, although deviations at certain points were authorized in 1851 and 1852. As an aftermath of the Hudson scandal, work here too was delayed, and it was not until 1 April 1857 that the line was ready for use throughout between Bishop Auckland and Leamside.

In its Act of 27 July 1846, the N&DJ was also authorized to build a line from Pensher (sic) to join the D&S at Sunderland. This was actually opened on 20 February 1852 for freight traffic and 1 June 1853 for passengers, and after the opening of the Leamside–Bishop Auckland branch in 1857 it provided an alternative route between Durham and Sunderland, without the need to travel to Shincliffe to join the Durham & Sunderland Railway. The Penshaw line was served by Fawcett Street station in the modern centre of Sunderland: this was replaced by the present station when the lines north and south of the Wear were joined in 1879.

On the day the Bishop Auckland branch was opened the short branch from Belmont Junction (on the 'old main line') to Durham Gilesgate was closed to passengers: this had been opened by the N&DJ on 15 April 1844, giving Durham City its first station, although the Shincliffe station of the D&S was just beyond the southern outskirts. The station buildings at Gilesgate were in use as the Durham goods station until November 1966.

EAST TO WEST BRANCHES

The Waterhouses branch was opened to freight traffic in 1858 under the Dearness Valley Railway Act of 30 July 1855. It was built by a nominally independent company, although about 20 per cent of the shares were held by NER directors, and the NER actually took it over in 1857, before completion. For the first nineteen years it was devoted solely to mineral traffic, not being opened to passengers until 1 November 1877. The sole intermediate station of Ushaw Moor was not opened until 1 September 1884. At its western extremity the line connected with a private colliery line to East Hedleyhope, and also with a tortuous line to Crook via the Stanley inclines of the S&D. An unusual feature of the Waterhouses branch was the wooden viaducts adjacent to Ushaw Moor. At one time wooden viaducts were common in the north-east but they have been gradually replaced. Passenger traffic ceased on 29 October 1951, and mineral traffic continued until 28 December 1964.

At Coxhoe Junction, one mile north of Ferryhill, the Clarence Railway Byers Green branch climbed up alongside the east side of the main line before crossing to the west on a girder bridge; immediately before the bridge the Great North of England, Clarence & Hartlepool Junction Railway line swings away to the east, whilst at main-line level the Coxhoe branch goes off to the north-east. Earthworks which once connected the GNEC&HJ to the Byers Green branch can be seen, and also the site of a curve connecting the Hartlepool line to the 'old main line'. It was here that the Hartlepool Company was involved in the long legal (and sometimes physical) battle with the Clarence

Railway over the crossing of the latter's line to reach the Byers Green branch (see Chapter VII).

The Byers Green branch was authorized by the Clarence Railway Act of 1 June 1829 and, as mentioned in Chapter VI, restrictions on the use of locomotives were imposed 'through Whitworth and the lands of Robert Eden Duncombe Shafto Esq.' Fortunately these restrictions were removed by the Act of 1837 – the year in which the Byers Green branch was opened to mineral traffic. Passenger services commenced in November 1845 but ceased in 1867, only to reappear again from 1 June 1878. Between 1845 and 1848, and also from 1865 to 1867, the passenger trains were extended beyond Byers Green to Tod Hills (actually on the West Durham Railway), and although the new service from June 1878 terminated at Byers Green this was actually at the former Tod Hills terminus, where a new station and engine shed were specially provided. From 1 December 1885, instead of terminating at Byers Green, the service was diverted over the new route into Bishop Auckland, via Coundon, and a third Byers Green station was opened on this line. Passenger traffic between Spennymoor and Bishop Auckland ceased on 4 December 1939 and the final portion, between Spennymoor and Ferryhill, lost its passenger trains on 31 March 1952.

On its route westwards the branch passed beneath the old Great North road north of Ferryhill village, with connections to the large Dean & Chapter colliery; east of Spennymoor were the Weardale Iron Company's Tudhoe Iron Works, opened in 1853; by 1885 they were producing 50,000 tons of steel a year, but they declined shortly afterwards, and were closed by 1914.

West of Spennymoor, the steeply graded Page Bank branch was opened c. 1855 to serve a colliery of that name (also known as South Brancepeth Colliery) on the north bank of the River Wear. From 1 January 1868 Messrs Bell Bros, who owned the colliery, rented the branch from the NER at £3 a week so that they could convey their workmen to and from Spennymoor. The NER supplied the two vans used, but it is not clear who supplied the motive power – if in fact locomotives were used. By 1891 the number of men carried daily had risen from between eighty and ninety to 250 and the charge was increased to £9 per week. By this time the NER was certainly providing the engine: the train consisted of three coaches and a brake van, the NER guard

being under the command of Messrs Bell's guard. The NER locomotive took the train down to the sidings alongside Whitworth
Park (on the level at the bottom of the bank) and from there the
colliery locomotive worked it across the river bridge to the
colliery platform. The coaches were stabled at Spennymoor overnight; the engine was supplied by Byers Green shed. The first
run was at 2.30 a.m. for the 'foreshift', then back to Spennymoor and to Page Bank again at 5.45 a.m. for the day shift;
then several times a day to suit the pit's shifts, the last run from
Page Bank at 4.30 p.m. taking home the 'backshift'. The branch
was 2¼ miles long and included 1¼ miles at 1 in 38 ascending
from the Wear; up this gradient the locomotives were allowed
to haul five wagons of coal at a time. The colliery was taken over
by Dorman Long c. 1921 and was closed in July 1931, when it
was dismantled and the branch lifted.

It was two miles west of Spennymoor, at its end-on junction
with the West Durham Railway, that the Clarence retained a
short stretch of line free from Parliamentary restraint, for the
use of which it could charge any toll it thought fit on traffic
bound for Hartlepool via the rival GNEC&HJ line via Wingate.
Naturally the Clarence preferred the coal to reach Hartlepool by
its own line and the Stockton & Hartlepool, and discriminated
against the Hartlepool Junction traffic. After two years the latter
company obtained an Act which included powers for the disputed section to be treated as a normal portion of the Clarence;
but even so their troubles were not ended, as the Clarence continued to put difficulties in their way until their disagreements
were finally settled.

At Relly Mill, south of Durham, a complicated network of
junctions developed based on the Durham–Bishop Auckland
line. From this the Dearness Valley branch struck off westwards
in 1858 and four years later the Lanchester Valley line to Consett was opened. In 1872 the Team Valley Extension opened
between Relly Mill and Ferryhill, and finally, in 1877, came two
connecting spurs to allow through running from Consett to the
south either via Ferryhill or via Bishop Auckland.

Two notable mineral lines cross the Team Valley main line
between Chester-le-Street and Gateshead. At South Pelaw, 1½
miles north of Chester-le-Street (not to be confused with the
Pelaw on the Newcastle–Sunderland line), the Stanhope & Tyne

– later the Pontop & South Shields – passes overhead. It was on this line that the well-known iron-ore trains made their strenuous journey from Tyne Dock to Consett, rostered to be hauled and banked by BR Class 9F 2–10–0 locomotives. At Ouston Junction, a few hundred yards further north, a connection is made with the Consett branch and this was used by a Newcastle–Consett–Blackhill passenger service until 23 May 1955.

A mile north of Birtley the Pontop & Jarrow line of the National Coal Board passes below the main line, but it is now rather difficult to see from the train because of the spread of the new Tyne marshalling yard. The Pontop & Jarrow (also known as the Bowes Railway) ran from collieries in the Marley Hill–Tanfield area to the Tyne and it can trace its roots to the first half of the eighteenth century when the 'Grand Allies' set up their monopolistic consortium of owners of coal-bearing lands in north-west Durham.

The Tyne marshalling yard is a British Railways' development to handle and sort freight traffic to and from Tyneside. Its sprawl has completely obliterated all traces of Lamesley station (between Birtley and Low Fell). There are four tracks between Ouston Junction and Low Fell, and only two between Low Fell and King Edward Bridge. Although primarily a freight route, the line from Low Fell through Dunston, across the Tyne at Scotswood and into Newcastle from the Carlisle direction is used for passenger trains in emergency. The all-electric signal box at Tyne Yard controls many miles of the main line, displacing a number of manually operated boxes; in addition the signal box at Newton Hall Junction has been demolished and the connections to the Leamside line removed.

Over the last few years the 'old main line' has declined in standards whilst the Team Valley and Relly Mill-Tursdale line has been improved to make it suitable for higher speeds. At Newton Hall, north of Durham, where the Team Valley line joined the Bishop Auckland branch, the curve has been completely realigned. However, the greatest changes are to be seen in the Relly Mill area, south of Durham (see plate 31), where all except the up and down main lines have been removed with the closure of the Bishop Auckland, Waterhouses, and Consett branches. Here again the main line has been realigned by cutting away part of the embankment which formerly carried the Bishop Auckland branch.

CHAPTER IX

West Durham

THE S&D WEST OF SHILDON

Even today people express surprise when told that the Stockton & Darlington Railway did not terminate at Darlington but that, even from the beginning in 1825, it continued some miles westwards beyond Darlington to Witton Park, within a mile of the River Wear, some four miles west of Bishop Auckland. Later, of course, it controlled lines as far north as Consett and as far west as Penrith, with through workings even farther west, to Cockermouth.

West Durham was, of course, the gathering ground for the S&D coal traffic, and this tempted other companies into the area to try for a share of the coal flowing eastwards. Limestone also played a great part in the development of the S&D, particularly in Weardale, although it was actually forestalled in the Stanhope area by the Stanhope & Tyne Railroad.

Beyond Shildon the original S&D line consisted of four inclines; all have long been dismantled but their course can still be traced and explored. From the pits at Witton Park the coal was hauled by horses to the foot of Etherley Ridge, the wagons being hauled up the ½-mile incline by a winding engine at the summit; they were then lowered down the other side, descending 312 ft in one mile, to St Helens (West Auckland from 1878). The wagons were taken over by horses for the 1½ miles to the foot of Brusselton incline, and were drawn up the 1¼-mile slope by another stationary engine. Finally they were lowered down the other side of the ridge to Shildon, from which point they were locomotive-hauled for the remainder of the journey to Stockton.

The area at the foot of Brusselton incline is now occupied by Shildon Wagon Works, but the outlet from the Works is still via Masons' Arms level crossing where *Locomotion No 1* was attached to the first train on 27 September 1825. Some two miles north of the crossing further pits were opened, but as they were separated from the railway by a ridge a further pair of inclines had to be constructed to reach them. Although the winding engine was not ready for use, these inclines, known as the Black Boy branch, were opened in July 1827, with horses hauling up two wagons at a time. The value of the Black Boy inclines was largely eclipsed by the opening of Shildon tunnel in 1842, but the northern portion of the Black Boy branch continued in partial use until the 1920s to serve a coal depot at the summit. Latterly access to it was gained by a connection with the line through the tunnel at a point near the northern portal.

Here again most of the branch is still clearly visible and worthy of exploration, although at the southern end alterations have been made on the site and the level of the land raised considerably.

The Stockton & Darlington made it a practice to construct lines in the names of certain directors of the company: if the venture failed the railway was not harmed and also, in cases where the directors between them owned all the land, the line could be built without Act of Parliament. This is what happened when Shildon tunnel was built through the ridge of land over which the Black Boy branch laboriously climbed. The object of the tunnel was not so much to reach the pits by an easier route as to tap the mineral wealth of the Wear Valley, and also to serve the towns of Bishop Auckland and Crook.

Work on the tunnel commenced in April 1839 and it was completed in January 1842, although passenger trains did not run through until 19 April 1842, when a service was provided to South Church, one mile beyond the northern portal and one mile short of Bishop Auckland. For a while passengers were then conveyed by road to Rainton Meadows to join the Durham Junction Railway for the next portion of their journey to Gateshead. The line through the tunnel left the original course of the s&d at a point $\frac{1}{2}$ mile east of Masons' Arms crossing and it was here that Shildon station was erected.

The line north of the tunnel was intended to run as far as Frosterley, with a branch to Crook, but because of fierce opposition from certain landowners in the Wear Valley only the section from the tunnel to the point where the Crook branch was to diverge, together with the Crook branch, was authorized by the Bishop Auckland & Weardale Act of 15 July 1837. The section between South Church and Crook was opened on 8 November 1843 and for the first time the important town of Bishop Auckland was served by railway.

The North Eastern gained entry to Bishop Auckland from the north-east later, and its branch from Leamside, through Durham, was opened on 1 April 1857. For a while this line used a temporary terminus at Tenter Street because of the delay by the NER and the S&D in providing a joint station. During 1857 discussions went on between the two companies and on 1 May the S&D gave 'consideration to amending the Plan and Estimate for an additional shed at Bishop Auckland coach station' and later the same month a timber shed costing about £400 was authorized. On 24 December 1857 the S&D appointed Henry Pease and Col. Stobart to join the NER representatives, Messrs Plews and Wharton, to form the Bishop Auckland Station Joint Committee. In 1864 extensive alterations were authorized, including the construction of connecting curves, thus forming the triangular layout as we know it today. The curves were opened on 21 December 1867.

ACROSS THE MOORS TO WASKERLEY

At Crook the Bishop Auckland & Weardale Railway terminated on the south side of the Willington–Wolsingham road, but when the Weardale Extension came to be built it was impossible to continue forward at this point and it had to strike off $\frac{1}{4}$ mile south of the original terminus. This necessitated a new station at Crook $\frac{1}{2}$ mile north of the original station. Beyond Crook the line had to climb the fearful Sunnyside incline, $1\frac{3}{4}$ miles long with gradients as steep as 1 in 13 and 1 in 16; this was, of course, worked by a stationary engine. From the summit, adjacent to the Willington–Tow Law road (B6299) locomotives were employed across the miles of wild moorland to Waskerley Park, where a junction was made with what had become known as the Wear & Derwent Railway. This had started life as the Stanhope & Tyne Railroad, but after the company had run into financial difficul-

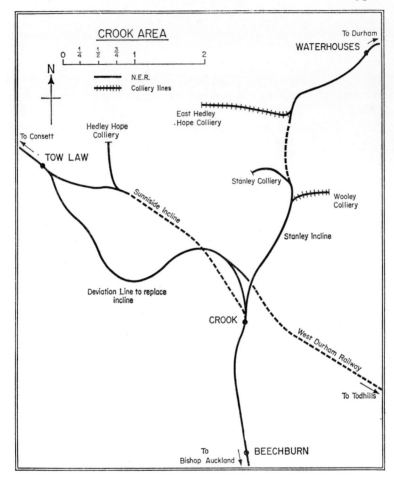

ties the western end was sold to the Derwent Iron Company (later Consett Iron Co. Ltd), which badly needed it to convey limestone from the quarries at Stanhope to its works at Consett. From 1 January 1845 this section was leased by the S&D, on whose behalf it was purchased shortly afterwards by Joseph Pease, Thomas Meynell, Henry Stobart, John Castell Hopkins and Henry Pease.

The Weardale Extension Railway from Crook to Waskerley was a project of the Derwent Iron Company but was actually constructed for that company by the s&D. Before the line was opened it was, apparently, purchased by Joseph Pease, Thomas Meynell and John Castell Hopkins and, together with the Stanhope–Carr House line, it became known as the Wear & Derwent Junction Railway, although it must be realized that the title had no Parliamentary sanction, no Act having been obtained for any part of the two sections making up the new line. The date when these gentlemen of the s&D purchased the two lines has not been established but it would appear to be between 1 January 1845 and 7 March 1845 when the first w&DJ Sub-Committee met.

Sunnyside incline was of course an obstacle to efficient and speedy working, and on 3 June 1862 the s&D obtained powers to build a deviation which could be worked throughout by locomotives. However, as locomotives improved during the 1850s the company considered the possibilities of using them on the incline, and in 1858 carried out tests using No 125 – one of the famous Bouch long-boilered 0–6–0 engines built in February of that year by Gilkes Wilson of Middlesbrough. The first tests were held in fine, dry September weather, five runs being made with varying loads and differing cut-offs. To test the performance in wet weather No 125 was used again on 18 October 1858; in Test No 1 on that day

the engine, weighing 27 tons 5 cwt, started from the bottom of the incline with 1,000 gallons of water (4½ tons) and a ton of coke in the tender (9 tons 5 cwt) attached to a train of four chaldron wagons weighing 19 tons 16 cwt, making a total weight of 61 tons 16 cwt. The steam pressure was 110 lb. per square inch and with the handle in the second notch from the end the speed reached 18 m.p.h. in 600 yds, and kept up this speed until it reached the top of the incline. Total run 1¾ miles at gradients of 1 in 32/19/16/13.4/16. The rails were sanded on the worst gradient.

Although the new engines could climb the incline it was decided to replace it, and an easier route was opened for mineral traffic on 10 April 1867 and for passengers on 2 March 1868. Even this was a tough proposition to work, as the four miles from Crook to Tow Law were all at 1 in 51 and 1 in 52.

As the lower part of the incline was surrounded by the extensive empire of the Pease family at Peases West, Roddymoor and Billy Row – an empire which included coal mines and drifts,

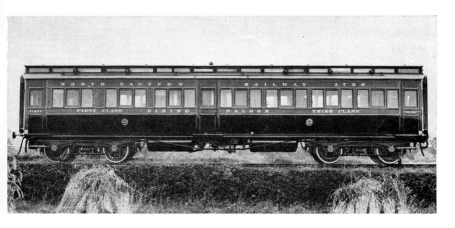

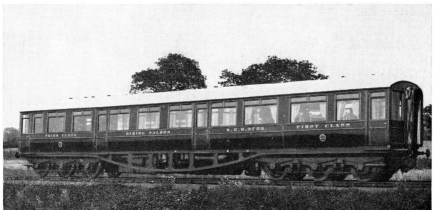

SPECIMEN ROLLING STOCK—I

(25) *Clerestory roofed composite dining saloon. Built 1905. Two vehicles of this type were sold to North British Railway: one in 1913 and the other in 1919*

(26) *Elliptical roofed composite diner. Built 1908*

(27) *40 ton hopper wagon*

BRANCH SCENES

(28) *Kirkby Stephen (looking east)*

(29) *Class A8 loco propelling its train from Whitby (Town) to Whitby (West Cliff)*

coking ovens and brickworks – it was left *in situ* for their use.

A passenger service still ran between Darlington and Crook until 8 March 1965, when it was pruned back to Bishop Auckland. Until 11 June 1956 the service continued beyond Crook to Tow Law and this section was served until July 1965 by a pickup goods train several days a week. The track on the upper part of Sunnyside incline was lifted after closure but the section from the summit to Tow Law remained in place until recently to serve a colliery. The passenger service north of Tow Law was withdrawn on 1 May 1939 but the track was not lifted until 1952, except for a short section beyond Tow Law left in place to serve some collieries. Approaching Burnhill the course of the line is now enclosed within a Government store, the northern extremity of which adjoins the now derelict Burnhill signal box; at Burnhill Junction the line divides, the left fork being the original Weardale Extension line to connect with the erstwhile Stanhope & Tyne at Waskerley, and that to the right the S&D deviation built to bypass Nanny Mayors incline and opened to freight traffic on 23 May and passenger traffic 4 July 1859.

From 1 September 1845 a passenger service was operated from Hownes Gill and Stanhope (uniting at Waskerley) to Crook, but from 31 October it ran between Crook and Waskerley only, for the rest of the winter. The full service was resumed again on 1 April 1846 but the Waskerley–Crawley (for Stanhope) service was withdrawn later the same year, never to be resumed.

Soon after the opening of the line between Shildon and Crook the S&D made another attempt to obtain powers to penetrate the Wear Valley, and this time was successful. The application was made to Parliament not in the name of the original company – the Bishop Auckland & Weardale – but in the name of another S&D protégé, the Wear Valley Railway. This section was only the first instalment of a plan to extend far beyond the confines of Weardale, in fact to Alston and Carlisle, but lack of support brought the line to a halt at Frosterley. It is described in the Weardale section later in this Chapter.

In 1846 the uncompleted Wear Valley Railway was chosen to swallow the Bishop Auckland & Weardale (Shildon–Crook), the Wear & Derwent (Stanhope–Carr House) and the Weardale Extension Railway (Crook–Waskerley), together with the Shildon

Tunnel Company, as a step toward bringing all these within the s&d fold. The Act for this amalgamation received the Royal Assent on 22 July 1847 and two months later the s&d invoked a section of the 1845 Wear Valley Act which allowed the take-over of the Wear Valley Railway. Thus five companies were gathered up in only two moves, together with the Middlesbrough & Redcar Railway. This arrangement came into force on 1 October 1847: the Wear Valley and the Middlesbrough & Redcar were leased to the s&d for 999 years, only to be amalgamated with it from 23 July 1858, when the Middlesbrough & Guisborough and the Darlington & Barnard Castle Railways were also absorbed.

From Crook the s&d built the Stanley branch, consisting of two inclines, climbing up from Crook for a mile at 1 in 16 and then dropping down the other side of the hill to join the Waterhouses branch in the Dearness Valley. Authorized in 1855 the line was completed in 1858: until it was demolished the engine house at the summit still carried the latter date over the door. Most of the northern section of the line was closed in the last century but a stretch at the top of the northern incline was retained to give access to two collieries – Stanley and Wooley, together with the southern incline. All is now closed and derelict.

THE WEST DURHAM RAILWAY

Into the picture immediately north of Crook (and crossing the Stanley branch just mentioned) intrudes the West Durham Railway. This was the outcome of the unsuccessful South Durham Railway (rejected by the House of Lords in 1836) and the New South Durham Railway (as modified in 1837), and it is not to be confused with an earlier West Durham Railway (developed from the Durham South-west Junction Railway) which did not materialize. Even before their line was opened, the West Durham and its predecessors had a hard fight against the s&d, which naturally objected most strongly to another company entering an area it regarded as its own.

When the New South Durham Railway changed its name to the West Durham Railway in 1837 it decided to go ahead with the line but to rely on wayleaves, and it was not until 1839, when construction was well advanced, that a bill was submitted to Parliament; this duly received the Royal Assent on 4 July

1839. Two token trains – one of coal and the other conveying local dignitaries – traversed the line from Willington Colliery to the Byers Green branch of the Clarence Railway on 12 June 1840, but as the Byers Green branch was unfinished, regular traffic did not commence until later.

Although nominally a separate concern the West Durham was really an extension of the Byers Green branch of the Clarence Railway. However, their common purpose did not prevent them from squabbling when the Clarence discovered that coal mined in the West Durham company's area was to be diverted to Hartlepool instead of Port Clarence.

The West Durham made an end-on junction with the Clarence near Byers Green and after a short distance on the level the steep-sided valley of the Wear was reached. Here a stationary engine handled the wagons on their journey down to the floor of the valley, via an incline $\frac{5}{8}$-mile long at a gradient of 1 in 18. A substantial bridge was built across the Wear and the line immediately began to climb two self-acting inclines – Sunnybrow and Helmington – to reach the high land east of Crook. The short stretch between the two inclines was later used to bring in a branch from Bowden Close colliery, and when the Durham–Bishop Auckland branch of the North Eastern was opened in 1857 it too connected at this point.

The line was opened from Byers Green to Tod Hills, down to the Wear, and up the other side as far as the summit of Sunnybrow incline, on 12 June 1840, and extended to its terminus at Whitelee Colliery, north of Crook, on 15 June 1841, making its total length almost $5\frac{1}{2}$ miles. The original opening of 1840 was only a formal occasion, as the Clarence Railway was using delaying tactics in completing its Byers Green branch, ostensibly through lack of funds. Consequently it was 19 October 1840 before traffic was moving regularly eastwards, only to be disrupted two years later when the dispute over the 'free' stretch of line at the extremity of the Clarence Railway flared up (see Chapter VIII).

The West Durham led a precarious existence for the first few years but as pits were opened on both sides of the line the coal traffic grew steadily until in 1846 the amount carried exceeded 200,000 tons; ten years later the company was paying a dividend of 10 per cent. This, unfortunately, was not to last; in the following year the opening of the Durham–Bishop Auckland branch by the North Eastern provided some of the West Durham's best customers with a more convenient outlet for their coal, and the amalgamation of the North Eastern and the Stockton & Darlington in 1863 soon had the West Durham in difficulties. In 1866 a working agreement was concluded between the West Durham and the North Eastern, and it was obvious that the days of the small company were numbered : it was finally extinguished by the NER Act of 4 July 1870.

The West Durham line continued to carry coal for another twenty years, but as it was almost surrounded by alternative NER and S&D routes it was really superfluous; this, together with the cost of operating the three inclines, led to its partial closure under the NER Act of 1891. The section between Burnhouse Junction and the top of the incline at Todhills remained in use to serve Byers Green colliery and also to enable the locomotives to reach the engine shed at Todhills (although the shed was actually known as Byers Green). The shed closed in 1922 and the remaining portion of the West Durham Railway ceased to operate in 1933. Since then opencast-mining activity has scarred the landscape and in some places it is almost impossible to discern where the railway was.

The West Durham Railway was purely a mineral-carrying line but passengers used its eastern end in connection with a Clarence Railway market-day train to Stockton on Saturdays. The position is extremely complicated as there have been three stations called Byers Green – all on different sites ! To illustrate the difficulty the changes are given in detail :

1. Service from Tod Hills (also quoted as Todhills) and Byers Green commenced November 1845.
2. Service cut back to Byers Green, and Tod Hills closed, August 1848.
3. Service extended to Tod Hills August 1865.
4. Service withdrawn from Byers Green and Tod Hills April 1867.
5. Service reinstated 1 June 1878 to new Byers Green station actually at Tod Hills.
6. Service withdrawn from Byers Green (5) 1 December 1885 on opening of Burnhouse Junction – Bishop Auckland line.

(Note: the station of 1878 existed until recently, adjacent to the former engine shed, now part of a brickworks.)

7. New Byers Green station opened 1 December 1885 on Bishop Auckland branch.

8. Byers Green (7) closed to passenger traffic 4 December 1939 and converted to public delivery siding.

9. Byers Green PDS closed to goods traffic 2 June 1958. (Note: the station buildings and yard are still extant: the yard is now used for timber.)

It is still possible to locate approximately the site of the length of line retained by Clarence to keep in check the West Durham Railway; in fact one of the obelisks erected to define the limits is still there, but instead of standing proudly by the course of the line it has been toppled into the undergrowth and lies there uncared for – a memento of stirring days in the history of the railways of Durham.

OVER STAINMORE

The final move to the west was the opening of the South Durham & Lancashire Union Railway for passenger traffic on 1 August 1863 between Spring Gardens Junction on the Haggerleases branch, 1½ miles west of St Helens station, and Barnard Castle. At the same time an s&d link was constructed between Bishop Auckland and Fylands Bridge Junction (later Fieldon Bridge Junction) where the Tunnel branch was joined. Thus a through route was completed from Bishop Auckland to Barnard Castle made up of five lines opened at dates between 1825 and 1863:

		Opened	
	Company	Freight	Passenger
Bishop Auckland–Fylands Bridge	s&d	1 Feb. 1863	1 Aug. 1863
Fylands Bridge–St Helens (part of Tunnel branch)	s&d	13 Sept. 1856	13 Oct. 1858
St Helens station	s&d	27 Sept. 1825	1 Dec. 1833
St Helens–Spring Gardens Junction	s&d	1 May 1830	13 Oct. 1858
Spring Gardens Junction–Barnard Castle	sd&lu	1 Aug. 1863	1 Aug. 1863

From 1 August 1863, therefore, the passenger service from Bishop Auckland to Lands via Tunnel Junction (which had replaced the service over the Brusselton inclines in 1858) was in turn replaced by the direct Bishop Auckland–Barnard Castle service, calling at Cockfield (renamed Cockfield Fell 1 July 1923) and Evenwood to serve the area formerly using the stations on the Haggerleases branch. However, a Saturdays-only market train continued between Bishop Auckland and Lands until 1872. Evenwood station was closed completely on 14 October 1957 and Cockfield Fell followed on 15 September 1958; through services between Bishop Auckland and Barnard Castle were withdrawn from 18 June 1962.

Engineering works on the SD&LU were heavy and included a large viaduct across the River Gaunless near Lands: this also crossed the Haggerleases branch which hereabouts ran along the river bank whereas the SD&LU climbed to cross Cockfield Fell. At Woodland Junction, at the east end of the viaduct, a private colliery line 5 miles long struck off to the north and ran in a large arc to Woodland Colliery, only some 3 miles beyond the Haggerleases terminus but about 550 ft higher in the hills. This was opened in 1873 and originally the NER worked it at 10s per hour per engine, but in 1911 the company purchased from the NER for £350 an 0–6–0 T engine (No 1293) which had been built at Darlington in 1876. The line is believed to have closed in 1921 and it was dismantled some two years later.

IN WEARDALE

The Wear Valley Railway was incorporated by the Act of 31 July 1845 which authorized a branch from the Bishop Auckland & Weardale line 'at or near the fifth milepost placed by the side of the said Branch Railway' to Frosterley, together with a branch from Broad Wood to Bishopley Crag. Here again it was intended that passengers and goods should be carried either in privately-owned vehicles or in those supplied by the company; in the latter case the company could charge 1d per mile extra for human beings, horses, mules and asses; ½d per mile extra for every ox, cow or bull, and ¼d extra for every calf, pig, sheep, or lamb! In addition an extra ¾d per mile per passenger or ton of goods could be charged 'for the use of engines for propelling carriages on the Railway'. The line was opened on 3 August 1847.

It was extended to Stanhope by another company nominally independent of the s&D, the Frosterley & Stanhope Railway, and the Royal Assent to its Act was received on 28 June 1861. This portion, after an amending Act in 1862, was opened on 22 October 1862 and worked by the s&D.

In the latter half of the nineteenth century Weardale was the source of a gigantic flow of minerals; but although agitation was strong for the line to be extended to the head of the valley ten miles beyond Stanhope, it wasn't until 1892 that powers to do so were obtained, and by this time the output of minerals was on the wane. This final section was opened on 21 October 1895.

The Bishopley branch, built under the 1845 Act, was purely a mineral line which ran up the valley of the Bollihope Burn at gradients of 1 in 43 and 1 in 57 to serve gigantic quarries. These produced originally limestone for agricultural purposes and little did the s&D imagine that its 1818 estimate of 5,000 tons to Yarm and 1,000 tons to Darlington per annum would be so greatly exceeded. By 1850 the amount transported had reached 66,706 tons, within five years it had reached 249,000 tons and by 1868 it had passed the 500,000 ton mark – due mainly, of course, to the development of the iron industry on Tees-side. The carboniferous limestone from the Frosterley and Stanhope areas proved to be an excellent flux for use with the ironstone of Cleveland and about $\frac{1}{2}$ ton of limestone was used for every ton of pig-iron produced. An unusual feature was that for many years the quarrying and lime-burning at Bishopley was let out on contract by the s&D, but the quarry eventually passed to Messrs Ord & Maddison. It was closed *c.* 1928.

When the line was extended to Stanhope in 1862 another large quarry was opened out at Newlandside, across the river from Stanhope, and Parson Byers quarry (midway between Frosterley and Stanhope) was opened ten years later. Both these had their own self-acting inclines to reach the working faces.

The passenger station at Stanhope was to have been on the south bank of the Wear but an amending Act of 1862 permitted it to be resited on the north bank; unfortunately when the line came to be extended further up the valley it was impossible to use the old station. When the Wear Valley Extension was opened on 21 October 1895 it struck off from the original line just south of the 1862 station, and a new one was built a few yards along the new line, leaving the old one to be used for goods.

Although sidings were established at various points on the final 9¼ miles between Stanhope and Wearhead there were no ventures as large as Bishopley, Newlandside and Parson Byers. The most interesting siding was that at Cambo Keels, midway between Eastgate and Westgate, installed during World War I by prisoner-of-war labour. Traffic from Heights quarry, on the northern side of the valley, was brought to it down a self-acting incline; at the foot the line branched into two and each leg turned at right angles to join the NER siding on the south bank of the river, crossing the water on two diverging wooden viaducts. The incline became disused c. 1922 and was dismantled in 1945.

Between the two World Wars the greatest activity in Weardale was near Wearhead, where a large reservoir was constructed for Durham County Council. Passenger services along the dale ceased on 29 June 1953 and from 2 January 1961 the freight service was cut back to St Johns Chapel. In the 1960s a large cement works was established at Eastgate, bringing much needed employment to the valley and traffic to the railway.

THE WEARDALE IRON COMPANY

Of Weardale – but not in it – was the fascinating privately owned mineral line of the Weardale Iron Co., which actually branched off the Waskerley–Weatherhill line at Parkhead – later Blanchland (Chapter X). The line was opened in 1846, striking westwards across the moors to the summit of Bolt's Law incline, down which the wagons were lowered to Rookhope, passing under the village street at the foot of the incline before crossing to the west side of the Rookhope Burn. The area around Rookhope has long been famous for its lead mining, and it reached its peak early in the nineteenth century, when a gigantic lead-smelting plant was established near the village. To disperse the poisonous fumes a flue a mile long was cut in the hillside nearby, leading to a chimney at the top. Further lead and ironstone mines were worked further up the Rookhope valley, served by both standard and narrow-gauge lines, and the whole area was a hive of mining activity.

From Rookhope the standard-gauge line climbed another incline to the crest of the hills forming the northern boundary of Weardale, and ran westwards parallel to the NER but 400 ft above it, to serve various mines and quarries. Heights quarry, previously mentioned, was on the course of the high-level line, but during World War I the restrictions imposed by Bolt's Law incline led to the provision of a separate incline down to the North Eastern.

The whole of the Weardale Iron Company's line closed in 1921, although the track remained in place until 1942, when it was lifted for war salvage.

West Durham is now almost devoid of railways, with only the Consett trains running up from South Pelaw, and the cement traffic along Weardale as far as Eastgate. North of Wear Valley Junction, through Crook, Tow Law, Burnhill and Rowley, together with the line to Waskerley and Weatherhill, all has gone, including even the station buildings at Rowley. These have been dismantled piece by piece, to be erected at Beamish Open Air Museum, where, eventually, there is to be a small railway system based on North Eastern practice, using a former NER locomotive and some NER coaches. Fortunately Hownes Gill viaduct still stands as a monument to the once busy railways of the area.

CHAPTER X

Tyneside

THE STANHOPE & TYNE RAILROAD

A few miles south-west of Gateshead stands one of the earliest relics of the Railway Age, the Causey Arch, scheduled in 1935 as an Ancient Monument. This stone bridge, crossing a deep gorge through which flows Beckley Burn, was erected in 1727 to carry a line of wooden rails to serve coal pits in the area.

For some 200 years horse-drawn coal traffic continued to be carried over wagonways with wooden rails until, in 1796, iron rails were installed on a line running from Walker to the River Tyne and this event, together with the almost simultaneous introduction of the steam locomotive, led to the development of railways as we know them today. Many lines continued to be built primarily for mineral traffic, but frequently passengers were carried as a concession, being looked upon as a necessary evil. In a number of cases the passenger traffic developed from the carriage of miners and their families to and from remote collieries.

The basic duty of the wagonways was, of course, to carry coal from the pits to the River Tyne for shipment, but as their potentialities became more obvious it was realized that they were also fitted for transporting normal goods traffic between towns, a duty which had hitherto been left to the canal system. During the eighteenth century various schemes were mooted for a canal between Newcastle and Carlisle and then, just before the turn of the century, William Thomas of Denton Hall suggested that a railway be built instead. Even in the 1820s a canal was still under discussion but in 1824 a definite swing in favour of a railway was observed and two meetings of interested parties were held in Newcastle in August 1824. From these meetings developed the Newcastle & Carlisle Railway, the first Tyneside

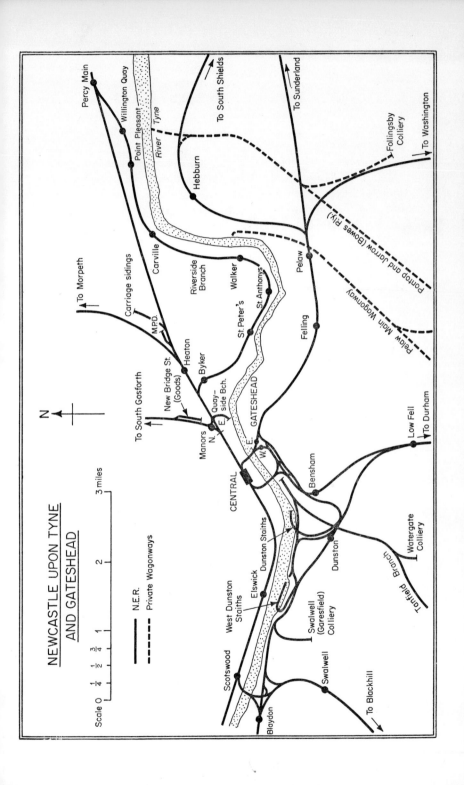

NEWCASTLE UPON TYNE
AND GATESHEAD

Scale 0 — ¼ — ½ — ¾ — 1 — 2 — 3 miles

N.E.R. ———

Private Wagonways - - -

N ←

Percy Main
Willington Quay
Point Pleasant
River Tyne
To South Shields
To Sunderland
Hebburn
Follingsby Colliery
To Washington
Carville
Carriage sidings
To Morpeth
Riverside Branch
Walker
Pontop and Jarrow (Bowes Rly.)
Pelaw
St Peter's
St Anthonys
M.P.D.
Pelaw Main Wagonway
To South Gosforth
New Bridge St. (Goods)
Heaton
Byker
Felling
Quay-side Bch.
N.E.
Manors
GATESHEAD
W.
CENTRAL
Bensham
Low Fell
To Durham
Dunston Staiths
Elswick
Dunston
Watergate Colliery
West Dunston Staiths
Tanfield Branch
Scotswood
Swalwell (Garesfield) Colliery
Swalwell
To Blackhill
Blaydon

line to carry passengers regularly : it was not the first public line
to be opened, this honour being claimed by the Stanhope & Tyne
Railroad, which commenced running to South Shields on 10
September 1834, six months before the first section of the Newcastle & Carlisle was opened.

The Stanhope & Tyne did not approach Parliament for an
Act but, under a Deed of Settlement dated 3 February 1834,
built its line on the wayleave system, so common in Durham
and Northumberland : the company paid each landowner for
the privilege of laying tracks across his land, and in most cases
he also received a toll based on the amount of traffic which
passed over those lines. But because of the excessive amount
paid out on wayleaves this company eventually became insolvent
and it was dissolved in February 1841.

The south-western extremity of the line was on the northern
slopes of Weardale, above Stanhope, where limestone was
plentiful, and coal deposits at various points between Consett
and South Shields were also tapped. Construction commenced
in July 1832 and as little was needed in the way of cuttings or
embankments progress was rapid : in many places the line was
simply laid across the moorland and much of it remained un-
fenced until it was closed.

From Stanhope lime-kilns to Annfield was opened on 15 May
1834, and the eastern section thence to South Shields on 10
September 1834. The line was 33¾ miles long and more than
half was worked by inclined planes, both self-acting and with
winding engine, with a few almost level stretches worked by
horses. It was only at the eastern end that locomotives were
employed.

The *Newcastle Journal* for Saturday, 13 September 1834 reported that the first shipment of coal

> took place on board the *Sally*, the property of Mr John Reed,
> lying at the Company's shipping berth, South Shields. The
> rejoicings and ceremonies commenced at day-break, by the
> discharge of a great number of carronades, placed on the
> banks of the Tyne and on the heights in the neighbourhood.
> At the same time a merry tune pealed from the bells of the
> parish church.

The first coals arrived from Medomsley about 2 p.m. and one of
the wagons was almost immediately lowered into the *Sally*

'amidst deafening cheers from the immense multitude, the firing of cannon, the ringing of church bells, and the waving of handkerchiefs by the ladies'. At this time there was almost incessant rain but 'this did not, however, damp the ardour of the people'. The day was rounded off by a dinner at the Golden Lion and '121 gentlemen sat down to a splendid entertainment, including an abundance of venison, and every other delicacy the season could afford'. Needless to say there were numerous speeches and toasts wishing success to the railway, the King, the Queen and the rest of the Royal Family, the British Navy, the Army, the Borough of South Shields, the landed proprietors through whose estate the railroad passed, the chairman, Medomsley Colliery – and many others. The assembled company was entertained with the songs 'How bright are the joys of the table', 'The Cork Leg', 'My temper is cheerful and mellow' – and no doubt many of the company were also mellow when they broke up at 10 p.m.!

The germ of the idea for a line from Stanhope is attributed to William Wallis of Westoe (South Shields) who, towards the end of 1831, signed an agreement to work coal at Consett and Medomsley, and limestone at Stanhope. To get the minerals to the River Tyne a line was first considered down the Derwent Valley, utilizing part of the old Pontop Wagonway, but this idea was dropped in favour of a completely new line. As the bridge at Newcastle limited the size of the vessels which could proceed upstream it was considered more economic to build a longer line to reach the Tyne below the bridge, where larger vessels could be used.

The engineer who surveyed the route was T. E. Harrison, later to become for many years one of the outstanding personalities directing the fortunes of the North Eastern Railway. Finance came mainly from speculators in London and eventually the company was formed with a capital of £150,000. Across the moors wayleaves were negotiated at about £25 per mile per year, but at the eastern end of the line it was a different story. Here the company was forced to pay £300 and more per mile and the total annual expenditure on wayleaves alone amounted to £5,600; as traffic did not come up to expectations, the amount paid out on wayleaves severely drained the company's resources; in any case its finances were so badly mismanaged that by the end of 1840 it was £440,000 'in the red'. Interest charges on various loans obtained amounted to approximately £20,000 and this, together with a falling revenue caused partly by the closure of the section between Carr House and Stanhope, put the company in difficulties.

The shareholders were responsible for the debts incurred and to cut their losses it was decided to dissolve the Stanhope & Tyne Railroad and to vest its assets in a new company, which was to be formed to liquidate the existing debts and to carry on the railway as best possible. The old company was actually dissolved on 5 February 1841 and the following year the Pontop & South Shields Railway obtained an Act to take over the northern end of its track. The section south-west of Carr House was sold to the Derwent Iron Company to transport limestone from the quarries at Stanhope to its furnaces at Consett. This section later passed into the hands of the Stockton & Darlington Railway and is covered in Chapter IX.

For its time, considering the difficult terrain over which it passed, the S & T was an extremely ambitious railway. Many miles at the Stanhope end crossed non-traffic-producing moorland and the main line was one long succession of changes of motive power: it comprised 10½ miles worked by horses, eleven miles worked by stationary engines (9), three self-acting inclines – and 9¼ miles worked by locomotives. In addition there was the deep ravine known as Hownes Gill to cross: the wagons were lowered one at a time down the side of the ravine on a horizontal platform and then, at the bottom, were transferred to a similar platform for the ascent of the other side. A winding engine in the bottom of the ravine did the haulage, the descending wagon assisting the one ascending. Only one wagon in each direction could be handled at a time, restricting the traffic to twelve each way per hour.

To reach the crest of the hill from the line's most southerly point – the lime-kilns on the northern slopes of the Wear valley above Stanhope, already mentioned – the wagons had to be hauled first up Crawley incline, a half mile long at 1 in 12 and 1 in 8, raising the wagons from 796 to 1,123 ft above sea level; at Crawley bank head the wagons were transferred to the rope worked by the Weatherhill engine, which drew them up to the summit 1,445 ft above sea level. Over the next eight miles to Hownes

Gill horses, stationary engines and self-acting inclines were used, perhaps the best known being Nanny Mayor's bank between Waskerley and Whitehall. The section south-west of Carr House was, of course, taken over in 1841 by the Derwent Iron Company, which in turn leased, and eventually sold it, to the S&D. William Bouch was asked to inspect the line and to report on it to the S&D directors: his report makes interesting reading as well as giving an excellent summary of the various inclines and stationary engines. For instance, the Crawley engine was 'on the George Stephenson plan' with cylinders 28 in. diameter and 72 in. stroke operated by steam from two tubular boilers 25 ft long by 6 ft diameter. The engine could haul two wagons at a time 'but can take three at a run'. A reminder of the difficulties encountered by the original company is provided by the comment 'the boilers have been erected about ten years and have worked about six years'.

It will be remembered (Chapter IX) that the Weardale Extension line from Crook arrived from the south to join the Stanhope to Carr House line (by then known as the Wear & Derwent Railway) at Waskerley on 16 May 1845 and on 1 September 1845 coaches commenced running from Crook to Stanhope and Hownes Gill. At the end of October the service was reduced for the winter to run between Crook and Waskerley only. The services beyond Waskerley were resumed on 1 April 1846 but the service to Crawley (for Stanhope) was withdrawn at the end of the year, never to be resumed. The Crook–Hownes Gill service continued to run, later extended to Carr House and eventually diverted to Benfieldside: from 1859, of course, it used the direct route from Burnhill Junction to Whitehall Junction. The service was withdrawn on 1 May 1939.

Although the line to Crawley (for Stanhope) and Hownes Gill was opened for passengers in 1845, no station at any of these points had even been considered. For instance the provision of a station at Waskerley was not discussed until 8 April 1846, when the engineer was authorized to advertise for tenders: only three weeks later he was instructed that work on this station should be suspended and a similar building erected at Cold Rowley instead.

The greatest obstacle on the line – Hownes Gill ravine — was eventually overcome when on 1 July 1858 a twelve-arch viaduct

730 ft long and 150 ft high was opened. The viaduct was actually built of firebricks made at Pease's Wear Firebrick Works at Crook, where they cost £1 6s 6d per 1,000; on the site they cost £1 11s 2d per 1,000. Altogether 2,655,000 bricks were used, and the bridge took sixteen months to build. The following year the Burnhill Junction–Whitehall Junction cut-off was opened, bypassing Waskerley and Nanny Mayor's incline, thus making possible through locomotive working from the summit of Sunnyside incline (between Crook and Tow Law) to Carr House. From 1 October 1868 trains from the south were diverted over a new curve to Benfieldside, where interchange could be made with the Lanchester valley trains to Durham and the Derwent valley trains to Newcastle. Benfieldside suffered numerous renamings after starting life as Blackhill; it became Benfieldside in 1867, Consett in 1882, Consett & Blackhill in 1885, and finally back to Blackhill again 1896.

The four Stanhope & Tyne inclines east of Carr House – Loud Bank, Stanley, Edenhill and Waldridge – as usual proved to be inconvenient and slow, and in 1875 powers were obtained to bypass that at Loud Bank by a new line which could be locomotive-worked. Nothing came of this scheme at the time but the NER Act of 19 June 1882 renewed the powers, with the line on a different course, increasing the length of the cut-off from $1\frac{1}{2}$ to 2 miles; this deviation line was opened on 1 January 1886. To replace the other three inclines, a $6\frac{1}{2}$ mile deviation was authorized on 23 May 1887, together with, at its east end, a connection between the S&T and the east coast main line, $1\frac{1}{2}$ miles north of Chester-le-Street. The connecting curve was opened on 16 October 1893 and the deviation followed on 13 November – both for mineral traffic only. Passenger traffic did not commence until 17 August 1896 and at the same time a new curve was opened at Consett, between the S&T and the Lanchester valley lines, making circular working possible from Newcastle, via Low Fell, Birtley, Beamish, Consett, Blackhill, and Rowlands Gill, and thence back to Newcastle. However, this was not exploited until much later; the Newcastle–Blackhill (via Rowlands Gill) trains continued on to Durham via Lanchester, with the Newcastle–Blackhill (via Birtley) trains returning the way they had come. The Derwent Valley passenger service to Blackhill was withdrawn on 1 February 1954 (by which time the

JUNCTIONS FOR CONVENIENCE

(30) *Coxhoe Junction looking south: train on flyover to Spennymoor line (now demolished)*

(31) *Connections at Dearness Valley/Baxter Wood/Relly Mill/Bridge House (south of Durham). Only the main lines (on extreme right) remain.*

EAST COAST MOTIVE POWER

(32) *4-4-0 class Q1 (introduced 1896)*

(33) *4-4-2 class V (introduced 1903)*

(34) *4-6-2 class A4 (introduced 1935)*

only intermediate station still open was Rowlands Gill) and the line has since been closed completely. The passenger service to Blackhill via Birtley and the 1896 deviation line was withdrawn on 23 May 1955.

Edenhill and Stanley inclines became disused about 1946, but Waldridge incline continued to serve collieries on Pelton Level.

Between South Pelaw Junction (where the curve from the east coast main line joins the s & t) and Consett, the 1896 line has become famous because it carries the iron-ore trains from Tyne Dock to Consett Iron Works. Until 1964 two class 9F 2–10–0 engines worked the nine-wagon trains, and the sound of them blasting their way up the 1 in 50 to Beamish was one not to be forgotten.

East of South Pelaw Junction the s & t route crosses the main line on an overbridge and almost immediately afterwards the site of the old Beamish wagonway can be seen on the left; the junction was controlled by a signalbox known as Durham Turnpike because of the proximity of the Great North Road (A1) now diverted to the east of Birtley. The present A1 crosses the s & t at a point known as Vigo : this was the summit of the most easterly of the inclines, which changed over to locomotive working as early as June 1857.

At Waskerley, on bleak Muggleswick Moor, a village sprang up to house the railway community employed on the line and at the locomotive sheds. The latter were established in 1846 and they continued to supply motive power to the area until September 1940, when they were closed and the three remaining engines transferred. The village, which had its own church and school – in 1855 the schoolmaster, John Langcake, was paid a salary of £2 18s 4d per month to teach fifty children – is now almost deserted; only one or two houses are still occupied; the church is used for housing chickens and the shed buildings have all disappeared, although the coaling-stage, built of stone sleepers, remains. One building was still used as an office by the goods agent who looked after the sand traffic originating at Weatherhill and Blanchland (renamed from Parkhead in 1923), and a goods train from Consett ran two or three times a week until April 1968. The line is now lifted.

THE BRANDLING JUNCTION

At its eastern end the Stanhope & Tyne–Pontop & South Shields line was (and still is) crossed on the level by the former Brandling Junction Railway line from Gateshead to Sunderland at a point some three miles short of South Shields, now known as Pontop Crossing. The Brandling Junction line was planned originally as a private venture by R. W. Brandling and his brother John to connect Monkwearmouth, South Shields and Gateshead. At the western end some conflict took place with the Blaydon, Gateshead & Hebburn Railway which, although authorized by an Act of 22 May 1834 to build for $16\frac{1}{2}$ miles, built only $1\frac{3}{4}$ miles. Eventually, after some squabbling, the Brandling Junction constructed part of its line on roughly the same course as the intended BG&H, whilst the Newcastle & Carlisle Railway constructed the western portion.

Although the Brandling brothers obtained an Act to purchase and take leases of land required for their railway, they relied solely on wayleaves, contracting to pay for these the total sum of £2,069 16s 6d per annum. On 7 September 1835 a company was formed to take over the assets of the Brandling Railway : the Brandling Junction Railway Company was incorporated by the Act of 7 June 1836. The new company agreed to pay the Brandlings £200 per mile per annum rent for the line, amounting to £3,434 5s 0d, thus producing for the brothers a handsome profit of £1,364 8s 6d a year on the wayleaves alone! Another difficulty appeared when the Stanhope & Tyne sponsored the Gateshead, South Shields & Monkwearmouth Railway, but duplication of interests was avoided by discussion between the companies and the idea was dropped. Work on the Brandling Junction line progressed steadily and it was opened in three sections : firstly the stretch from the Newcastle & Carlisle Railway at Redheugh, up the 1 in 23 stationary-engine-worked incline through Greens Field to Oakwellgate, together with the self-acting incline down to Gateshead Quayside, was opened on 15 January 1839; this was followed by Monkwearmouth to South Shields on 19 June 1839. The lines between Gateshead and Cleadon Lane, and Brockley Whins and Green Lane, were opened to mineral traffic on 30 August 1839 and to passengers six days later. Finally the Newton Garths branch between East Boldon Junction and West Boldon Junction in the south-east angle at Pontop Crossing (which never carried a passenger service) was opened on 9 September 1839.

A second connection between the Stanhope & Tyne and the Brandling Junction was opened at Pontop Crossing, in the north-west angle, on 9 March 1840 as the outcome of an agreement between the two lines and the Durham Junction Railway to provide through services between their various termini at Gateshead, South Shields, Monkwearmouth and Rainton Meadows: although opened on 24 August 1838 this was the first passenger service over the Durham Junction line.

It was probably on 9 March 1840 that the direct Brandling Junction service between Sunderland and South Shields via the Harton branch was withdrawn and traffic worked by interchange at Brockley Whins. The Harton branch was abandoned by the Newcastle & Darlington Junction Act of 21 July 1845 but it was eventually relaid, and it opened for traffic for the second time on 1 January 1867. The curve in the south-west angle at Pontop Crossing, provided to allow through running from the south to Gateshead, was opened on 19 August 1844, although a special train from London to Gateshead had run via the curve in the north-west angle on 18 June 1844. The south-west curve was built mainly on a wooden viaduct and although main-line traffic was diverted away from it when the Washington–Pelaw cut-off was opened to passengers on 1 October 1850 it was not demolished until 1940.

THE NEWCASTLE & CARLISLE

During the development of the Stanhope & Tyne and the Brandling Junction Railways the Newcastle & Carlisle Railway was steadily building the first line across England. Following the two meetings held in Newcastle in August 1824 a committee was formed and it called upon William Chapman to prepare estimates for the construction of a railway and a canal between Newcastle and Carlisle: on 27 October 1824 he reported that the cost would be £252,488 and £888,000 respectively. In March 1825 it was decided to have a railway, and a company was created immediately – so quickly in fact that the directors were appointed on 9 April. To meet contingencies the estimate was increased by £40,000 and the round figure of £300,000 was announced as the capital required. It was hoped to apply to Parliament in 1826 for the necessary powers, but because of discrepancies in the survey the bill was withdrawn and not submitted again until 1828. The Act became law on 22 May 1829 and authorized a main line from the west end of the Close at Newcastle to the north-west corner of the Canal Basin at Caldewgate in Carlisle, together with a branch from Elswick to Thornton Street in Newcastle.

Unfortunately the Act prohibited the use of locomotives – a fact which led to much trouble when the first section of the line was opened with great jubilation on 9 March 1835. Due to an objection by a landowner – Mr Bacon Grey – to the use of steam locomotives, traffic had to be suspended from 28 March, and it was not resumed again until 6 May, after the objector had been persuaded by public opinion to withdraw his opposition. Parliament did not actually sanction the locomotives until 17 June 1835. Dates of opening for the various sections of the Newcastle & Carlisle are :

9 March 1835	Hexham–Blaydon
28 June 1836	Hexham–Haydon Bridge
19 July 1836	Rome Street (Carlisle)–Blenkinsopp Colliery (Greenhead)
1 March 1837	Blaydon–Redheugh
9 March 1837	Canal Basin–Rome Street (Carlisle)
18 June 1838	Blenkinsopp Colliery–Haydon Bridge

On the day the line was opened throughout, great festivities were held, including a civic reception by the Mayor of Newcastle to his opposite number from Carlisle, who had travelled in one of the five trains which left the Solway early in the morning. From Gateshead a procession of thirteen trains set off in the opposite direction with some 3,500 passengers. Because of a number of mishaps they did not return until sixteen or seventeen hours later, with many of the passengers soaked to the skin as they sat unprotected from the weather in the carriages of the day.

It must be remembered that at this time the line had not reached Newcastle but had to be content with a terminus at

Redheugh (Gateshead) on the south bank of the Tyne, with transport across the river by barge. Eventually, on 21 May 1839, a temporary terminus was established near the Shot Tower in Newcastle but it was not used regularly until 21 October 1839. Redheugh station continued in use until 1850. The line was extended eastwards to another temporary station at Forth Banks on 1 March 1847 and finally into the new Central station on 1 January 1851, three months after the east end of the station had been opened by Queen Victoria.

The Newcastle & Carlisle managed to remain independent until 1862, but by the Act of 17 July in that year it passed to the North Eastern, after four years of bitter fighting.

At its eastern end the Newcastle & Carlisle runs on the north bank of the Tyne, passing the famous engineering works of Vickers-Armstrong and Armstrong-Whitworth: in the 1930s the latter concern pinned its faith to diesel traction and built a number of locomotives for home and overseas. When the gauge was suitable a number of these were tried on the LNE in the Newcastle area, and in fact the LNE purchased three diesel-electric railcars and a diesel railbus.

At Scotswood the Scotswood, Newburn & Wylam Railway had its separate platforms; it branched off to the north at the eastern end of the station and rejoined the N&C route west of Wylam. The N&C crosses the Tyne on a girder bridge built in 1868 to replace the original wooden structure which was destroyed by fire. On the south bank of the river the present route is joined by goods lines which originally carried the passenger service to the temporary terminus at Redheugh, and it was from this complicated area that the line to Blackhill via the Derwent Valley was opened on 2 December 1867. The valley of the Tyne hereabouts was the site of numerous small coal mines which could load their coal direct into the ships, but this trade has now all but disappeared.

Engineering works on the Carlisle line were not particularly heavy, although two tunnels were necessary – at Farnley Scar, ¾ mile east of Corbridge, and at Whitchester, a mile east of Haltwhistle – 170 yd and 202 yd long respectively. Originally a cutting was planned at Farnley, but it was actually built as a single-line tunnel, only to be doubled in 1846–7. Certain types of vehicles were forbidden to be passed by other trains in the tunnel and this, together with its physical condition, led British Railways to open it out; it thus became a cutting 130 years after it was first planned as such.

Hexham, with its beautiful Abbey, is the first station of note, serving a thriving town; until 1959 it warranted a small locomotive depot to provide some of the engines for the frequent service to and from Newcastle – a service now worked by diesel railcars. Following the valley of the South Tyne the line then passes through Fourstones, Haydon Bridge and Bardon Mill before reaching Haltwhistle, where the Alston branch strikes away to the south from the east end of the station. Brampton Junction, 11½ miles west of Haltwhistle, in fact ceased to be a junction for the interchange of passengers more than fifty years ago. From Brampton Junction the line descends all the way to Carlisle, and eastbound freight trains had to be assisted by a second engine up the first twelve miles from Carlisle.

The line between Newcastle and Carlisle is the sole surviving cross-country branch of the NER, and under the scheme for the development of the main lines it is planned to play an important part in feeding traffic from the east coast on to the west coast main line between Euston and Glasgow.

On 26 August 1846 the Newcastle & Carlisle company was authorized to build a branch southwards from Haltwhistle to Alston, but three years later a further Act was obtained to amend its course at six points, and also to build a branch from Lambley to Haltonlea Gate – later known as the Lambley Fell branch. The line was opened throughout from Haltwhistle to Alston on 17 November 1852 and it is one of the few country branches in the North East still open. However, it has recently been announced that when the roads in the area have been improved the line to Alston—reputed to be the highest market town in the country—will be closed.

In 1865 the Hexham & Allendale Railway received powers to construct a branch between the two points mentioned in the title, and also a line from Allendale to 'The Dead Heap' at Allenheads. The former was opened on 13 January 1868 for freight traffic and on 1 March 1869 for passengers. The Allenheads extension was not built. The branch terminated nearer to the village of Catton than Allendale; in fact, until 1898 the station was known as Catton Road. Passenger traffic ceased on 22 September 1930 but freight continued to be carried until November 1950, when the line was completely closed and the track lifted. The terminus at Allendale is now a caravan site!

The name of the signal box controlling the branch to Allendale was Border Counties Junction and it took its name from the Border Counties Railway, opened in 1862 from this junction to Reedsmouth, Bellingham and Riccarton. Before it was opened it was taken over by the North British Railway and, as a concession for not opposing the Newcastle & Carlisle and NER Amalgamation bill, the NBR was granted running powers between Border Counties Junction and Newcastle. These powers also included the provision by the NER of goods warehouse accommodation at Redheugh or Newcastle, with the NBR having the option to build its own goods depot if required, full running powers to any wharves, collieries, etc., in the Newcastle area, and provision by the NER of engine stabling and use of turntables at an agreed price.

An ambitious scheme for development on the north bank of the Tyne west of Scotswood Bridge was authorized by the Scotswood, Newburn & Wylam Railway & Dock Act of 16 June 1871. In addition to the line from Scotswood to Wylam (with a connection to the Newcastle & Carlisle Railway at each end) a dock was to be constructed adjoining the suspension bridge at Scotswood, served by a branch from the company's $6\frac{1}{4}$ mile main line. By April 1876 most of the line had been completed but 'whereas the construction of the said dock has become useless by reason of the River Tyne not having been dredged upwards to such a distance as to allow access thereto it is necessary that it be abandoned'. The abandonment of the dock was authorized and the company was allowed to drop the '& Dock' from its title.

Part of the line was laid along the site of the Wylam wagonway, alongside which stood the house in which George Stephenson was born and spent his childhood. There is no doubt that the horse-drawn wagons trundling past the door kindled his interest in railways – an interest which was destined to play its part in changing the face of the world.

EARLY WAGONWAYS

On the south bank of the Tyne west of Gateshead some of the earliest wagonways were constructed and it seems probable that at least one was working by 1530. However, it was not until a century later that they developed sufficiently to lay wooden rails and sleepers, and not until 1660 that they became an established method for transporting coal.

The Ravensworth wagonway ran from coal workings on the estate of the same name northwards to the Tyne at Dunston; its approximate date of construction was 1632 and it is from this early line that the Tanfield wagonway developed. As the coal seams nearest to the river were exhausted the mines and drifts gradually moved southwards, until by the end of the seventeenth century the centre of mining activity was approaching the Pontop and Tanfield areas. To reach the Tyne at Derwenthaugh a wagonway was laid early in the eighteenth century; from various accounts it is obvious that this, known as the Main Way, was a difficult and expensive line to construct, although no doubt justified. Branches fed coal to it from the adjacent pits.

In June 1726 a group of mining families – including the Montagus, the Liddells and the Bowes – banded together to purchase and work collieries, to share the cost of extending the Ravensworth wagonway, and to make branches to serve new pits and drifts. To carry one of these branches across a gorge the famous Causey Arch was erected, as recorded at the beginning of this chapter. About 1820 a new route to Tanfield East and Tanfield Lea was constructed and twenty years later the whole line was relaid with iron rails under agreements signed by John and Robert William Brandling in their efforts to divert coal mined in the Tanfield area from the Stanhope & Tyne on to their own line – the Brandling Junction Railway. The Tanfield branch eventually passed to the NER via Newcastle & Darlington Junction, the York & Newcastle, and finally the York, Newcastle & Berwick. Traffic continued to be worked over most of the line until August 1962, when the southern section was closed, leaving in use the Lobley Hill self-acting incline to serve Watergate Colliery. When this ceased using rail transport on 18 May 1964 the remaining portion of the branch was closed, bringing to an end more than 300 years of continuous operation.

Other major wagonways in the area which remained in private ownership until taken over by the National Coal Board were:

Beamish wagonway. Originated in 1763, serving pits in the Beamish area and it was connected to the Stanhope & Tyne near Birtley. At one time the S&T actually planned to purchase it to form the basis of its main line.

Pontop & Jarrow wagonway. This was an extension of the Springwell wagonway, which ran from Springwell colliery (south-east of Gateshead) to Jarrow. The first extension (to Kibbles-worth) was opened in 1842, followed twelve years later by a further extension westwards to Marley Hill, where connection was made with the NER Tanfield branch. The wagonway was latterly known as the Bowes Railway.

Pelaw Main wagonway. Opened in 1809 from Urpeth Colliery to the Tyne at Hebburn, and included the first stationary engine for hauling wagons. It was later extended to Ouston (near Birtley) and parts of it are in use to this day.

Sacriston wagonway. Ran from Charlaw and Sacriston (north-west of Durham city) to join the Stanhope & Tyne at Pelton. It was opened in 1839.

Burnhope wagonway. Developed by William Hedley from 1826, it ran eventually from Burnhope again to join the Stanhope & Tyne at Pelton Level. Known also as the Craghead wagonway.

Far to the west of the above was the Earl of Carlisle's wagonway, running south-eastwards from the Cumberland market town of Brampton, originally to Hallbankgate but later to Lambley colliery, where it connected with the Lambley Fell branch of the Newcastle & Carlisle Railway, which in turn branched off the Haltwhistle–Alston branch at Lambley. Here again the winning and carriage of coal was the reason for the building of the line, which was opened in 1799.

In 1837 the railway and collieries were leased to a company formed by James Thompson who, up to that time, had been operating them as the Earl of Carlisle's agent. The new company continued to work the line for seventy years, but the decline of the coal trade in East Cumberland forced it to sell out in 1908. Thenceforward the line was run by the Naworth Colliery Co.

Ltd until taken over by the National Coal Board in 1947. Under NCB management the system lasted for a few years, but traffic ceased in March 1953.

With the coming of the Newcastle & Carlisle Railway the course of the Brampton Railway, by which title the Earl of Carlisle's line was also known, was changed at its western end and connection was made with the N&C at Milton (renamed Brampton in 1870). In 1836 a horse-drawn coach for passengers was provided between Milton and the Brampton terminus of the private line. In 1881 this was replaced by a locomotive-worked service, but in 1890 this ceased due to conditions imposed by the Board of Trade after an inspection. In October 1912 the branch was taken over by the NER, and it was reopened to passenger traffic on 1 August 1913 after the track had been relaid. The service was withdrawn again in 1917 because of wartime conditions, but it was reinstated from 1 March 1920, only to close for good on 29 October 1923.

In the middle of the nineteenth century the good citizens of Newcastle must have looked on in wonderment as new railways were constructed right into the heart of their city. Now the same thing is happening again, but this time it is motorways that are being built, not railways! Certainly Newcastle Central station stands where it did and fortunately the architectural merit of the portice looks like keeping it that way.

CHAPTER XI

Northumberland

FROM THE TYNE TO THE TWEED

Although not strictly within the boundaries of this volume it should be mentioned that the first railway in Northumberland to obtain an Act was the Berwick & Kelso Railway, first projected in 1809 and authorized by Parliament in 1811. The line was actually to have commenced at Spittal, near Tweedmouth, *in County Durham,* but this was one of the detached portions of the Palatinate which remained separated from County Durham proper until 1844. The scheme was unexpectedly abandoned in 1827, although in 1836 the estimates were revised and re-issued, and a figure of £100,000 quoted for the twenty-two miles planned.

There were numerous schemes for railways between the Tyne and the Tweed but the two main contenders were the Newcastle & Berwick (backed by George Hudson, with the technical support of George Stephenson) and the Northumberland Railway, supported by Lord Howick. His lordship's antagonism to the Newcastle & Berwick was aroused because its line, as surveyed by Stephenson, passed close to his residence. Hudson did eventually agree to alter the route, but by this time Lord Howick was too far committed to the opposing line and the two schemes were fought out in Parliament. The Northumberland Railway was planned to use the atmospheric method of working, whereby the vehicles were attached to a piston drawn along a tube under the rails by the creation of a vacuum in front of the piston; this did not find favour at Westminster and when it was decided to consider both as locomotive-worked lines the Northumberland Railway bill was withdrawn, leaving Hudson victorious with an Act which received the Royal Assent on 31 July 1845.

The main line as authorized was from a junction with the

Brandling Junction Railway at Gateshead, passing across the Tyne on a bridge to Neville Street in Newcastle, thence joining the Newcastle & North Shields Railway near Manors and, after using this line as far as Heaton, striking off northwards to join the North British Railway 'near the ruins of Berwick Castle'. In addition there were to be three branches :

1. Bilton to Alnwick. Opened to freight traffic on 5 August 1850 and to passengers a fortnight later.
2. Cramlington to Newsham. Not constructed.
3. Tweedmouth to Kelso. Opened to Sprouston 27 July 1849 and extended to join the NBR 1 June 1851.

The section between Heaton and Morpeth was opened on 1 March 1847 and on 1 July trains commenced running through between Newcastle and Tweedmouth, using at Newcastle the terminus of the Newcastle & North Shields Railway in Carliol Square.

From 29 August 1848 trains began crossing the Tyne on a temporary bridge reached from Manors by a reversal outside Central station, then under construction. The next step was the completion of the permanent bridge on 15 August 1849, followed by its formal opening by Queen Victoria on 28 September, and Her Majesty visited Newcastle again on 29 August 1850 to open the magnificent Central station. Commenced in 1847 this was designed by John Dobson and cost some £100,000 to build; it is still in use today although extensions have been carried out at various times.

By the time work on the station commenced the York, New-castle & Berwick Railway had been formed by the amalgamation of the York & Newcastle (which had within the past three years swallowed the Durham Junction, the Brandling Junction, the Durham & Sunderland, the Pontop & South Shields, the Great North of England, and the Newcastle & Darlington Junction) and the Newcastle & Berwick.

The industrial area comprising Newcastle on the north bank of the Tyne and Gateshead on the south was the goal of many early railways and it was a notable day when the first passenger train ran through from Euston Square (London) to Gateshead in 1844. In those days the journey was slow and uncomfortable but as conditions improved, the journey time decreased, until in

1935 it was covered in four hours by the *Silver Jubilee* stream-lined train, which was steam-hauled. Under British Railways, with diesel traction, this time has been bettered by twenty-three minutes.

Over the years many shipyards were opened on both banks of the Tyne to repair and construct vessels employed in the coal trade and from these developed some of the largest and most famous shipbuilding firms, such as Sir W. G. Armstrong Whitworth & Co. Ltd, Swan, Hunter & Wigham Richardson Ltd, Wallsend Slipway & Engineering Co. Ltd, and R. & W. Hawthorn Leslie & Co. Ltd. As the steamship developed, companies were formed to manufacture the machinery and many of these branched out into other forms of engineering, including the manufacture of large naval guns and locomotives. In the 1930s Armstrong Whitworth & Co. Ltd made a determined attempt to capture the diesel locomotive and railcar trade, but although a number of successful units were built for British and overseas railways the venture was not entirely successful and the company eventually dropped the railway side of its business.

Until 1906 there were only two railway bridges across the Tyne – Scotswood bridge for Newcastle and Carlisle trains, and the High Level bridge for all other traffic. The three tracks of the latter had to handle the east coast main line trains, the local passenger services to South Shields, Sunderland, and Durham, local freight traffic between collieries, works and yards on both banks of the river, and numerous light engine movements to and from the large locomotive depot at Gateshead. East coast trains had to reverse at Newcastle until the King Edward bridge was opened and although at one time a curve was planned to enable trains to run from the High Level bridge direct to the north they would then have missed Newcastle station – an unthinkable proposition, although from 1928 the summer *Flying Scotsman* passed through Newcastle without stopping. The King Edward bridge allowed east coast trains to work through without reversal, but another important feature was the triangular junction at its Gateshead end which (together with a similar layout at the south end of the High Level bridge) allowed trains from north, south, east or west to join any of the other routes. Unlike its predecessor the KEB has only one deck, carrying four tracks, whereas the High Level has three railway tracks on its upper deck and a roadway below where, for many years, a toll was collected by NER employees.

Newcastle Central was the most important station on the North Eastern Railway and at one time handled almost 1,200 arrivals and departures daily. Many of these passed over the famous crossing at the east end of the station, where the local trains using the bay platforms on the north side (and bound for stations in County Durham) crossed the main lines. For fifty years the movement of trains was controlled by an electro-pneumatic signalling installation operated by three signal boxes, with similar boxes on the Gateshead side, but these have now been replaced by two all-electric signal boxes. In addition much of the main line southwards is controlled by a new all-electric box at Tyne Yard – the new marshalling yard which sprawls across the Team Valley between Low Fell and Birtley. Running under this large yard is a reminder of how it all started : descending the western slope of the Team Valley is a rope-worked incline owned by the National Coal Board, which carries coal from Marley Hill and Kibblesworth collieries to the Tyne for shipment. To surmount the eastern side of the valley the wagons are attached to another rope and this changeover takes place *below* the BR yard.

THE BLYTH & TYNE

The Blyth & Tyne Railway, an important predominantly mineral line in the Newcastle area, managed to remain independent for much longer than the other companies; in fact it did not fall to the North Eastern until 1874. The first step in the formation of the B&T came when the owners of Seghill Colliery became dissatisfied with the transport of their coals to the Tyne over the Cramlington wagonway. In 1839 they decided to build their own wagonway, using wayleaves, and it was opened on 1 June 1840 for minerals and in August of the following year for passengers. The water at Blyth was not deep enough for the larger vessels then coming into use and in 1843 a line direct from Blyth to the Tyne was planned. It was decided to construct only the northern portion of this and to use the Seghill Railway south of Seghill. The connecting link from Blyth was opened for mineral traffic in 1846 and for passengers on 3 March 1847. In 1850 a privately owned line from Bedlington made connection at New-sham and this later formed part of the B&T Morpeth branch.

In 1851 Parliamentary sanction was sought to incorporate the various wagonways forming the route from Blyth to the Tyne, under the title of The Blyth & Tyne Railway, and an Act was obtained on 30 June 1852. The section between Blyth and Earsdon Junction (near Backworth) lost its passenger traffic on 9 December 1963; south of Earsdon Junction the line lost its passenger trains on 27 June 1864, but it is still in use for its original purpose – mineral traffic down to the Tyne.

Next came the Act for the branches to Morpeth and Dairy House (south of Hartley) on 4 August 1853, followed on 3 July 1854 by the Act for an extension from Dairy House to Tyne-mouth. The privately owned section between Newsham and Bedlington was purchased in 1855 and subsequently formed part of the Morpeth branch opened to mineral traffic in October 1857 and to passengers on 1 April 1858.

Between 1621 and 1662 John Dove and his son were obtaining coal in the Whitley area and this was transported to the coast at Cullercoats by means of a wooden wagonway. In 1732 the mines were flooded and it is believed that at this time they were abandoned, but further mines were sunk in the area in the early part of the nineteenth century and in 1811 a wagonway was constructed from Whitley southwards to the Tyne. It was on the course of this wagonway that the B&T built its line to Tyne-mouth, authorized by the Act of 3 July 1854 and opened on 31 October 1860.

The northern portion of the Tynemouth branch was closed to passengers between Hartley and Monkseaton on 27 June 1864 and traffic to the north from stations east of Backworth had to travel by a train bound for Newcastle (New Bridge Street) and at Backworth change into a train bound for Blyth or Morpeth. However, with the electrification of the coast lines the direct service between Monkseaton and Hartley was restored, although the intermediate station called The Avenue was not reopened.

Also on 27 June 1864, at the southern extremity of the line, an extension to Tynemouth was opened and the original Tyne-mouth (B&T) station was renamed North Shields, but these two stations and the railway south of Monkseaton were replaced from 3 July 1882 by a line running nearer the coast. On the same date (27 June 1864) a line was opened from Monkseaton to Newcastle, with a connection to the former Seghill Railway at Backworth. It crossed a number of wagonways, including the famous one at Killingworth on which George Stephenson carried out many of his early experiments with locomotives. The terminus at Newcastle was at Picton Place, where the buildings were erected to the designs of John Dobson, architect of the splendid Central station some fifteen years previously. The B&T terminus eventually became known as New Bridge Street until, in 1909, a connection was put in between the former B&T line and the east coast main line at Manors, whereupon New Bridge Street was closed to passengers, although the yard remained open until recently as a coal depot. Picton House, part of the B&T terminus, was until recently used by various Government departments, including a branch Post Office, but this has now been demolished.

At the eastern end of the B&T the new coast route between Monkseaton and Tynemouth was authorized by an Act of 27 June 1872 but no construction was done before the NER took over the B&T in 1874. On 29 June 1875 the NER was granted modified powers. The line was opened on 3 July 1882 and on that date a fine new station was opened at Tynemouth. Less pretentious buildings were erected at Cullercoats and Whitley Bay, although the latter was replaced by a larger station on a slightly different site in 1910. At Monkseaton (actually called Whitley from its opening in 1860 until 1882) a station was opened on 25 July 1915 on a new site; three spurs had to be provided to reach it, and one to reach the existing goods depot situated on the 1860 route to Tynemouth.

At the southern end the new line was extended beyond Tynemouth station, under the main Newcastle road, to join the extended Newcastle & North Shields Railway line between North Shields and the 1847 Tynemouth terminus; from 3 July 1882, therefore, the old terminus became the goods depot. Part of the line to the B&T Tynemouth terminus was retained to provide a link between the new line and the B&T North Shields terminus, which continued in use as the North Shields goods depot. This was reached by a reversal, part of the 1860 route to Monkseaton being used as a shunting neck.

Thus, except for a short stretch of a few hundred yards at

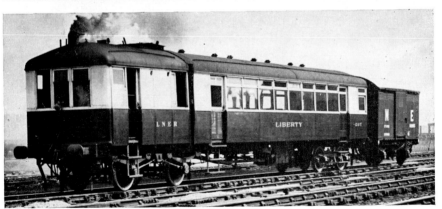

ROLLING STOCK—2

(35) *GN & NE vehicle used between Newcastle and King's Cross*

(36) *ECJS No. 24*

(37) *Sentinel steam railcar: extensively used in NE area of LNER*

VIADUCTS—2
(38) *Yarm*
(39) *King Edward Bridge, Newcastle.*

New Bridge Street, there was a complete loop and trains ran from New Bridge Street to Central via Backworth, Monkseaton, Tynemouth and North Shields, and vice versa. The practice continued for some time after electrification, but the link at New Bridge Street was finally inserted and opened on 1 January 1909 and it became possible to run through from Central to Central in either direction. This will be dealt with more fully in the section on electrification.

In the meantime the Quayside branch was authorized on 28 July 1863 and opened on 1 June 1870, and the Riverside branch was authorized on 13 July 1871 and opened on 1 May 1879. The former was a steeply graded branch dropping down at 1 in 30, through tunnels and cuttings, from Manors to the Quay at Newcastle. For the first thirty-five years of its life the branch was worked by steam locomotives and the smoke, steam and noise produced as they battled up the steep gradient can well be imagined. In 1905 the duties were taken over by two specially built electric locomotives, the line being electrified at the same voltage (600v. D.C.) as the passenger lines. These two continued here until 1964, when they were replaced by diesels, but the branch was closed in June 1969.

The Riverside branch diverges from the main line at the north end of the Ouseburn viaduct, between Manors and Heaton stations, and it largely follows the northern bank of the Tyne serving numerous shipyards and works before joining the North Shields line at Percy Main. The passenger service was withdrawn in July 1973.

Before leaving the Blyth & Tyne section, mention must be made of various curves put in by the N E R :

1. Benton south-west curve between Benton Quarry (on the east coast main line) and Benton station. Opened 1 May 1903. Not used by passengers but by empty electric and diesel trains to and from Gosforth car sheds.

2. Benton south-east curve between Benton Quarry and Benton East junction. Opened 1 July 1904 and used by express electric trains from the coast to Newcastle.

3. Benton north-west curve between Benton North junction (on the east coast main line) and Benton station. Originally authorized 1902 but not built until 1940 as a wartime

emergency route. Still used in emergencies and for diversions when engineering operations are being carried out on the main line between Manors and Benton North junction.

4. South Gosfoth East to South Gosfoth West, between the Gosforth & Ponteland light railway and the former B&T line. Opened 1905 and used for access to Gosforth car sheds.

The B&T had visions of extending northwards and at various times obtained powers to do this, but was never able to carry out its intentions. However, a number of the proposed lines were planned solely to keep out other companies who were thinking of invading the area. The Acts were:

1. 3 July 1854. From Bedlington Colliery to a junction with the YN&B at Longhirst. Not built.
2. 10 August 1857. The Longhirst Extension (above) abandoned and in substitution a branch to Warkworth Harbour. Built as far as North Seaton.
3. 29 June 1861. Branch from (2) to Newbiggen [sic]. Not built.
4. 15 August 1867. From end of the Warkworth Extension at North Seaton to Warkworth Harbour, together with the Newbiggin branch. The Warkworth Extension built only as far as Ashington and the Newbiggin branch constructed throughout.

Although many of the B&T schemes came to nought there was still development in the area, culminating in 1961 with Blyth shipping more coal than any other port in Great Britain. Mines to the west of Ashington were opened in the 1860s and connected to the NER east coast main line north of Pegswood, although there was actually no station of that name until 1903. The journey to Blyth was very roundabout, via Morpeth and Newsham, with a reversal at each. From 1867 coals were also shipped to a small extent at Cambois, on the north bank of the River Blyth, and to reach this branch (authorized by an Act of 15 August 1867 and opened the same year) reversal was necessary at Bedlington instead of Newsham.

When the NER took over the B&T in 1874 coal shipments at Blyth had fallen seriously, due mainly to the silting up of the harbour and approach channels. Nothing was done until 1881, when a start was made in dredging the channel to take larger vessels; in the following year a Board of Commissioners was set up to take over the running and improvement of the harbour and its approaches. As an added incentive the NER obtained powers in 1882 to put in two curves, one at Morpeth and one at Newsham, which would have allowed through running from the Ashington area to Blyth. Neither of these was in fact built and to reach the new staiths opened in 1884 reversal was still necessary at Morpeth and Newsham.

In 1886 the Ashington collieries obtained an outlet to the east by building a line to connect with the former B&T line at a point where the Newbiggin branch turned away eastwards from the uncompleted Warkworth Extension. Further staiths were opened in 1888 and at the same time a second line from Newsham to Blyth was opened : this connected with the south end of the new staiths, whereas the original line served the north end.

The next move in the development of the port of Blyth was in 1893, when powers were obtained to widen and extend the Cambois branch of 1867, and to construct extensive staiths at North Blyth; an additional curve at the junction of the branch with the Bedlington–Newbiggin line (Marchey's House junction to Winning junction) at last gave a direct route for Ashington coals, without a single reversal being necessary. These extensions were opened on 13 July 1896.

The NER started work on further staiths prior to World War I, but the task was then suspended until 1926 and they were eventually opened on 16 April 1928. Over 6,000,000 tons of coal a year were shipped at Blyth in the 1930s, a total surpassed in 1961 when 6,889,317 tons were 'teemed' – a term covering the unloading of the coal into the holds of the ships.

Year	Coal Shipped
1880	234,708 tons
1890	1,758,134 do
1900	3,177,659 do
1910	4,163,750 do
1961	6,889,317 do

Blyth's expansion has resulted in less traffic on the Tyne, where the longer haul necessary adds to the cost of the coal. In fact almost 90 per cent of the coal shipped at Blyth is from collieries within a radius of six miles.

The colliery complex around Ashington was one of the last to run its own passenger service. The trains suited the various shifts and were worked by National Coal Board locomotives; former main-line bogie stock was used, most of it being ex-NER, as might be expected. It was at Ashington, too, that NER forty-ton bogie coal wagons were introduced in 1903 to run solely between the colliery and North Blyth staiths : each train of twenty-five wagons averaged three round trips per week.

At Morpeth the B&T's own passenger station appears to have remained in use until 24 May 1880, when B&T trains commenced using the extensively altered NER station via a curve laid down under the original Act of 1853. The B&T station remained in use as the goods depot.

When the NBR-sponsored Wansbeck Valley line reached Morpeth from the west in 1862, the B&T was asked to allow it a route to Newcastle independent of the NER; the NBR line originally crossed the NER main line on an overbridge to connect with the B&T. Although a curve between NBR and NER was authorized by the original Wansbeck Valley Act it was not built until *c*. 1871-2, by which time the original powers had lapsed. It was, therefore, constructed under an agreement dated 8 August 1871, each of the two companies building part of the curve and installing signals at its own end. The NBR trains then deserted the B&T station for the North Eastern.

TYNESIDE ELECTRIFICATION

The NER was always willing to experiment, particularly when faced with competition, and a result of this was the electrification of certain lines north of the Tyne early in the century.

Towards the end of the nineteenth century it became fashionable for Newcastle businessmen to live at one of the resorts on the coast – Tynemouth, Cullercoats, Whitley Bay or Monkseaton – and to travel to Newcastle daily. To cater for this traffic, and also to offset competition from the rapidly developing electric street-tramway systems, the NER decided to electrify an almost circular route from Newcastle Central, via Heaton, Percy Main, Tynemouth, Whitley Bay, Monkseaton, Backworth and South Gosforth, to the former B&T terminus at New Bridge Street. This involved the whole of the former Newcastle & North Shields Railway (plus a portion of the 1847 Tynemouth extension), the

1882 coast route proposed by the B&T but actually built by the
NER, and the 1864 B&T line between Monkseaton and New
Bridge Street; and also the east coast main line from Heaton
to Benton Quarry, together with the south-east and south-west
curves, the Riverside branch and goods-only Quayside branch.

The total number of passengers booked in the Newcastle area
in 1901 was 9,847,000 but by 1903 the trams had cut this to
5,887,000, of which 2,844,000 originated in the proposed electrified area. However, the electric services brought the passengers
back again and by 1913 the total had topped 10 million.

First trials of the electric trains were carried out on the Riverside branch in September 1903 and the first passenger service
commenced on 29 March 1904. By the end of the year the whole
scheme was in operation. Over a period of six months in 1905
the passengers booked on the electric lines showed an increase
of 24.8 per cent, bringing an increase in gross receipts of 17.1
per cent, with an increase in running costs of only 11.7 per cent.

All went well and the electric trains continued to give a
regular and reliable service until in August 1918 a disastrous
fire occurred at the electric car sheds at Walker Gate; thirty-four
cars were completely destroyed and many others badly damaged.
A hurriedly introduced mixed service of steam and electric trains
carried on, but it was not until 1922 that things were back to
normal as the last of the thirty-four replacement cars began
work. Another result of the fire was the opening of spacious
new car sheds at South Gosforth, adjacent to the spur joining
the B&T line to the Ponteland branch. These sheds maintained
the electric stock used on the North Tyneside services, together
with the whole of the diesel railcar fleet based on Newcastle.

In 1909, as mentioned earlier, a connecting line was put in
between the east coast main line at Manors and the former B&T
line at New Bridge Street. This meant that trains could run
round the circular route in either direction from Central station
but, in fact, the connection was not used in this fashion until
1 March 1917. Until then it was used only for trains between
Central and Benton, and the coast trains continued to start from
Central and terminate at Manors North (and vice versa).

On 1 June 1905 the Ponteland branch, which had been built
under a Light Railway Order, was opened to passengers; it
was to be electrified when traffic had been sufficiently built up.

However, this never happened, and the line continued to be worked by a 'steam autocar' until it was closed to passenger traffic on 17 June 1929, together with the later branch (opened 1 October 1913) from Ponteland to Darras Hall.

A branch was also planned from the Avenue branch, one mile north of Monkseaton, to Seaton Sluice – a small village on the coast where the Seaton Burn enters the sea. As the name Seaton Sluice was not considered appropriate for a residential area it appeared as Collywell Bay on the indicators of the electric trains! The construction contract was let in December 1912 for £25,483 0s 10d but Seaton Sluice – or Collywell Bay – was never to see an electric train. The line had almost been completed when in August 1914 the Great War broke out and work ceased. During the war the rails were removed for use elsewhere, but later a temporary track was laid to enable a rail-mounted naval gun to approach the coast. In 1924, when the scheme was re-examined by the LNE, it was stated that rehabilitation, with a single electrified track, would cost £50,000; it was not proceeded with. In 1931 the scheme was abandoned completely, leaving things as they stood, and thus the line can still be traced where it has not yet been built over.

The electrified system was abandoned in 1967 and the electric trains replaced by diesel railcars. However in 1973 the newly formed Tyneside Passenger Transport Authority announced plans for re-electrification as part of a rail rapid transit network, new underground lines and new bridge over the Tyne.

Not a single branch remains on the west side of the main line between Newcastle and Berwick. This was a poorly served area, even when railways were at their peak, with only the NER's Alnmouth–Coldstream and Tweedmouth–Kelso lines, and the NBR's Wansbeck Valley and Rothbury branches.

On the east side the decline in coal production has led to the closure of the Amble branch, and a reduction in facilities at Blyth, where some of the large wooden staiths have been demolished. However, the former Blyth & Tyne line from Morpeth through Bedlington and Seghill to Percy Main is still open to mineral traffic, and forms a useful emergency route for passenger trains if the main line is blocked for any reason between Manors and Morpeth.

CHAPTER XII

Some Features of Operation

The locomotives and rolling stock used in North Eastern England provide an endless source of study and research. In the early days steam locomotives were built by private firms, but both the Stockton & Darlington and the North Eastern decided to build their own, and from these decisions sprang the famous works at Darlington (North Road) and Gateshead – the sources of many famous classes. Smaller works also existed at Shildon, York, Leeds, Hartlepool, Stockton and Hull but these were gradually closed down and the work concentrated at Darlington and Gateshead. Even Gateshead works ceased to build new engines in 1910 but continued to carry out repairs until 1932. The works were reopened during World War II but closed again in 1959.

A few of the larger colliery concerns built their own locomotives, and a typical example is the Earl of Durham's Lambton Engine Works at Philadelphia (near Houghton-le-Spring in Co. Durham) which are still in operation, carrying out major repairs and overhauls to National Coal Board locomotives. However, most of the privately owned engines were built by North Country builders, such as Robert Stephenson Ltd, Black, Hawthorn & Co. Ltd, Chapman & Furneaux Ltd, Hawthorn Leslie & Co. Ltd, Manning Wardle & Co. Ltd, Hudswell, Clarke & Co. Ltd, and Hunslet Engine Co. Ltd. A feature of colliery operation in the North East was the number of locomotives purchased from main-line railway companies. Naturally the NER predominated and this tradition was carried on by the North Eastern Area of the LNE and to a lesser extent by British Railways, so that between 1890 and the present time more than 100 locomotives passed into private ownership, and although most of them continued to work in Northumberland or Durham some found their way to strange places. For instance, a Class 964A 0–6–0 T finished its days at Milford Haven, and a Class H2 0–6–0 T worked at Norwich until a few years ago. An example of this longevity in private ownership is provided by the two Class 964 six-coupled saddle-tanks scrapped by the Seaham Harbour Dock Co. in 1963: the last engine of this class on the NER was withdrawn in 1909!

In the 1930s it was possible to see in Durham and Northumberland engines which had originated on the London, Brighton & South Coast, Cardiff, Rhondda & Swansea Bay, Barry, Great Eastern, Great Northern, Glasgow & South Western, London & North Western, Midland & South West Junction, and Metropolitan railways. In fact some of the more impecunious colliery concerns were much like working museums, using to the last cast-off locomotives they had purchased cheaply from one railway company or another. Under the National Coal Board most of these old engines have been swept away and a fleet of powerful 0–6–0 saddle-tanks has been built up, although these are now being replaced by diesel locomotives, some ex-British Railways.

A miscellaneous collection of coaches was inherited by the NER in 1854, many of them being nothing more than boxes on wheels. About 1880 a 32 ft 6 in. standard six-wheel coach was evolved, with differing compartment arrangements, and approximately 1,000 of the five-compartment 3rds were built; 257 of these survived at the grouping of 1923 and they finally became extinct in 1930, although a few are still to be seen in departmental use. The NER was very early off the mark with bogie vehicles, and after turning out an eight-wheel directors' saloon in 1891 it commenced to build the familiar clerestory-roofed vehicles in quantity in 1895. These were of two varieties, 45 ft and 52 ft over headstocks, and at the same time a quantity of 49 ft low-roofed coaches was built. In 1906 a change was made to elliptical roofs and these remained standard into LNE days. The NER colour for coaching stock was crimson lake, changed to teak by the LNE.

Many of the early bogie vehicles had internal corridors, but it was not until 1908 that the NER commenced building trains of fully vestibuled stock for its Newcastle–Liverpool and Leeds–Glasgow services. The normal length of this stock was 52 ft over headstocks, but there were also some magnificent dining-cars 65 ft 6 in. over headstocks and weighing over 40 tons. Corridor

coaches to NER basic designs continued to be built during the
first few years of the LNE, and they have only recently been
withdrawn. The NER vehicles could be distinguished by the two
windows in each end of the coach – one on either side of the
vestibule. It gave nervous old ladies a shock to see the next coach
bucking and swaying as though about to jump the rails at any
moment, and the feature was not perpetuated in the LNE's
coaches.

Once through trains had started running between London and
Edinburgh on the east coast main line the inconvenience of
keeping separate the vehicles belonging to the three east coast
partners soon led to the use of jointly owned vehicles which ran
under the legend, 'East Coast Joint Stock'. When the scheme was
prepared by the GNR in June 1860 it was estimated that fifty
coaches costing £13,450 would be sufficient for a start, each
company paying its share in proportion to its mileage, thus:

GNR mileage Kings Cross–York, 191.

$$\text{Prop. amount} \quad \frac{191}{400} = £6,422 \ (24 \text{ vehicles})$$

NER mileage York–Berwick, 151.

$$\text{Prop. amount} \quad \frac{151}{400} = £5,077 \ (19 \text{ vehicles})$$

NBR mileage Berwick–Edinburgh, 58.

$$\text{Prop. amount} \quad \frac{58}{400} = £1,950 \ (\ 7 \text{ vehicles})$$

$$£13,449$$

The scheme was approved in principle by the NER directors
in July 1860 and Seymour Clark of the GNR was informed 'it
will be necessary, however, that the plans and details of the
colours be approved by us, as we wish that the distinctive colours
of each of our companies' stock should be avoided, and another
colour be adopted, so that the public may see at once that they
are Joint Stock and not exclusively the property of either of the
three companies'. It was also agreed that the new coaches should
be used only in the traffic of the three companies and that they
must run through from London to Edinburgh and not be
stopped short at any intermediate point. They began service in
1861 and it was soon found advantageous to deal with the stock
as a whole, each company paying its mileage in proportion to

the entire cost. In 1880 it was decided that the stock should be shared on a fixed percentage basis, namely GNR 40 per cent, NER 35 per cent and NBR 25 per cent. Over the years the number of vehicles gradually increased, until at the grouping in 1923 there were almost 400 carrying the letters ECJS. When they were displaced from the Joint Stock by more modern vehicles they were shared out amongst the three partners and renumbered into the new owners' ordinary stock.

The ECJS vehicles were considered to be the best in the British Isles, and they certainly were imposing, many of them being carried on two six-wheel bogies. Pullman cars were introduced on east coast trains in 1878 but only three – *Columba*, *India* and *Iona* – were used for any length of time. *India* was destroyed in the Manor House collision on 2 November 1892 and the other two were transferred to normal ECJS usage from 1 January 1895. One of these became NER 2933 in 1901 and ran between Scarborough and Leeds as a refreshment car until about 1907.

In 1905 the NER and GNR agreed to provide joint stock for certain London–Newcastle services, again on a percentage basis depending on the mileage, namely NER 30.75 per cent and GNR 69.25 per cent. Eventually a total of thirty-six vehicles was built for the GN&NE Joint Stock. Both ECJS and GN&NEJS were in the teak livery used by the GNR, and to distinguish between them the lettering was on GNR vehicles shaded blue, on ECJS red, and on GN&NEJS green.

In 1903 the NER commenced experimenting with a couple of petrol-electric bogie railcars. Extensive teething troubles were experienced and the two cars were not revenue-earning until August 1904, when they started running between Scarborough and Filey. Although painted crimson lake when first turned out, they were put into traffic painted red (lower panels) and cream (upper panels). They were also unusual for NER stock in having vertically slatted sides, although this feature was soon afterwards used for normal coaches, both NER and ECJS. The combination of slatted panels and red and cream livery was then used on the whole of the NER Tyneside electric stock. Red and cream remained the standard livery until 1920, when a change was made to the crimson lake of the normal coaching stock. The LNE painted all the coaches in its standard teak livery, but this was abolished in 1937 when new all-metal stock was ordered for the North Tyneside lines, and red and cream was reintroduced. During World War II the stock was repainted blue and off-white, and finally, under BR ownership, it became green.

The electric stock built between 1904 and 1915 was all clerestory roofed but that built in 1920–2 to replace the vehicles lost in the Walker Gate fire was elliptical roofed, although the slatted lower panels continued to be used for new vehicles until 1938. Electric parcels vans were used on the system and at times of pressure two of these would work trains of ordinary coaches which had been specially fitted with 'jumper' cables – one parcels van at each end of the train.

A title peculiar to the NER was 'steam autocars', used to denote an obsolescent 0–4–4 T coupled to one or two coaches, the whole being capable of being driven from either end. These push-and-pull units, first used between Hartlepool and West Hartlepool in 1905, became a familiar sight throughout the system. Some of them ran for quite long distances and many put in extremely long hours. When the Class BTP engines were ready for scrapping it was planned to fit the ubiquitous Class O 0–4–4 T with push-and-pull gear but at that time the 'Sentinel' steam railcars came on the market.

From 1925 'Sentinel' cars of various types were purchased by the LNE, being introduced extensively in the North East from 1927. The two-cylinder variety was mainly used in the Hull area where the countryside is flat; the more powerful six-cylinder type was to be found throughout the North Eastern area; whereas the twelve-cylinder cars (except for *Phenomena*) were used between Middlesbrough and Scarborough over the hilly coast route. Due to their unreliability and uncomfortable riding the 'Sentinels' were never popular with the public, and most passengers were thankful to see push-and-pull working reintroduced in 1937. Since 1954 BR diesel railcars have been introduced throughout the Region on all but east coast main line and Newcastle–Liverpool services and they, like the 'Sentinels' before them, have tended to drive passengers away because of their mechanical and heating troubles, coupled with a high noise level.

And what of NER locomotives? Until the early years of the present century they were resplendent in a livery of Brunswick green with, wherever possible, the brass and copper fittings highly polished. The green was obtained by mixing equal parts of Prussian blue and chrome yellow, but it must be admitted that the results varied between different works. Large elliptical brass number-plates were fitted to all engines and from 1904 the engine classification was carried below the number on the vermilion-painted front buffer-beam.

NER engine classification was extremely simple: all engines built by T. W. Worsdell, Wilson Worsdell and Vincent Raven were allocated a letter class in alphabetical order of appearance. T. W. Worsdell's first design – a 2–4–2 T of 1886 – was allocated Class A, and every letter of the alphabet was used by the time the NER went out of existence. Modified or improved designs were denoted by a figure 1, 2 or 3 suffix to the class letter of the basic design. Engines built prior to the accession of T. W. Worsdell were given a class number, which was usually the number of the first engine built (or, sometimes, rebuilt).

For many years the locomotive engineer was Edward Fletcher, who received his early training with George Stephenson, and he remained in office until 1883. He was followed for a short period by Alexander McDonnell. In 1885 the NER directors appointed T. W. Worsdell, who left his mark on NER locomotives for many years: in fact many of the NER locomotives running up to 1967 had features he introduced. Whereas Fletcher's engines had been rugged in appearance, Worsdell's were graceful of line, with continuous splashers on the big-wheeled coupled passenger engines, and double-window cabs on all tender engines.

Wilson Worsdell succeeded his brother in 1890 and for twenty years he designed locomotives with the same graceful lines, in spite of their gradual increase in size. Vincent Raven followed in 1910 and, except for Government duties during the Great War, he reigned at Darlington until 1923. Raven was an NER-trained man and yet again the same lines were followed: his locomotives included some that were perhaps the most handsome ever to run on any British railway, namely his green three-cylinder 'Atlantics' of Class Z.

At grouping, almost exactly half of the tender locomotives were suitable for freight, mineral or mixed traffic duties as there were 230 0–8–0, 752 0–6–0 and 103 4–6–0 engines. The locomotive stock also included thirteen electric engines – two for the Newcastle Quayside branch, ten for the Shildon–Newport mineral workings, and the experimental engine built in 1922 in readiness for possible electrification of the main line between York and Newcastle.

In spite of intensive dieselization many Worsdell and Raven engines were running until the end of steam in 1967 : the Class J27 (NER P3) 0–6–0s were the mainstay of the coal traffic on the north bank of the Tyne, around Blyth and Percy Main, while the Class Q6 (NER T2) 0–8–0s were to be seen hard at work in the Tyne Dock and Sunderland areas. In 1949–51 twenty-eight engines were built by BR to a design which first appeared in 1898, (Class J72) and one of these engines is preserved.

In County Durham, particularly in the west, the gradients were too steep to allow the use of locomotives, and rope-worked inclines were built to collieries in the hills. Most of the inclines were worked on the self-acting principle, the descending wagons hauling up those ascending; in some cases steam winding-engines were used, and in others the rope merely passed over a braked drum at the top, in the charge of a brakeman. On certain banks the descending wagons (and coaches, for that matter) were allowed to run free, controlled only by a guard with a primitive brake. This dangerous practice died out about 100 years ago, but rope-worked inclines are still to be found in County Durham, mostly operated by the National Coal Board; British Railways inherited a few. Most inclines, however, have by now been converted to electric winding. Many were, of course, converted to locomotive haulage long ago, and some were abandoned after being bypassed by a line on easier gradients.

Yorkshire also had two famous inclines, one used by both passenger and goods vehicles, at Beck Holes on the Whitby & Pickering Railway, and one at Ingleby. The latter served the Rosedale ironstone mines, and though purely a mineral line the staff used to turn a blind eye to local inhabitants stealing a ride across the bleak and hostile moorland at the top of the incline.

A few of the more famous inclines on the NER were:

Brusselton
and Etherley   S&D 1825 Near Shildon   Abandoned

Black Boy	S&D 1827	Near Shildon	Abandoned
Weatherhill			
and Crawley	S&T 1834	Near Stanhope	Abandoned
Hesleden	HD&R 1835	Near Hartlepool	Realigned and in use as locomotive line
Beck Holes	W&P 1836	Near Goathland	Abandoned; replaced by locomotive line
Sunnyside	S&D 1845	Near Crook	Abandoned; replaced by locomotive line
Stanley	S&D 1858	Near Crook	Abandoned
Ingleby	NER 1861	Near Battersby	Abandoned

The Durham & Sunderland Railway, the Stanhope & Tyne Railroad, and the Tanfield branch of the Brandling Junction Railway all relied largely on inclines.

The inclines bred a particularly tough type of railwayman, who had to work long hours, sometimes in biting winds with rain and snow, and frequently on the crest of some exposed hill with no shelter. It was an arduous and also a dangerous life, particularly for the bankriders who rode every set of wagons up and down. Run-off switches were provided at various points to divert and derail any wagons which broke away (or 'ran amain') but accidents did happen, often resulting in a derailment and a resounding breaking up of wagons at the foot!

But the NER still had 127,616 wagons in use at 31 December 1922, of which almost half were devoted solely to the carriage of coal, coke, ironstone and limestone. Even more significant is the fact that almost 20,000 of these mineral wagons had a capacity of 20 tons or over. When it is remembered that in 1863 the chaldron wagon of 4 tons capacity was still in common use – at that time there were 26,372 in service on the NER and S&D – the great increase in capacity and economy can be appreciated. The NER was a pioneer in the use of large capacity mineral wagons, but although it did introduce 40 tonners between Ashington Colliery and Blyth it had to standardize on 20 tonners because of the restrictions on size imposed at the older collieries and shipping points. The 20 tonners with their high sloping sides became a familiar sight throughout the North

East, and a few are still used by the National Coal Board.

By its Act of 11 August 1905 the NER was empowered to run its own 'omnibuses, coaches, cars and other road vehicles, to be drawn or moved by animal, electric or any other mechanical power, and may therein convey passengers' luggage, parcels, merchandise and goods'. The company provided petrol and steam lorries to collect and deliver goods in villages remote from the railway. Both passenger and freight services are known, in fact, to have been running before the Act was passed : the first passenger service was introduced between Beverley and Brandesburton on 7 September 1903, whilst an experimental freight service commenced between Tollerton and Brandsby on 11 October 1904. This was later altered to run from the Easingwold terminus of the Easingwold Railway.

In addition to running all-the-year-round bus services between Beverley and Brandesburton; Thirsk Town and station; Ripon Market Place and station; and in the Blyth, Monkseaton and South Shields areas, the company introduced in 1905–6 a series of summer day and half-day tours by char-à-banc in the Bridlington and Scarborough areas. Even today the luxury coaches of United Automobile Services set off on similar tours from the station yard at Scarborough, direct descendants of the NER tours of almost 70 years ago. In 1912 a network of passenger services in the Durham area was instituted and this became the major centre for NER buses until in 1930 they were disposed of by the LNE to United Automobile Services and Northern General Transport.

The char-à-bancs used on the summer tours had interchangeable bodies so that during the winter a van or lorry body could be fitted. Motor parcels vans were used in the Newcastle district from 1906 and the company's road fleet also included some steam traction engines for working heavy loads. At the grouping the NER owned more than a hundred road vehicles of various types, including a Leyland bus fitted with rail wheels for use on light local passenger services around York. It was later transferred to Selby where, in 1926, someone inspected the contents of the petrol tank using a paraffin torch lamp with a naked flame !

In 1900 the NER obtained powers to operate steamships between Hull and Rotterdam, Amsterdam and Harlingen and this was accomplished by subscribing £120,000 to the Hull & Netherlands Steamship Co. Five years later it obtained another Act, by virtue of which it became joint owner of Wilson's & NER Shipping Co. Ltd, with powers to run services between Hull and Dunkirk, Ghent, Antwerp, Hamburg etc. A company was formed to purchase and operate seven ships : these were not the first vessels owned by the NER, as for many years the company's own fleet of tugs, dredgers, lighters, etc had been working at Tyne Dock, the Hartlepools, Middlesbrough and (from 1893) Hull.

The NER also operated jointly with the LYR a summer passenger service between Hull and Zeebrugge; to connect with this a daily 'Continental Boat Train' was advertised between Liverpool (Exchange) and the Riverside Quay at Hull. However, Hull never succeeded as a passenger port, although mention must be made of the many thousands of emigrants handled there. These people came from northern European countries, and their route was from Hamburg to Hull by sea, then across England by rail to Liverpool, where they embarked for the last leg across the Atlantic to a new home in the United States of America. This traffic continued for many years prior to World War I and reached its peak in 1903, when 61,278 passengers were conveyed from Hull to Liverpool via four routes :

L&Y via Normanton, Todmorden, Rochdale and Wigan.
MR and CLC via Pontefract, Sheffield and Chinley.
LNW via Leeds, Huddersfield and Stockport.
GCR via Doncaster, Penistone and Stockport.

NER engines and men, with NER coaching stock, worked through and returned empty after the men had rested at Liverpool.

Emigrant traffic was also handled at Tyne Dock, the Hartlepools and Newcastle, but the numbers were insignificant when compared with those at Hull. In 1907 the Hull & Barnsley Railway attempted to obtain a share of the traffic, using a passenger station erected on Alexandra Dock. However, its four-wheel coaches without lavatories were unsuitable for the long journey across England, and after the locomotive superintendent, Mr Stirling, had reported that it was impracticable to fit these necessities the H&B tried to hire stock from other companies; no one would oblige.

IN SEARCH OF ECONOMY

(40) *Londonderry steam wagon operated by NER on Plain of York.
Standing at Easingwold (Alne & Easingwold Railway)*

(41) *NER Leyland road bus fitted with rail wheels for operation in
York area 1922*

(42) *Petrol-electric railcar put to work between Scarborough and Filey 1904*

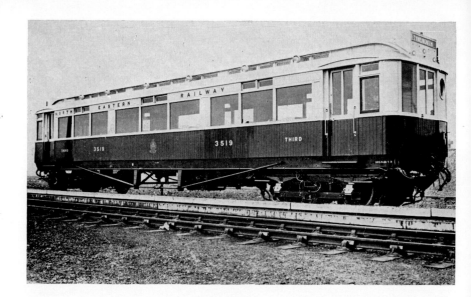

A NEW FORM OF TRACTION

(43) *Motor coach for North Tyneside electrification (600V. D.C.)*
(44) *Electric loco for Shildon–Newport electrified freight service*
(1,500V. D.C.)

Of its engineering features the NER could boast of the High Level bridge at Newcastle, the Queen Alexandra bridge at Sunderland, and the King Edward bridge, also at Newcastle. Magnificent stone or brick viaducts also exist at Yarm, Berwick (the Royal Border bridge), Arthington, Whitby, Crimple, and Thorpe Thewles to name a few, while a feature of the southern portion of the line was the number of large swing bridges, including two on the main line at Selby and Naburn.

Some of the larger stations are still in their original form except for extensions. Newcastle (1850), York (1877), and Darlington (1887) are good examples, although in each case the introduction of colour light signalling has greatly changed their appearance by doing away with the forest of semaphores which cluttered most North Eastern stations.

The largest marshalling yards on the NER were at Gascoigne Wood (near Selby), Newport (near Middlesbrough), and Hull. Gascoigne Wood was the collecting yard for coal from the South Yorkshire coalfield, which was then worked to Hull for shipment as required: similarly this yard handled the distribution of empty mineral wagons on their return from Hull. It was closed in 1959. Newport Yard has been completely modernised by British Railways and is now known as Tees Yard. The Hull yards were improved by the LNE when the Inward Yard was opened in 1935. The new Tyne Yard has replaced a number of small and obsolete yards around Newcastle and Gateshead and its control tower also houses the all-electric signal-box controlling movements on the main line.

And what of the future for the railways of the North East? The only lines which appear to have a definite future are:

Shaftholme Junction–Newcastle
Hull–Goole–Doncaster
Hull–Selby–Leeds
Middlesbrough–Stockton–Sunderland–Newcastle
Newcastle–Carlisle

It will be noted that these few lines serve all the major centres of population and, another important point, their traffic is steady and not greatly affected by seasonal flows.

The main line north of Newcastle was not to be developed,

according to one plan, but this now seems to have been forgotten. That once important alternative to the main line – the Leeds Northern route – closed in 1967 between Harrogate and North-allerton, and the York–Hull line, via Market Weighton, closed in 1965. Some of the remaining branches (heavily subsidised) are still carrying passengers but their future is not secure. Much of the trouble has been poor management, in particular the slow-ness in appreciating the implications of the motor age.

From 1 January 1967 the Eastern and North Eastern Regions of BR amalgamated, and the headquarters of the enlarged Eastern Region was moved from London to York. Extensive new office blocks were built in the yard of the old station and were used in addition to the former NER headquarters offices, and the offices in the old station buildings and hotel. Now, after only seven years, further reorganization is to take place in 1974 with the replacement of Regions by smaller 'territory' manage-ment areas based on York and Newcastle. Under the Grouping of 1923 the old NER system remained intact, and even in the first stages of Nationalisation the North Eastern Region of BR was only the North Eastern Area of the LNER under another name!

Over the last twenty years, however, the North Eastern has been decimated, losing hundreds of miles of track, thousands of passengers, and countless tons of traffic; many lines have been swept away so thoroughly in some places it is difficult to realize that a railway ever existed there.

Diesel railcars serve the branches which remain open, but they are noisy and smelly and drive away more passengers, and so it goes on. The only bright spot is the standard of speed on the main line between York and Darlington, over a line laid on an excel-lent course by the Great North of England Railway more than 130 years ago – long before the North Eastern Railway was ever thought of!

Author's Notes and Acknowledgments

In any work with historical content concerning the North Eastern Railway the first acknowledgment must always be made to W. W. Tomlinson's monumental work *The North Eastern Railway: Its Rise and Development*. Published in 1914 it is still a necessity for anyone interested in north eastern England. I have been privileged to inspect the material collected by Tomlinson, which was held in the British Railways Board Archives at York, and often, when checking dates and references in the wonderful collection of Stockton & Darlington and NER Minute Books, I have come across pencilled notes of his on doubtful or obscure items. Two other particularly useful volumes have been consulted over the years, both by H. G. Lewin, himself a North Eastern man. These are his *Early British Railways* and *The Railway Mania and its Aftermath*.

The files of practically all the many railway periodicals have been consulted at one time or another but this work is based mainly on the Minutes and other official documents in the Archives at York, where help was forthcoming from Mr E. H. Fowkes, later Archivist, British Railways Board, London, and from his successor at York, Mr W. MacDonald.

For the sake of continuity and clarity in the index a few small items proper to two chapters have been repeated, in an attempt to make the work readable by both tyro and expert.

A number of place names (particularly in County Durham) have changed slightly over the years and occasionally in the text use is made of various forms of the same name. An example of this is Sim Pasture and Simpasture. Another item which may occasion surprise is the use of the name Chaloner Whin for the well known junction south of York, usually referred to as Chaloner's Whin. In the first NER Appendix to the Working Timetable (1873) it appears as Chandler's Whin, but in the final edition of 1922 it had become Chaloner Whin and it is this form that has been used throughout.

The word freight may be distasteful to some readers but after the visit to America by certain NER officials early in the twentieth century it was used frequently by the company and has thus found its way into this work.

The countless references to the NER have not been included in the index.

Unfortunately, in 1972 all the invaluable Stockton & Darlington and North Eastern records were moved from York to London and transferred from the care of the British Railways Board to the Public Record Office. This was a reversal of a previous decision to house the railway records at the new Railway Museum at York, and it has led to the ludicrous situation of the relics being moved from London to York and the records from York to London!

From many years' experience it is obvious that by far the greater number of .people deeply interested in Stockton & Darlington and North Eastern matters live in north-eastern England, and they have thus been deprived of easy reference to the records of their own territory through the whim of officialdom.

Index